Ethical Behavior in Sport

Ethical Behavior in Sport

Herb Appenzeller

CAROLINA ACADEMIC PRESS

Durham, North Carolina

Library of Congress Cataloging-in-Publication Data

Appenzeller, Herb.
Ethical behavior in sport / Herb Appenzeller.
    p. cm.
Includes bibliographical references and index.
ISBN 978-1-59460-421-8 (alk. paper)
1. Sports--Moral and ethical aspects. I. Title.

GV706.3.A95 2011
796.01--dc23

2011031378

Carolina Academic Press
700 Kent Street
Durham, North Carolina 27701
Telephone (919) 489-7486
Fax (919) 493-5668
www.cap-press.com

Printed in the United States of America

Dedication

Every so often, a person comes along who touches the lives of countless numbers of people without fanfare or publicity. This was Jack Jensen, golf and basketball coach at Guilford College for 45 years, who was a role model for ethical behavior in life as well as sport. Jack, in a quiet, modest and humble way, exemplified all that is good in sport today.

When a local coach lost her husband to an unexpected heart attack, she took time off to take care of her duties at home. At Jack's recent memorial (having suddenly passed away in May 2010), she told me of the day she returned to school and, opening the door of her classroom, found Jack standing there with a rose in his hand and words of encouragement.

We never knew that the parents of a close friend at Wake Forest University invited Jack to live with them when he coached at the local high school. The husband died and the woman developed a serious illness. She lived a lonely life so Jack traveled 110 miles to bring her roses two or three times a month.

When one of our former basketball players died suddenly of a heart attack, Jack immediately got in his car to be with the grieving family in Atlanta. He stayed for several hours to comfort the family and then left to make the six-hour return trip home. When a former basketball player had his leg amputated after a motorcycle crash, Jack was the first to see him prior to and after surgery, and stayed in close contact in the ensuing years.

Story after story was told during the record crowd visitation in Alumni Gym (Crackerbox), where his teams played and won exciting and often nail-biting games, and took him to a NAIA National Basketball Championship in 1973, with three members later playing in the NBA.

It was after that championship that I asked Jack to take on an impossible task of reviving a defunct golf program. The rest is history: the Golf Association of America installed Jack into its Hall of Fame in January 2008 (one of six Halls of Fame) for a career that included 26 national tournament appearances and four national titles, making him the second coach in NAIA history to win two national championships in two major sports: basketball and golf. After Jack's passing, at the conclusion of the academic year, his grief-stricken golf team lost the Division III National Tournament by one stroke!

All who knew Jack Jensen feel that they are better today because he touched their lives and made a difference. *Atque in perpetuum, frater, ave atque et vale!* Until eternity, Jack Jensen, hail and farewell, and thanks for a life well-lived!

Contents

Acknowledgments

Ethical Behavior in Sport has been a "labor of love" because it has given me the opportunity to relive 70 years of memorable events in my long involvement in sport, first as a participant in football and track from junior high school to high school and then college. I then had the wonderful opportunity to coach four years in high school, five years at a junior college and six years at a small, liberal arts college with high academic standards and Quaker values. I also had administrative duties for 39 years with an opportunity to teach and initiate a sport management program that received national attention. For 46 years, I had "hands-on" experience in every aspect of academics and athletics.

Guilford College gave me the opportunity to speak on the local, state and national levels. The institution supported my publishing in athletics and sport and risk management during my long tenure at this special place. Much of the material in this book uses my personal experiences to explain the various ethical situations that confronted me throughout my career.

I thank the students at Rolesville High School, Wakelon High School, Chowan Junior College (Chowan University) and, for 37 years, Guilford College students. In these four schools, the students performed in the classroom and on the athletic fields with determination, integrity, dignity and a spirit of cooperation.

I invited only one author to write a chapter in the book, Colleen McGlone, professor of sport administration at Coastal Carolina University, who is one of the experts in the country on hazing. Her chapter is one of the most informative and well-written on the topic and I am grateful for her willingness to share her expertise for the good of our readers.

I want to thank Linda Lacy and Keith Sipe at Carolina Academic Press for encouraging me to write a very informative book on ethics in sport. Because of their vision and dedication, their series on sport and risk management, and sports in general, has been an important asset to the coaching and teaching profession. Their consistent assistance has been rewarding and appreciated. I also appreciate their willingness to let me use material from many of my previous books that add to the present book.

To my wife, Ann Terrill Appenzeller, I want to express my deep appreciation for her willingness to go beyond the call of duty to be a part of every phase of the book. Her suggestions, guidance, encouragement and outstanding ability have hopefully made a good book even better. On a personal note, Ann saved my life on several occasions and then made life worth living.

Appreciation is due several people who gave permission to include valuable material to this book. They are as follows:

- Dr. Tom Appenzeller "A New Crisis in Youth Sport"
- Paul Batista "Balancing the Establishment Clause v. the Free Exercise Clause"
- Wilt Browning "Chicken Little: The Sky is Falling"
- Michael Carroll and Daniel P. Connaughton "Review of *Patterson v. Hudson Area Schools and Malnar*: 10 Tips to Prevent Hazing"
- Chicken Soup for the Teacher's Soul "Roses in December"
- Linda Carpenter and Vivian Acosta "Title IX in Nutshell"
- Gil Fried "Can Sports Kill?"
- Dennis Haglan "A Letter to the Washington Post"
- Bill Martin "Sports Kids Play" Article by Dr. Kendall
- Dr. Robert Malekoff "Agents Aren't the Only Threat to College Sports"
- Dr. Frederick O. Mueller "Heat Stress and Athletic Participation"
- James Schmutz "Testimony on Concussions before the U.S. House of Representatives"

Prologue

"The most personal experiences are the most universal." —*David Bills, Pastor, New Garden Friends Meeting*

After seven decades as a teacher, coach, administrator and author, R.H. Jordan put the role of sports in its correct position in 1928 when he wrote:

> If one wishes to know the soundness or weakness of a school, he or she should examine the athletic program of the school. This is the touchstone. No other will do as well. If there is dishonesty, weakness, selfishness, hypocrisy, the story will be told in athletics. If there is truth, honor, courage, self-control, these will be manifested in the games.

It has been written that "ethics in sport" has seen the most growth and activity of any area today. There are numerous research studies in philosophy and social science that deal with ethical behavior in sport. Philosophers and social scientists produce a wealth of material on the topic. Some writers point out that ethics is the study of human conduct with an emphasis on what is right and wrong. In many texts, the words fair play and morality stand out and references are made to morality, justice, righteousness and virtue. Emphasis on ethical behavior in sport evolves around basic principles of right action in a particular profession.

As a participant in sport on the high school and collegiate level, a coach on both levels, a sport administrator for 40 years, and an author on sport management and law, I have a special purpose for *Ethical Behavior in Sport*. Quintilian, a Roman educator, wrote centuries ago that "education is not what you are able to remember, but the things you cannot forget." This book is about the things I cannot forget after 70 years in the sport industry.

The book is different from other books that deal with the important issues of ethics in sport. It was designed that way and uses meaningful experiences from the on-the-job experiences of the author starting with my first varsity high school football game in which I was a part of bigotry and harassment never before experienced. The book uses anecdotes and personal stories that fill the pages. Thomas Peters and Nancy Austin note in their best seller *A Passion for Excellence* that stories, as nothing else, reveal what is important to an institution. They believe, as do I, that stories convey to the reader the mistakes and successes of the past so that others can profit from them. Bob Gingher, a book editor for the *Greensboro News & Record*, writes that "no one develops learning tools by rote, but again by examples and by the story." He concludes "stories are the indispensable tools of teachers and students, without them there is no such thing as moral imagination."

It is my hope that the stories recalled that raise ethical questions will enable the reader to relate to moral dilemmas and ethical questions encountered in his or her life. I hope the reader will form opinions on the decisions made and profit from the experiences presented in the book.

Ethical Behavior in Sport

Chapter 1

The Sport Administrator

"The Ole Coach cannot take over as AD as was once the case." — *Tom Gleason, National Association of Collegiate Directors of Athletics (NACDA)*

Michael Blackburn, Associate Executive Director of the National Interscholastic Athletic Administrators Association (NIAAA), described athletic administrators:

> Their dedication to school, community, patrons and athletes is unparalleled in any other field of endeavor. The countless hours spent away from family while serving the needs of others often go unnoticed. But the results in human terms cannot be questioned. The life lessons taught to young people in athletics can never be duplicated in the classroom. Leadership shown to young people is often returned by the formation of future leaders as a result of what they learned during athletic competition. (*Interscholastic Athletic Administration*, 2009)

Until the late 1970s, most National Collegiate Athletic Association (NCAA) and National Association of Intercollegiate Athletics (NAIA) athletics directors were former head coaches in football and basketball (and occasionally baseball) promoted on the basis of service and merit. In some instances, however, this hiring method was an attempt to assign administrative responsibilities to a coach whose teams could not win (Appenzeller, 2003).

On the secondary level, most athletics directors also coached and taught in addition to administrative duties. In some instances, colleges assigned dual roles to the athletics director who coached a sport. The late Paul "Bear" Bryant held a dual position at the University of Alabama, as did the late Jim Valvano at North Carolina State University. In 1991, George Perles held a dual position as head football coach and athletics director at Michigan State University. Trustees, unhappy with Perles' record as the football coach, developed criteria to end dual appointments. Former MSU President John DiBaggio argued that holding a dual position as athletics director and football coach led to "insufficient oversight of the football program." When Perles was retained after the 1991 season to coach football but not administer the athletics program,

DiBaggio commented that "the jobs are separate and distinct and a mistake was made when they were joined over my objections" (Appenzeller, 2003). The Board of Governors of the University System of North Carolina adopted a policy prohibiting dual roles for athletics directors. Valvano and others, like Clarence "Big House" Gaines of Winston-Salem State University and Jeff Mullin of UNC Charlotte, elected to coach rather than remain as athletics directors. Dual positions were eliminated in state universities and many private schools in North Carolina in the 1990s. Today, dual positions on the major college level are a rarity and practically no athletics director is expected to teach and coach (Appenzeller, 2003).

The Changing Role of the Sport Administrator

Today in the 21st Century, sport administration has changed so dramatically that I would be fortunate to be hired for the same position I held years ago. I accepted my first job in a small rural high school totally unaware that I lacked experience and knowledge to administer the tasks at hand. The positives that enabled me to survive and succeed in my work were energy, enthusiasm and love for students. I taught six different classes, coached basketball and baseball and was the athletics director for the sport program. My duties as athletics director were limited to scheduling, purchasing and maintaining equipment. There were no formal requirements for administering a sport program, no methodology to guide me. I, like most athletics directors in those days, followed John Dewey's education theory of "learn by doing."

The role of the athletics director has changed at many colleges and universities, and men, and in some instances women, now enter the field with a background in sport administration and a master's degree in business administration. In 1967, James Mason developed a sport administration program at Ohio University and other institutions followed suit. In 2003, there were nearly 200 institutions with sport administration programs that provide training for the sport administrator. John Swofford, a graduate of the University of North Carolina, was one of the first graduates from the Ohio University sport administration program. Swofford represents a new breed of sport administrators schooled in finance, marketing, time management, personnel management, fundraising, promotion, legal affairs and other areas previously neglected in sport administration. After a very successful tenure at his *alma mater*, the University of North Carolina at Chapel Hill, Swofford was chosen to be Commissioner of the powerful Atlantic Coast Conference (ACC). His skills as an athletics director made him a viable candidate for the position (Appenzeller, 2003).

Muddy Boot Soldiers

In a profession that is changing rapidly, one thing remains constant. Most athletics directors on the secondary and collegiate level still remain in the background, leaving the spotlight for coaches. My goal as a college administrator was to perform administrative duties, allowing time for coaches to coach. I have always believed that the best administrators do not care who gets the credit when their programs achieve success. These administrators work behind the scenes to ensure a smooth operation for coaches and athletes alike. When General Norman Swarzkopf, Jr. was asked to name his heroes, he named his father (who was also a general), Civil War generals Ulysses S. Grant and William Tecumseh Sherman, and World War II and Vietnam General Creighton Abrams. His reason: all were "muddy-boot soldiers" and "none of them ever worried about who got the credit. They just worried about getting the job done" (Appenzeller, 2003).

Going back to the sport administrator as a "behind the scenes operator," consider this for a minute. Can you name the renowned basketball coaches at Duke University, Temple University or the University of Arizona? Can you name the football coaches at Penn State University or the University of South Carolina? Now, can you name the athletics directors or the presidents of those schools? I routinely pose this question to my students and the results are always the same. They name Duke's Mike Krzyzewski, Temple's former coach John Chaney and Arizona's former coach Lute Olsen. They respond quickly with Joe Paterno at Penn State and Steve Spurrier at South Carolina, but draw a blank on the athletics directors or presidents at these universities.

It is apparent that the "Ole Coach" will not be hired or promoted to administer an athletics program in the new century. More and more, dual positions of athletics director and coach will be relics of the past. A new breed of sport administrator has emerged since 1967, when James Mason, with the help of Los Angeles Dodger Walter O'Malley, started the sport administration program at Ohio University. The present-day administrators, however, will still remain in the background as they let the spotlight shine on the coaches and athletes in their programs.

Status of Sports Today

Dr. William Friday, a member of the Knight Commission, commented on his view of the current "big-time college athletics these days." Friday said, "I think a judgment, if I may put it that way, is approaching because of the excessive costs of the whole business right now." He then alluded to the problem today's escalating costs of athletics when he said:

> I think the difficulty lies in the fact that trustees and administrators have lost control. Too often, the demands are dictated by television—playing any night of the week. They're in complete control of when games are played. (*News & Record*, 2010)

Knight Commission

The National Collegiate Athletic Association (NCAA), at its 2010 Convention in Atlanta, called for "a national overhaul in athletics that would include transparency on program budgets," as described in the Knight Commission's 2010 Report, *Restoring the Balance: Dollars, Values, and the Future of College Sports*. The Knight Commission based that call on the concerns of 95 university presidents who "blamed most of the economic challenges on excessive salaries for football and basketball coaches." The Report expressed concerns that the solution to the financial crisis may be to eliminate sports. The presidents want to make changes themselves, but feel that "some oversight and authority is needed to address the challenges of the influences of alumni, boosters, politicians, and commercial entities" (Knight Commission on Intercollegiate Athletics, 2010).

Nancy Hogshead Maker, Director of the Legal Advocacy Center for Women in Sports, cautioned that sustaining football and basketball could lead to dropping other sports. She also believes that blaming Title IX and women's sports for the escalating costs of all college athletics is a mistake (Knight Commission on Intercollegiate Athletics 2010).

USA Today (2010) recently conducted a survey of 120 coaches in NCAA Division I athletics and found that 25 of the coaches surveyed made $2 million or more during the 2010 season and that nine earned $3 million or more. It noted that an exhaustive analysis of athletics department budgets would be required to begin to understand both income and expenses generated by college athletics.

Technology for the Sport Administrator

Authorities in the field of sport administration observe that the job of today's sport administrator is complex because of expanding sport programs, but decreasing budgets. They predict that technology will play a major role in the sport industry in the new century and help the administrator manage a successful program (Appenzeller & Appenzeller, 2008).

Dr. Todd Seidler and Dr. David Scott, professors of sport administration at the University of New Mexico, predict that "new procedures, design ideas, or tools that may allow for an increase in efficiency or productivity of staff can be invaluable and may prove to be the difference between success and failure." Seidler and Scott identify trends and innovations that are available for the sport administrator, such as "ticketing technology, conjoint analysis, data mining, virtual signage, access control, building controls, energy efficiency, on-line video conferencing, and high tech applications in planning for the future" (Appenzeller & Appenzeller 2008).

The late Mark McCormack, CEO of International Management Group (IMG), agreed that technology is important in today's world of e-mail, Palm Pilots, laptops, digital communicators, World Wide Web and cell phones. McCormack also cautioned the new century sport administrator that "technology is wonderful and seductive. But it is also insidious, especially if it chips away at our appreciation of the value of constant human contact—because without these moments of face-to-face exchanges, we lose a vital regulator in our lives." He added, "Remember this ... no matter how tempting it is to hide behind technology, there's more to be gained by looking into another person's face than staring at a screen" (McCormack, 2000).

Regulating Sports Agents: A Problem

Atlantic Coast Conference Commissioner John Swofford commented on the problem of improper conduct by sports agents. Swofford said:

> As an [athletics director] for years, it is something I know you feel vulnerable to, because it's a very difficult thing to control. You have to do everything you can do, in terms of knowing what's going on in your program and educating your student athletes ... and yet it still happens on occasion. (*News & Record*, 2010)

Swofford continued when he remarked:

> The NCAA rules are clear enough, but the risk associated with agent contact isn't shared equally. The athletes have a lot to lose. The people who don't have a lot to lose are the ones instigating and creating the problem in the first place. That's the agents and their runners. We

need to push harder to develop more cooperation from places like the NFL, or the NFL Players Association, who have the capacity to sanction agents and suspend agents, which hits them right in the pocketbooks. (*News & Record*, 2010)

Swofford concluded that "in reality, it's like a lot of things. It gets down to individual ethics. It's people's individual behavior and the choices they make. That's always a difficult thing to legislate" (*News & Record*, 2010).

Josh Adams, a star running back at Wake Forest University, told reporters that his football coach, Jim Grobe, constantly talks to his players about unethical agents. Adams said that Grobe tells all of his players to not accept a Snickers bar or candy from anyone (*News & Record*, 2010).

In 2010, the top wide receiver, A.J. Green, sold his 2009 Independence Bowl Jersey to an agent for $1,000. As a result, the NCAA punished him by ruling him ineligible for the first four Georgia games. Marcell Dareus, an Alabama star, accepted $1,787 for improper trips to Miami and received a two-game suspension from the NCAA. The defensive end is expected to pay $1,787 to a charity of his choice. The NCAA "has also been looking into possible agent-related violations at Florida, North Carolina, South Carolina and Georgia" (*The Associated Press*, 2010).

Deborah Yow Issues Warning to Agents

Just as she did when she was Athletics Director at the University of Maryland, Dr. Deborah Yow, now Athletics Director at North Carolina State University, issued a warning to any sports agent who gets their athletics program in trouble.

In a conversation with the *Raleigh News & Observer*, Yow said, "I'm going to protect NC State University from any agent abuse." As a deterrent against agent abuse, Yow has written to agents, who are required to register with the NC State Department, to discourage agents from offering prospective high draft choices any promise of value to them. In North Carolina and Maryland, the Uniform Athletic Agents Act specifically mentions that an educational institution can seek damages, including lawyers' fees, from an agent or former athlete who injures the school.

Yow emphasizes that the loss of a Bowl game can cost a school more than $1 million in revenue. Besides agent abuse, a lack of institutional control can be costly when dealing with the NCAA. Sending a letter to sport agents shows that the institution cares (*News & Record*, 2010).

"Agents Are Not Only Threat in College Sports" by Robert Malekoff

Dr. Robert Malekoff, associate professor of sport studies at Guilford College, wrote an intriguing article about the problems of agents in the *Charlotte Observer* (2010):

> College football coaching icons Nick Saban and Urban Meyer are upset. The NCAA is looking into alleged improprieties at Alabama and Florida—not to mention our own University of North Carolina among others.

Both Saban and Meyer have no problem identifying the real villains here—unscrupulous sports agents. Saban compares them to pimps and threatened to ban them from the Alabama campus. Meyer equates these player representatives to predators and sees their recruiting of college stars as a "dirty part of our business." As Robin, the Boy Wonder might say … holy hypocrisy, Batman!

The courting of star college athletes by agents is nothing new. In 1983 University of Georgia Heisman Trophy winner Hershel Walker signed a multi-million dollar contract to play for the fledgling United States Football League's New Jersey Generals despite the fact that he had a year of eligibility remaining. College football coaches were up in arms about the early defection and were quick to label agents as a threat to the college game. Fast-forward 25-plus years later and star football players leaving a year of eligibility on the table is commonplace. Some might even call it progress.

But let's get back to Meyer and Saban whose concerns sound remarkably familiar. Perhaps this is because similar charges can be leveled against some college football recruiters regarding their insatiable pursuit of high school stars. And nowhere in the country has the conduct of recruiters been brought more into question than the powerful Southeastern Conference (SEC) which typically sees more schools on NCAA probation than any other grouping.

The fact of the matter is that too many big time college coaches tend to live by the adage "do as I say, not as I do." Saban didn't let the fact that he was under contract with the Miami Dolphins stop his agent from negotiating with boosters and university officials at Alabama. Likewise, Meyer happily left Utah for what he saw as a better situation at Florida.

Apologists (they won't be lacking) will correctly argue that neither coach did anything illegal and that we all have the right to better ourselves professionally, but too many overlook the fact that in college football it is the rank and file "employees" (the players) that put coaches in the position to pit organizations against one another in order to raise the bidding.

Why should anyone be surprised when college stars fall prey to the enticements offered by agents? After all, it is Saban, Meyer and their coaching brethren who treat 16- and 17-year-olds as if they are princes in hopes that the teens will attend their schools (and make the university and the coach millions).

The brightest of these stars are wined and dined while in high school and often treated like a whole different class of citizen once they arrive on campus—complete with special dining privileges, luxury living accommodations, private tutoring, opulent locker rooms, etc. Given this preferential treatment and the fact that they see everyone around them—most notably their coaches—getting rich, can we really blame the players for being susceptible to agents who want to curry favor by bankrolling a vacation or weekend of partying?

SEC Commissioner Mike Slive raised concerns about the agent "problem," and called for the development of a "national strategy to improve this issue." While Slive is at it, he may want to think about an approach that might prevent SEC coaches from running off scholarship athletes (see basketball coach John Calipari at Kentucky, where some players have said their athletic scholarships were revoked to make room for other players Calipari had recruited) and recruiting eighth graders (Calipari's predecessor, Billy Gillispie), or the fact that we have a 400-plus page NCAA rule book largely in response to ongoing coach misconduct. And if the compliance police make it difficult to break rules, you can bet that many coaches—like the agents they decry—will figure out ways to bend them.

If agents are about money and greed, what are we to make of university presidents and trustees who throw tradition and loyalty to the wind to form superconferences that offer increased television revenue? Saban, Meyer, Slive, et al. should look in the mirror before being so quick to delegate blame.

Institutional Subsidy Rises in Athletics

The NCAA's annual report of athletics revenues and expenses "painted a bleak financial picture for intercollegiate sports and reinforces critics' charges that the current pattern of sports spending is unsustainable" (Maltz, 2010). The report also noted that athletics programs, rather than achieving self-sufficiency, are depending on subsidies from their institutions. This comes at a time when pressure to reduce the costs of athletic budgets is a source for discontent on college campuses. The report concluded that only 14 of the football programs from the Football Bowl Subdivision (formerly Division I-A) generated more revenues than expenses, and that no programs in the Football Championship Subdivision (formerly Division I-AA) generated net revenues in 2009. In the 2006–07 and 2007–08 seasons, 25 programs made a profit. The gap between the "haves" and "have-nots" continued to widen in the 2007–08 season. In the 2008–09 season, the median institutional subsidy rose from $8 million to $10 million. Other data from the 2010 report is as follows:

- Ticket sales and donations from alumni and other supporters make up more than half of the revenues generated by FBS programs.
- Salaries and benefits for coaches and athletic scholarships for players make up nearly half of the total expenses of FBS programs.
- The highest median head coaching salaries in the FBS are, in order, football ($1.2 million), men's basketball ($911,000) and women's basketball ($313,000).
- Only 2% of football programs, 6% of men's basketball programs and 2% of women's basketball programs in the FCS generated surpluses. (Maltz, 2010)

Too many schools in the FBS depend on football and men's basketball to support their own programs, as well as other sport programs. However, in the past six years, only 60% of the FBS programs generated surplus revenue. It is obvious that revenue in these high-profile schools is failing to generate funds needed to maintain such programs. (Maltz, 2010).

NCAA Addresses Academic Concerns

The NCAA's Division I board of directors recently responded to a request by school presidents and proposed legislation as an attempt to keep football players from "coasting in the classroom during the season" (Wieberg, 2011). The board adopted the following legislation, which was voted upon by NCAA members in January 2011:

1. Football players will be required to pass nine hours in the fall to be eligible for all games in the following year. Failing to do so will lead to a four-game suspension.
2. The academic abilities of all incoming freshmen and transfer basketball players at most Division I schools will be assessed. Those players in need will be required to attend summer school.
3. Returning basketball players will be required to pass six hours for them to play at the start of the season, and summer school will be "encouraged" for those players who need the extra class time. (Wieberg, 2011)

The Struggle to Reform

In 2003, Chancellor Gordon Gee left Ohio State to become president of Vanderbilt University. Gee, in an unprecedented move, placed Vanderbilt's athletics program under the umbrella of student affairs. Gee reassigned athletics director Todd Turner to student affairs, stating that there would be no need for an athletics director in his reorganization of the athletics program. Intramurals, physical education, club sports and athletics were mixed together under a vice-president. The unusual reorganization gave college and university presidents hope that Gee's action would signal reform in athletics that would give presidents control of their institutions' athletics programs.

As an athletics director for 40 years, 30 of them on the collegiate level, I did not believe Gee's plan would work. After several years of Gee's administration, Vanderbilt announced that the athletics program would spend $60 million to upgrade and make its program competitive in the strong Southeastern Conference. Gee then returned to Ohio State, where reportedly he became the highest paid administrator in the United States. His salary is thought to be over $1 million per year.

Gee was faced with a dilemma when five outstanding members of Ohio State's football team were punished by the NCAA prior to the 2011 Sugar Bowl. The five players could play in the Sugar Bowl, but had to sit out for five games during the 2011 season. The players had sold championship rings, jerseys and other memorabilia to the owner of a tattoo parlor, which was against NCAA rules. Many administrators waited to see if Gee would punish the athletes additionally. Neither Gee nor head football coach Jim Tressel did anything and played them in the Bowl game, which Ohio State won.

In March 2011, Jim Tressel came under fire for allegedly violating NCAA Bylaw.10.1. "According to *The Columbus Dispatch*, since 2006, the NCAA has sanctioned 27 schools for violating bylaw 10.1, which requires coaches and others to be truthful and forthcoming about possible violations. Of the 12 coaches involved, one kept his job. The others resigned or were fired" (Whiteside, 2011). Tressel sent an email to a mentor of his quarterback Tyrell Pryor, telling him that Pryor had sold championship rings and other Ohio State material to the owner of the tattoo parlor. He did not comply with the NCAA's requirement and did not notify university officials. When Gee was asked if he would fire Tressel, Gee tried to be funny and said, "I'm just hopeful that the coach doesn't dismiss me." Gee's comments did not go over well with educators and members of the Knight Commission, who want university presidents to control the excessive spending of athletics programs. David Ridgpath, an assistant professor at Ohio University and a member of the Drake Group that advocates changes for academic integrity in today's athletics programs, said, "As asinine as [Gee's] comment was, it's not as stupid as it sounds … It was dumb, a poor attempt to humor, but I think we all know what he's really saying. Jim Tressel can have him out of office tomorrow, but it would be tougher to get Jim Tressel fired" (Whiteside, 2011).

Ohio State officials suspended Tressel for two games this fall and fined him $250,000. Tressel asked the administrators to penalize him for five games, the same as his players. Hodding Carter, a professor of public policy at the University of North Carolina and former member of the Knight Commission, replied to Gee's remarks about Tressel: "I realize now why I had my doubts about trusting presidents with the responsibility. Of course the comment was in jest. The problem was that it was in the context of standing tall." Carter also said, "I expect shrimp to fly before I expect the NCAA to inflict a major penalty and they should." (Whiteside, 2011).

The slap on the wrist for Tressel reflects a major problem facing college presidents today: they want to control the athletics programs, but lack the power to get the programs under their control.

Christine Brennan, an Ohioan who writes for *USA Today*, wrote that people have repeatedly asked her if Tressel is "the real deal." She now can give her opinion of the man they believed went by the rules. She notes that Tressel writes advice on how to live your life. His latest book, *Life Promises for Success: Promises from God on Achieving Your Best*, is a collection of inspiring readings from the Bible. Brennan concludes that people who once believed Tressel was an Eagle Scout know now that he is like all the other coaches in big-time college sports who have cheated. She adds, "He actually might be worse, based on the depth of the deception. Tressel set himself up as someone better than the rest, and thrived on that image." Brennan says that if he follows the terms of his contract, he should have the dignity to resign (Brennan, 2011).

There has been a tremendous reaction to Tressel's failure to go by the rules, and people everywhere are upset over Gee's and other Ohio State officials' failure to fire Tressel right away. Gee had the rare opportunity to reform college athletics and try to give presidents the power to control college sports when he went to Vanderbilt, but now he has joined the crowd at the top of the programs and let others manage and control college athletics.

NCAA's Action Questioned

Former president Grimsley Hobbs wanted Guilford College to be a member of the National Collegiate Athletic Association (NCAA). He believed that the governing organization would place us in a group of notable universities. Our Faculty Athletic Committee (FAC) was very happy about our affiliation with the National Association of Intercollegiate Athletics (NAIA). Therefore, we decided to have dual membership in the NCAA and NAIA.

We were accepted by the NCAA in November 1973 and received welcome letters from UNC-Chapel Hill, NC State, Duke and Wake Forest. We were pleased with these letters from our neighboring colleges and looked forward to our membership in the NCAA. I decided to take our coaches to the January NCAA meeting so they could learn about the NCAA and its operation.

Our policy was to start spring football practice in January so we could let our athletes join the track, baseball and lacrosse teams. We had just practiced for two days when we went to the NCAA Annual Meeting in Chicago. We were going to be a Division III (no athletic grants) member of the NCAA. At the meeting, Division III members passed a rule that would prohibit spring football practice. I met with the NCAA Compliance Director and told him that we had started spring football for two days, but would turn in the equipment when we returned to campus. The compliance director said, "Well then, since you had two days of practice, you will be on probation." I said, "How can we be penalized for a rule you just passed for next year?" He would not listen and kept saying, "You're on probation." You can imagine our frustration—the year before, our basketball team had won the NAIA National Championship in Kansas City and now everyone would think we had violated a rule and were punished by the NCAA. Our FAC and Hobbs called the NCAA to get them to rectify the unfair ruling that they had retroactively made. When they refused to listen to our appeal of a rule that was not in effect when we joined, we withdrew from the NCAA, in February 1974. Our four-month membership was, in all probability, the shortest in NCAA history. Thirteen years later, Guilford College joined the NCAA again and became a member of the Old Dominion Athletic Conference (ODAC). It now has a great relationship with the NCAA and has achieved much success in athletics. However, I never regretted our withdrawal from the organization in 1974 after the ruling that a retroactive action was not changed.

It's the Peanuts, Popcorn and Cokes!

Another situation developed that posed an ethical question to a very strong academic institution that was also a member of the NCAA. Their athletics director was an outstanding administrator who served on several NCAA committees. One day he thought he would check on a question he had posed. Every year, this outstanding university hosted a banquet for its prospective students, among whom there were usually 10 or 12 who were interested in athletics. The athletics director called the NCAA to ask if athletes attending the banquet at a country club would present a problem for the university. "Yes, definitely," he was told. He persuaded the school to move the banquet to a church basement, where the food would consist of peanuts, pretzels, popcorn and soft drinks. He was given permission to move the banquet, to the disappointment of many departments that looked forward to the country club environment each year.

After the gathering at the church, the athletics director again called the NCAA and asked if this change of venue was acceptable to them. "No," they replied, "any athlete who attended the get-together will be ineligible for sports if they enroll at the university." The university president, an attorney by profession, was angry over the proposed penalty to the athletes who might enroll. He threatened a lawsuit and the NCAA offered a compromise to settle the issue. The NCAA proposed that the prospective student-athletes who attended the get-together at the church sign an affidavit that stated that their decision to attend the university was not influenced by the "cokes, peanuts, pretzels and popcorn they ate that night." In return for this signed statement, the men were eligible to participate in the sports program at the university. Unbelievable, but true! With the many problems facing college athletics today, NCAA officials decided to act on such a minor problem, which they had created.

Rules and Regulations that Govern College Sports Are a Problem

Dennis Haglan was a highly successful football coach at Guilford College and an assistant football coach at Duke and Wake Forest Universities. In addition to his coaching, Haglan was in charge of compliance for the athletics department at one of the schools where he was an assistant coach. The following is a letter Haglan wrote to a sports reporter at *The Washington Post* (2011). His observations about the NCAA's rules and regulations stem from the recent Ohio State coach Jim Tressel scandal:

Dear Ms. Hamilton,

First, you should understand that I have no affiliation with Ohio State and basically could care less about their programs. Secondly, since I have been a coach/athletic administrator/fundraiser, and now (small) donor at the NCAA DI level for many years (retired now for seven years), with one of my duties in the mid-80's as compliance officer for our athletic department, I feel that I have some insight into NCAA rules—from several perspectives—that most people do not have. What I am about to say is not to defend Tressel—whom I don't know from Adam—but rather to try to bring some added perspective into the rules and regulations that govern all collegiate sports.

Without getting too long-winded, let me begin by saying that my primary experience in athletics was at a small, private, Division I (DI), football playing university in the southeast—one that prided itself on following the rules and for never having received a sanction from the NCAA. Our athletics director would have fired a coach on the spot for any significant wrong doing. This 'culture' notwithstanding, however, I would add that all of our coaches were very conscientious. Yet, that does not mean that they knew all the rules.

When our athletics director, who also served as the department 'compliance officer' at that time, asked me to assume this responsibility, I agreed. Although I had served as an assistant coach for a number of seasons prior to becoming his assistant—and was very conscientious about following the rules—I have to admit that most of us took our lead from what we were 'told' about the rules, rather than taking the time to 'read' the rulebook for ourselves; we also naively assumed that 'common sense' and 'civility' would serve our needs. I soon learned how wrong I was about these two 'day-to-day guides' to reasonable human existence in the athletic world.

As I assumed the added responsibility of compliance officer, I began reviewing the rulebook. The thing that amazed me then, and still stands out in my mind today, was the very first paragraph: O.I 600. I read it, tried to digest it, and when I got to the end—which consumed virtually the entire page with very small print—I realized that this was 'one sentence': ONE SENTENCE!

Now, I am a reasonably smart guy, but this book was filled with these 'one sentence' paragraphs that most normal folks would have a hard time understanding. To be fair, however, it was around that time that the NCAA rulebook was about to be revised (I believe that the Auburn president was the one leading the charge on these revisions). I am not sure, however, that reading the new rulebook still does not require an 'interpreter,' or someone with the sense and reading skills of a lawyer.

I don't feel that our university was any different than most universities and coaches at that time. What I mean by that is, as soon as I was

asked to serve in this capacity—along with my other operational duties—my days became overrun with coaches calling to ask for rules interpretations. That alone told me two things: one, that coaches, in
fact, are very conscientious, and two, that understanding and having
confidence in one's own interpretation of the rules was lacking. In the
last 20 years, as I am sure you are aware, we have gone from my era
of compliance being a 'part' of one's duties within an athletic department, to nowadays having a full-time compliance officer with at least
one assistant, and in some cases, several assistants. Believe me, most
colleges and universities WANT to do what is right. However, let me
cite just a few examples of what a normal person would consider 'fair
and equitable,' or the 'right thing to do,' and I think one will begin to
realize as I have over these past 35 years or so, that too often coaches
reputations are diminished—and sometimes ruined—because of 'infractions' that really are nothing more than 'misdemeanors,' so to speak,
and do not apply to anyone on campus—EXCEPT ATHLETES!

First, however, one needs to understand that coaches are like parents to their athletes. Whereas a professor on campus might have
his/her students for a semester, or a year, a coach has them for four,
or five years—and most likely got to know the student-athlete and
his/her family during the recruiting process, which probably extended
back several years prior to matriculation. Consequently, the word
'family,' in the best sense of the word, exists among virtually all teams.
With this in mind, let me paint a few scenarios for you.

Say you are the coach of a DI athlete that just happens to live in a
neighborhood several hundred miles from campus; it is spring break
and you, as the coach, will be spending your spring break recruiting
in this same area. This particular athlete, like many athletes, comes from
a family that is less than comfortable financially. He/she asks you for
a ride home since you are going this way anyway. Can you give him/her
a ride? NO! However, you can give a ride to any other student that
lives in this area without giving it a second thought!

Or how about this: A musician, or artist (or math or engineering student, or practically any other student on campus that is highly skilled,
and usually on some sort of scholarship) that has exceptional skills is
soon discovered by the community; on weekends, or evenings, this
student can earn extra money by offering his/her services to various
groups or organizations. That's okay, but a student-athlete cannot use
his/her skills to do the same (except in certain summer/off-season
camps, etc.).

Or, how about this: Let's say a debate team (or some other campus group other than an athletic team) wins some grand competition and receives not only monetary compensation, but also some 'hardware,' like watches/trophies, etc. Some of these students decide that they do not want the 'hardware' and decide to sell it. That's perfectly alright. However—and you know where I am heading—if student-athletes want to earn some money from selling similar-type 'hardware,' they are prohibited from doing so; it is a NCAA infraction, just as the other examples I have cited. The NCAA rulebook is filled with rules that seem to defy common sense and civility—and do more to 'separate' the 'student' from the 'athlete,' than to make him/her more like a normal student.

All that said, I am not excusing anyone—coach, athlete or administrator—that commits a crime, or a serious rules infraction. However, when the public is seemingly constantly bombarded with news of athletes breaking the rules, or of coaches breaking the rules, or of coaches 'covering' for their athletes, I would hope that the media would begin separating, so to speak, 'the wheat from the chaff,' and go easier on those coaches and athletes whose infractions are nothing more than 'misdemeanors' in the grand scheme of things, and would agree that this is nothing different than what they (the media) would do—were they a 'good parent' trying to exercise civility, common sense, and good judgment in dealing with their 'own children.' Thanks for allowing me to share this opinion with you.

Sincerely,
Dennis Haglan

Could NCAA Division III Be the Answer?

When Guilford College decided to reenter the NCAA in a non-scholarship Division III program, I wished them well and decided to put my time and effort into the development of a sport management program. Guilford College has prospered in the Division III program and in the past three years, the basketball program has won more games in the state of North Carolina than any other college or university, including the University of North Carolina, Duke, Wake Forest and NC State. Guilford's record was 104–19 for a winning percentage of 84.6%. And two of its players were named players of the year for Division III teams. The team played in the Final Four of the NCAA Division III Tournament two years in a row.

On September 4, 2010, I attended an opening football game between Guilford College and local rival Greensboro College. The setting of the game was special—the stands were full, with people ringing the field. The fans on each side were excited and enthusiastic, but cheering both teams for outstanding play. Sportsmanship was evident on both sides and the game came down to the final play, as it has for most of the previous games. Greensboro won 17–15 to even the series at 7–7. But best of all there was no charge for admission to the game—all you needed to do was to donate two cans of food, particularly soup. After all, this was the "Soup Bowl." The Homeless Bank received 7,000 cans of food for the homeless. Everyone won at this game! I have become a believer in college sports at the non-scholarship Division III level, where it seems everyone wins.

Ethical Questions

1. How has the role of the sport administrator changed from the past to today?
2. What are the duties of the athletic administrator in today's program?
3. What is the characteristic of the "muddy boots soldiers"?
4. Who started the sport administration program? When? Where? Why was the program started?
5. What does the Knight Commission advocate to complete an overhaul of college programs?
6. Discuss the role of technology for the present athletic administrator.
7. How can the problem of sports agents be resolved?
8. Discuss how the Jim Tressel situation was handled.

Chapter 2

Coaching Issues

"There's a special bond between a coach and an athlete and it can lead to a lifelong influence as they grow into adults."—*Kevin Charles, as quoted in* Athletic Management *(2009)*

Coaches have always faced issues that never seem to change. Issues that deal with their employment (often triggered by the number of wins and losses), their role in the classroom and community, salary, tenure, training and problems that are present when a coach is assigned to coach a different gender team. In this chapter, some of these issues will be considered, particularly those involving ethical behavior in the coaches' approach to the various issues.

A Coach's Influence

Alphonso Smith, an outstanding student-athlete at Wake Forest University and All-America who was drafted by the Denver Broncos, discussed the influence a coach had on his life. In *Tribute to Wake Forest* (2010), Smith said:

> Coach Hood, the person who was the most vital influence regarding my development as a man, once told me that he would know whether he was a great coach ten years from now, when we became husbands, fathers, and contributing men in our communities. It was simple, Coach Hood clearly cared more about me and my teammates as people than players.

Smith concluded, "His message changed my life and I try to care more for others than I care for myself. I made the right choice in coming to school here, and I will always cherish the Black and Gold."

Coach and Athlete Have Boundary Lines

In *Athletic Management* (2009), Abigail Funk reported on a problem that exists when a male coaches a female team or vice-versa. The article noted that parents and administrators alike have concerns when an adult (male or female) is in a position of authority over a student-athlete of the opposite sex.

The article reported that a male coach was arrested for having sex with two 16-year-old girls he coached in ice hockey for several years. The coach was put on a paid-leave from his position as coach of the girls ice hockey team for the private prep school.

Most states require high schools to do a background check on teachers before hiring them. However, coaches are not "subject to a more extensive check." *The News Journal* reported on a 2001 survey from the American Association of University Women Educational Foundation that teachers ranked first and coaches second in sexual misconduct in schools.

Kevin Charles, Executive Director for the Delaware Interscholastic Athletic Association, commented to *The News Journal* on the sensitive subject:

> There's a special bond between a coach and an athlete and it can lead to a lifelong influence as they grow into adults. We all look back on coaches who had an influence on our lives in a positive way. If you have that, there's an opportunity for it to go in a negative way, too ... In an educational setting, these coaches are teachers. Boundaries have to be drawn, and it has to be the adult who draws the boundaries. (Funk, 2009)

Robert Shoop, a Kansas State University law professor and author of "Sexual Exploitation in Schools: How to Spot It and Stop It," lists four points of emphasis:

1. Schools should have a clear policy describing the appropriate boundaries for sexual harassment and abuses.
2. Schools should require training for all personnel, from principals to custodians.
3. Every student must undergo comprehensive training to understand the nature of sexual harassment and abuse.
4. Each school should have someone trained to investigate reports of abuses, preferably two people, a man and a woman. (Funk, 2009).

As an athletics director for 40 years, I made it a point to thoroughly discuss this problem with our staff. I always cautioned our coaches to be "friendly but not familiar" with our students.

Letters of Intent and Releases

The practice of releasing an athlete from a signed Letter of Intent after a coaching change at the school can lead to problems and is being called into question. Zack Maynard, an outstanding quarterback under Turner Gill, formerly at the University of Buffalo, attempted to transfer to another school following Gill's acceptance to coach the University of Kansas Jayhawks for the 2010 football season. The university agreed to allow Maynard to transfer under certain conditions, one being that he could transfer to a Division I program with their permission. Maynard sought a Division I program that would also offer his brother a scholarship. His brother, Keenan Allen, was an outstanding high school player who was highly recruited and offered a football scholarship to the University of Alabama. He was named to the All-America team by *Parade* (2010). He later committed to the University of California at Berkeley.

Abigail Funk, writing in *Athletic Management* (2009), questioned the legality of a Letter of Intent if it is signed by a minor and points to the controversy surrounding the release of athletes who signed Letters of Intent. The NCAA Eligibility Center has reviewed several cases in which the athlete who signed an agreement wanted a release to sign with another school. As an example, University of Memphis Athletics Director R.C. Johnson gave all the basketball recruits letters promising them that they could be released if John Calipari left. When Calipari left Memphis for the University of Kentucky, two of the highly regarded recruits got the release Johnson promised (Funk, 2009).

In early October 2009, the NCAA's Policy and Review Committee adopted a policy to clear up any confusion. The policy renders "null and void any letter of intent that contains any advance agreements that would release the prospect in case of a coaching change or other circumstances" (Funk, 2009).

On a personal note, in 37 years as an athletics director at Guilford College, I turned only one player wanting permission to transfer down, in agreement with the coach. Lloyd "World" Free, MVP of our 1973 NAIA National Championship Team, requested a transfer to an NCAA Division I school. Lloyd was contacted by an assistant coach from a nationally prominent school the night we won the 1973 Championship. The coach of that school was under fire because of alleged recruiting violations and was under investigation by the NCAA. I called this coach and told him that Lloyd Free could get a release to any other school but not his institution because he tried to illegally recruit him after we won our national championship. His reply was, "I don't even know the athlete you are talking about." Free remained with us that year, was named All-America NAIA and then signed a lucrative contract with the Philadelphia 76ers of the National Basketball Association (NBA).

Attorneys for the student-athletes who want to receive a release from a letter of intent believe it is a legal issue if the signee is a minor. Richard Gusler, an attorney, said, "The law believes minors suffer a disability and that the disability prevents them from executing binding contracts … I can't imagine a minor not being allowed out of a contract" (Funk, 2009). It is apparent that this can be an ethical issue, but it also may be a legal issue, one that the NCAA is investigating.

In North Carolina, Kelsey Evans signed a Letter of Intent to play basketball at Western Carolina University (WCU). When Kellie Harper left WCU to coach Elon University, Evans sought a release of her Letter of Intent. Evans' request was denied and she filed a lawsuit after WCU refused to release her. Two weeks later, WCU granted her request to transfer to Elon University. In North Carolina, "a minor can back out of a contract upon turning 18 unless a Superior Court judge had approved the contract. (Currently, North Carolina Superior Court judges do not review National Letters of Intent)" (Funk, 2009).

Coaches Cutting Scholarships

Several schools in our conference instituted a policy regarding student-athletes who had athletic grants and wanted to transfer to other schools. The basketball and football coaches required the athlete to repay his/her scholarship for as many years he/she received the financial aid before they would authorize the Dean's office to send a transcript to the school the athlete wanted to attend. Our coaches accepted my refusal to adopt such an unethical policy.

In addition, some coaches would reduce a student-athlete's scholarship when there were violations of team rules, academic problems or other reasons the coach decided were subject to a reduction of the student's athletic scholarship. Once again, our coaches chose not to implement such a policy. Our school would never permit such a practice by our coaches.

"I'll Be Suing You, Coach"

Coaches reflect on the days when coaches were respected by their athletes, parents and community. Decades ago, coaches were rarely questioned about their strategies or starting lineups. Lawsuits were rare and when a disgruntled athlete or parent sued a coach, they were criticized by teammates and parents alike. Coaches were not required to defend themselves in court.

Today, coaches are sued in record numbers for just about anything and everything. They describe the feeling as devastating, causing them to feel anxious, nervous, disappointed and distracted from their jobs. A coach recently commented that from the time he was sued until he went to court two years later, he never slept through the night. As a result of the flood of lawsuits against them, coaches are leaving the profession in large numbers in a time when they are needed to guide our children. Coaches feel that, win or lose, lawsuits damages their reputations. Lawsuits are expensive for coaches and school districts. A student-athlete in Chicago sued the team doctor, his football coach and the school district for $32 million after he was rendered quadriplegic in a regular season game. He settled for $23 million at a time when Chicago's schools were facing a budget shortfall.

Coaches are signing up for insurance to protect themselves from expensive litigation, only to find that the price of insurance has escalated to unheard of costs. Team morale and community spirit are affected when divisive lawsuits are filed. Team values, a sense of sportsmanship and togetherness have become things of the past.

Non-injury lawsuits continue to increase by as much as 200 per year, according to Gil Fried, sport law authority at the University of New Haven. Fried estimates that the threat of lawsuits reach the thousands each year. John Sadler, who insures over 4,000 sport organizations, said, "Parents sue when they get their feelings hurt." According to a 2003 report on *ABC News*, a father whose son failed to get his ice hockey team's most valuable player award "hired a lawyer and sued his son's ice hockey league to the tune of more than $200,000."

The parents of many athletes in various states have sued because their sons and daughters were placed on junior varsity teams when the parents believed they belonged on the varsity teams. A family in Comsewogue, New York, filed a lawsuit against the school district because their daughter was dropped from the varsity to the junior varsity soccer team. In other situations, parents sue when they believe that their sons or daughters were denied college athletic scholarships because a coach hindered their progress athletically. In New Haven, California, the Rubin family sued the New Haven Unified School District for $1.5 million, alleging that their son Jaween was dropped from the varsity basketball team. The parents felt that Jaween's coach not only caused him to lose a college scholarship but also an NBA career. Marc Martinez sued his son's baseball coach because he dropped him from the varsity team, which he alleged cost his son a college baseball scholarship. The coach, John Emme, appeared on *Good Morning America* (2003) and reported that he was suing Martinez for defamation of character.

In a remarkably similar case, parents in Houston, Texas, sued several coaches and a school principal for not pitching their son in a quarterfinal state playoff game. They attributed his lack of scholarship offers to the action of the baseball coach who cut him from the team. A federal judge in the highly publicized case made some important comments when he said, "A judge should not get involved in second guessing a coach's decision on who plays and who does not … A judge is not a super referee over high school athletics. They give opinions not starting lineups" (*Rutherford v. Cypress Falls Independent Sch. Dist. Court*, 1988).

Dyed Hair and Playing Time Problems

In another case against coaches, parents sued when a coach dropped their son from the wrestling team in Oregon because he dyed his hair green (*From the Gym to the Jury*, 1999). In another, a coach kicked a senior basketball player off the high school team for having pink dyed hair. He did say the student could return if he peroxided his hair blonde (*From the Gym to the Jury*, 1999). A soccer coach in Omaha, Nebraska, quit when parents threatened to sue because of lack of playing time for their daughter. The coach said it was difficult to coach when parents brought stop watches to practice to record the minutes their daughters got to play. A youth baseball coach was taken to court when his Babe Ruth Baseball Team lost every game. A father sued for $2,000 on the basis of alleged gross negligence on the part of the coach. The coach won the case and then quit.

Parents Suing Coaches Mirrors Society

These cases are just the tip of the iceberg but illustrate the time in which we live. On *Good Morning America* (2003), I noted that parents suing coaches "mirrors society today. Everyone feels that if they are wronged, they need compensation." One thing appears certain: there will continue to be a proliferation of litigation in the days ahead and coaches will be named defendants in record numbers. The challenge will be to find solutions through cooperation and communication between all parties concerned. More opinions by federal judges who hold that the courts should not try to name a starting lineup will help curb lawsuits. Solutions need to be found before this serious dilemma becomes epidemic.

Mississippi Court Gives Coaches Latitude to Motivate

A student at Jefferson County High School in Mississippi suffered heat stroke that left him with permanent injuries. The athlete sued the school district and his football coach for his heat stroke. He claimed that his coach had the team practice in the hottest month and allowed one water break during the two hour practice. When he requested a rest, his coach refused and called it "whining."

Both the school and coach raised immunity defenses under the Mississippi Tort Claims Act (MTCA), and contended that decisions such as when to hold practice and how to handle players' complaints during football practice are within the coach's discretion. The court agreed with the defendants, stating:

> Coaches have to know what motivates their players and what does not. Coaches know that in order to discipline football players each one is a different human being—one player may be disciplined by a mere stern look from the coach, while a military-style drill sergeant chewing out will not phase another player. Coaches will know their players well enough to know who may holler "wolf" and who will not. (*Harris v. McCray*, 2003)

The court concluded that it was reasonable for the coach to tell the player he was "faking it" when the player said he felt weak and needed water. The court felt that his injuries were regrettable, but pointed out that it was not helpful to second guess the coach. Because a coach needs to be able to motivate his players in the way he knows the best, the court held, a coach needs to use his "discretion" as he sees it—even if it means ignoring a boy's request on a hot summer day (*Harris v. W. McCray*, 2003).

I was coaching football at a junior college when our coaches believed an athlete was "faking it" and avoiding contact. I left for a district meeting and asked our coaches to scrimmage the team. They decided to put the player they thought was faking an injury in the contact scrimmage. At the last minute, they decided not to use him in contact work. The following day the athlete was taken to his home town in an ambulance for serious back surgery. His surgeon told me that if he had participated in contact drills or scrimmages, he probably would have been in a wheelchair for life. In this case, believing the student athlete was "faking it" could have led to disaster and permanent injury.

Motivational Techniques Cause Problems

A middle school basketball coach in Pleasantville, New Jersey, was fired after he told a boy he was getting an award at the school banquet. At the banquet, the coach presented the boy with the "Cry Baby Award," saying he begged to get in and all he did was whine. The award featured a baby atop a pedestal with the boy's name incorrectly spelled. The coach said he got one as a boy and it helped him (*From the Gym to the Jury*, 2004).

Alleged Misconduct Leads to Dismissals

Today, ex-coaches try other courts for wins as dismissals lead to litigation. Many coaches in this era have seven-figure salaries and much is as stake. The modern coach is reluctant to go away quietly, and in 2010, six coaches in football, men's and women's basketball sued claiming racial discrimination against the school.

Mike Cleary, executive director of the National Association of College Directors of Athletics (NACDA), said, "The coaches have agents, and agents say, 'Sue,' because if somebody gets money, they get a part of it." Cleary describes it as "the Old West, where everybody would pull their guns out ... Now they pull their attorneys out" (Carey, 2010).

Dr. Gary Roberts, dean and law professor at Indiana University, says that "coaches now are sometimes being fired for off-field issues and behavioral patterns, things that in past years might not ordinarily lead to dismissals. So the coaches are pushing back." Roberts adds, "You're seeing more dismissals for cause, so coaches will come back and say, that's not cause, or I didn't do what they said I did" (Carey, 2010).

Mike Leach, Texas Tech head football coach, who was accused of allegedly mistreating a player who had a concussion, filed a lawsuit against the school, citing libel, slander and breach of contract. Jim Leavitt, former South Florida head football coach, was fired over allegations that he grabbed a player by the throat at the halftime of a game. Leavitt argued in his suit against the school that the school's investigation was flawed and his reputation had been damaged. Bobby Gonzalez, Seton Hall ex-basketball coach, sued the school claiming that he did everything he was required to do as coach and was fired without cause. Seton Hall officials contended that he was fired for his behavior on and off the court. They later settled out of court. Robin-Potera Hoskins, former women's basketball coach at Montana State, sued after she was fired, alleging sexual discrimination because she complained that the women's programs were not treated equally with the men's programs. The university denied her complaint and said that she mistreated her players. She filed a wrongful dismissal lawsuit. Former Texas Southern women's basketball coach Surina Dixon sued claiming that the university retaliated against her because she complained of gender inequity and wanted equity for women in the athletics program (Carey, 2010).

Binghamton basketball coach Kevin Broadus was put on a paid leave in October 2009 "after his starting point guard was arrested on drug charges and five teammates were dismissed for other violations." Broadus claimed that racial discrimination was the reason for his firing (*From the Gym to the Jury*, 2009).

In response to the trend of suing when fired, Jim Haney, executive director of the National Association of Basketball Coaches, cautions coaches to negotiate rather than sue because filing lawsuits can "become an obstacle in getting a job, at least on the collegiate level" (Carey, 2010).

Winning Titles Leads to Ballooning Salaries

Clemson football coach Tommy Bowden was fired mid-season after Wake Forest defeated Clemson, and he was given a settlement. Dabo Sweeney was named interim head coach for the remainder of the season. Sweeney was later hired as the head football coach for the 2009 season, and when he led his team to the Atlantic Coast Conference Championship Game, he and his assistant coaches were compensated with massive increases in salaries. Clemson's Board of Trustees Compensation Committee increased the guaranteed compensation of its ten-man football staff by more than 56%, from $2.6 million to $4.005 million. This was accomplished despite budget deficits in 2008 and 2009, in which university employees, including athletics department personnel, had to take furlough days because of state budget costs (Berkowitz, 2010).

Bill Surver, a biology professor at Clemson and president-elect of Clemson's faculty senate, commented on the raises of defensive coordinator Kevin Steele and offensive coordinator Charlie Harbison. Steele's salary went from $200,000 to $575,000, leading Surver to ask, "Where does this end?" Athletics Director Terry Don Phillips said:

> There's going to have to be one university out there that says, "We're going to be fair, we're going to be competitive, but there is a point we're not going to move over." It could be tied to net revenue off what football or basketball does ... The problem is if you've got a very suc-

cessful, highly popular coach, you've got a problem with the people that support that program. (Berkowitz, 2010)

Salaries Rise for Assistant Football Coaches

What is fast becoming a trend among successful football coaches, salaries have also been increasing for the offensive and defensive coordinators by 38% or more. This trend comes at a time when most institutions of higher education are experiencing "financial distress" (*USA Today* 2010). In 2009, two assistants, Monte Kiffin (Tennessee) and Will Muschamp (Texas), received more than $650,000 (Kiffin, $1.2 million and Muschamp, $900,000). The University of Georgia has agreed to pay Todd Grantham, former Dallas Cowboys defensive line coach, $750,000 as its new defensive coordinator, which is 130% more than what Georgia paid the defensive coordinator it fired (Berkowitz, 2010).

Bowl Games Lead to Millions for Football Coaches

Games of the pre-bowl major college football season will determine champions, bowl assignments and the distribution of millions of dollars to conferences, schools and coaching staffs.

As reported in *USA Today* (2009), "the coaches' payouts come in the form of myriad incentive bonuses that are available for victories against rivals, in conference title games and those that increase impressive win totals. In one case, there could be further enhancement of a seven-figure annual salary increase that already has been earned" (Berkowitz, 2009).

All of this is on top of possible payments for other types of achievements, as well as guaranteed compensation and perks that by themselves place head football coaches—and some top assistants—among the USA's highest-paid public employees. For example, Bo Pelini at Nebraska got $150,000 for winning the Big 12 title game and $100,000 for entering any bowl game (Berkowitz, 2009).

Vince Vawter, retired editor and publisher, wrote an editorial for the *Knoxville News-Sentinel* (2010) about the huge salaries some coaches receive: "College coaches supposedly love what they do. Let them do it for a fair salary that doesn't in some cases dwarf that of the president of the United States."

Auburn Coaches' Payday

Successful coaches are rewarded with huge financial gains. As predicted, coaches who win national championships, Bowl Games and Conference Titles gain financial rewards (Berkowitz, 2011). Auburn University has the highest paid assistant football coaches following its 2011 National Championship. Gus Malzahn, Auburn's offensive coordinator, received a raise of $800,000 and the nine full-time football assistants are guaranteed nearly $4.085 million for the 2011 season. Malzahn will be paid $1.3 million. Head Coach Gene Chizik's salary increased from $2.1 million to $3.5 million (Berkowitz, 2011).

Basketball Coaches Whose Teams Qualified for the 2009 NCAA Tournament Rewarded

A 2010 *USA Today* study revealed the salaries of coaches whose basketball teams qualified for the 2009 NCAA tournament. A sampling of the coaches revealed that the average salary at the 65 schools is $1.3 million, not including benefits, perks and incentives. The average for coaches at the power conferences, the Atlantic Coast Conference, Big East, Big 10, Big 12 and the Pac 10, is $1.9 million, or five times the lower conferences. Several private schools did not send their replies to the study (*USA Today*, 2010).

The study defined guaranteed income to include "base-salary, annualized deferred payment, annuities and contractual expense accounts ... It also includes television, radio, Internet deals; apparel contracts, public relations, camps and other income that the university guarantees." Not included in guaranteed income were "incentive payments, bonuses and benefits" (*USA Today*, 2010).

The five highest salaries, as expected, are: Mike Krzyzewski (Duke) $4,095,909; Rick Pitino (Louisville) $4,073,093; Bill Self (Kansas) $3,675,656; Tom Izzo (Michigan State) $3,083,300; and Thad Matta (Ohio State) $2,662,000 (*USA Today*, 2010).

Coach K's Salary Tripled over Three Seasons

Duke University's basketball coach Mike Krzyzewski's "pay nearly tripled over four recent seasons—rising from about $1.3 million to more than $4 million" (Curliss, 2010). This increase came prior to the 2010 NCAA National

Championship. Coach K's salary may be the highest of all NCAA Division I basketball coaches.

In a Final Four news conference, Coach K commented that coaches are paid what the market will bear. "If you're at a program for a long time, if you're at a school for a long time, you become much more than just a basketball coach at the school," Coach K said. "You become an ambassador for the school" (Curliss, 2010). Coach K concluded that he turned down several multi-million dollar offers from NBA teams because his decision to stay at Duke was not all financial. He remarked, "The allure of coaching in college has no price at all" (Curliss, 2010).

By comparison, Roy Williams, head basketball coach at the University of North Carolina at Chapel Hill, has a contract that paid him $1.6 million in 2009. Head football coach at UNC Chapel Hill, Butch Davis received $1.7 million, according to his contract. Duke's commitment to upgrade its football program meant David Cutcliffe got paid $1.54 million, or three times as much as former coach Ted Roof was paid.

Athletics directors are also sharing in more attractive contracts. Kevin White, Duke University's athletics director, was paid $1.5 million in 2008–09. Much of White's salary came from incentive bonuses. UNC Chapel Hill athletics director Dick Baddour was paid $295,000, plus potential bonuses of $150,000. Lee Fowler, NC State's former athletics director, was paid $280,000, which he will receive for the remaining years on his contract (Fowler was fired in 2009) (Curliss, 2010).

Do Coaches' Salaries Compare to Entertainers?

The Knight Commission members met at a conference in Atlanta in 2010 to discuss their position on sport as it relates to higher education. The main problem today, as seen by the Commission, is the huge salaries paid to college basketball and football coaches. It is interesting to look at others who receive huge incomes for their annual work:

- Mark Zuckerberg—$3 billion (Facebook owner)
- James Cameron—$50 million (movie director)
- Jay Leno—$32 million (entertainer)
- Johnny Depp—$25 million (actor)
- Glenn Beck—$23 million (TV analyst)
- John Stumpf—$18.7 million (CEO of Wells Fargo)
- Wolfgang Puck—$18 million (chef)

- Taylor Swift—$17.2 million (singer)
- Kristen Stewart—$16 million (actress). (*News & Record*, 2010)

When compared to the amount of money listed above, the $4 to $5 million salaries for coaches seem less significant, particularly when their colleges raise over $80 million per year due to the success of their sport programs. Granted, these successful coaches are subject to incredible pressure to win every year.

Pepper Rodgers' 1980 Perks

Today's coaches in football and basketball receive incentive bonuses for victories over rivals, conference titles and lucrative Bowl Games. Other types of compensation are built into contracts that include perks. It is interesting to recall the perks (see below) given to former Georgia Tech head football coach Pepper Rodgers, who was fired in 1980. If these were the perks in 1980, consider what perks go to the football coaches who have base salaries of $4 and $5 million per year.

A. Benefits and perquisites received by Rodgers directly from the Georgia Tech Athletic Association:

(1) gas, oil, maintenance, repairs, other automobile expenses;

(2) automobile liability and collision insurance;

(3) general expense money;

(4) meals available at the Georgia Tech training table;

(5) eight season tickets to Georgia Tech home football games during fall of 1980 and 1981;

(6) two reserved booths, consisting of approximately forty seats, at Georgia Tech home football games during the fall of 1980 and 1981;

(7) five season tickets to Georgia Tech home basketball games for 1980 and 1981;

(8) four season tickets to Atlanta Falcon home football games for 1980 and 1981;

(9) four game tickets to each out-of-town Georgia Tech football game during fall of 1980 and 1981;

(10) pocket money at each home football game during fall of 1980 and 1981;

(11) pocket money at each out-of-town Georgia Tech football game during fall of 1980 and 1981;

(12) parking privileges at all Georgia Tech home sporting events;

(13) the services of a secretary;

(14) the services of an administrative assistant;

(15) the cost of admission to Georgia Tech home baseball games during the spring of 1980–1981;

(16) the cost of trips to football coaches' conventions, clinics, and meetings and to observe football practice sessions of professional and college football teams;

(17) initiation fee, dues, monthly bills, and cost of membership at the Capital City Club;

(18) initiation fee, dues, monthly bills, and cost of membership at the Cherokee Country Club;

(19) initiation fee and dues at the East Lake Country Club.

B. Benefits and perquisites received by Rodgers from sources other than the Georgia Tech Athletic Association by virtue of being head coach of football:

(1) profits from Rodgers' television football show, "The Pepper Rodgers Show," on Station WSB-TV in Atlanta for the fall of 1980 and 1981;

(2) profits from Rodgers' radio football show on Station WGST in Atlanta for the fall of 1980 and 1981;

(3) use of a new Cadillac automobile during 1980–1981;

(4) profits from Rodgers' summer football camp, known as the "Pepper Rodgers Football School" for June 1980 and June 1981;

(5) financial gifts from alumni and supporters of Georgia Tech for 1980–1981;

(6) lodging at any of the Holiday Inns owned by Topeka Inn Management, Inc. of Topeka, Kansas, for the time period from December 18, 1979 through December 31, 1981;

(7) the cost of membership in Terminus International Tennis Club in Atlanta for 1980 and 1981;

(8) individual game tickets to Hawks basketball and Braves baseball games during 1980–1981 seasons;

(9) housing for Rodgers and his family in Atlanta for the period from December 18, 1979 through December 31, 1981;

(10) the cost of premiums of a $400,000.00 policy on the life of Rodgers for the time period from December 18, 1979 through December 31,1981.

Rodgers sued for all these perks after he was fired. The issue was resolved by an out-of-court settlement between Rodgers and the Georgia Tech Athletic Association (Appenzeller, 1985).

Does Football Cost Too Much?

The new Cowboys Stadium, home of the Dallas Cowboys of the National Football League (NFL), may be the worst yet best of today's NFL experience. Sally Jenkins, writing in *Parade* (2009), describes the arena as "a technological marvel of glass and steel." However, the cost for a family of four to attend a football game at the new Cowboys Stadium is $758.58, as compared to $412.64 for an average NFL game.

Parking is plentiful, but at $50 to $60 for a space. The $2.15 billion stadium has set the bar high regarding cost, but may be the model stadium for future teams in the NFL. One fan estimated that on the way to his seat he paid $50 for a sweatshirt, $22 for a T-shirt, $8 for a chicken sandwich, $5 for french fries and $6 for a soda. Ticket prices for a game run from $59 to $500,000 for a luxury box (Jenkins, 2009).

Season tickets for football at the University of Tennessee increased from $19 up to $315 for the 2008 season. Athletics Director Mike Hamilton said that the increase in ticket prices was necessary to fund the budget. He noted that the "rising costs of student-athletic scholarships, travel and increased operating costs in addition to the expense of rewarding successful coaches who achieve success on a national basis, is essential to the overall success of the program" (*News-Sentinel*, 2008). University of Tennessee's Student Government Association President John Rader called the raise in ticket prices for students "outrageous and lunacy."

It is interesting to note that only Vanderbilt and South Carolina of the Southeastern Conference (SEC) admit students to football games for free. However, Tennessee is the only SEC school "that doesn't use student fees to fund their men's sports." Auburn University receives $49 million in student fees for its athletics department, while Florida gets $25 million in student fees (*News-Sentinel*, 2008).

An Unusual Proposal

Doug Elliott, writing in the *News & Record* (2007), expressed his view on coaches salaries when he said, "As a fan of the free market I have a plan that 'would revolutionize college sports.'" He suggested the following:

Let's create a true incentive-laden contract by depositing the coach's $2 million salary in an account at the beginning of the season; then for every loss suffered by the team, the university will withdraw $100,000

from the account and distribute it evenly among the top-rated pro-
fessions, based on teacher evaluations collected from the students. At
the end of the season, the coach will collect the remaining account
balance as his salary.

Elliott noted that professors are protected by tenure, while coaches face media
abuse and a lack of job security. He insists that he does not worry about high
salaries for coaches who win, and believes that outstanding coaches like the late
Everett Case of North Carolina State University are worth every penny they get.

Crisis on Campus

The escalating increases in salaries for football and basketball coaches in
Division I NCAA schools are creating a crisis that is evident in many schools.
In some schools, "the football salary increases could have political ramifications for the athletics department on campus and financial consequences for
the department internally" (Berkowitz, 2010).

Point Loma Nazarene University (PLNU) in San Diego dropped "its men's
golf, men's track, men's cross country and women's softball programs to resolve
issues involving federal gender equity regulations" (Schrotenboer, 2010). PLNU
plans to add women's golf in 2011. The school had been using a seaside park
facility to play its softball games. However, San Diego officials' decision to return the facility back to its natural habitat, Sunset Cliffs Natural Park, left
PLNU without a place to practice and play softball. Therefore, the university
regrettably eliminated three men's sports and women's softball to meet Title
IX guidelines and avoid gender-related litigation. Women's softball is one area
of Title IX where many collegiate and interscholastic programs fail to provide
facilities for the women's team as good as those for the men's baseball team. PLNU
plans to honor softball scholarships promised and also help students find other
schools where they can finish their athletic careers. At the time this decision was
made, PLNU had a 6–0 record in softball (Schrotenboer, 2010). More schools
will be confronted by situations similar to that of PLNU.

Running Up the Score

Yates High School of Houston, Texas, was the defending state 4A champion
in basketball. It played cross-town rival Lee High School. Rivals.com ranked
Yates High School No. 1 in the country, while Lee High School entered the
game with a 1–12 record. Yates set a single-game scoring record and led 100–12

at halftime. Yates played all 15 members of its squad, but kept pressing throughout the game. In the third quarter, a fight erupted after an intentional foul was called on a Lee player. The final score was Yates 175, Lee 35. The game ended in a brawl and raised questions regarding sportsmanship and coaching ethics (Phelps, 2010).

Yates coach Greg Wise said that he was not "scoring on other teams out of disrespect." His team scored over 100 points in eight games that season and won six games by more than 60 points. He answered his critics by saying, "We practice running, passing, trapping everyday … If we get to a game and I tell them not to do what we do in practice, I am not coaching well."

The league had a mercy rule, but both teams wanted to continue to play. Many coaches and administrators suggested various ways to keep the score under control. It is interesting to think of ways to control the score and whether or not a coach should attempt to alter his/her game to keep from a 175–35 victory (Phelps, 2010).

Bobby Bowden, who had only one losing season and 33 winning seasons coaching football at Florida State, had a coaching philosophy about running up the score. Bowden felt that it was his responsibility to encourage his players to score whenever they could and let the opposing coach try to stop them. Bowden did not believe in trying to limit his substitutes to hold back, but rather to play as they practiced when they were in the game.

On two occasions, one in high school and the other in college, I coached teams who played exceptional opponents on their home courts. Late in one of those lopsided games, the hometown fans began screaming for 100 points. I called time-out and decided to use an offense that we used when we were trying to run out the clock to preserve a win. We used the clock every time we had possession of the ball and went into our stall. It gave us good practice and drove the opposing fans into a wild frenzy. Neither opponent reached 100 points, even though they did everything they could to do so.

The question of running up the score in any sport is determined by the coaches and their coaching philosophy. It appears that this issue will be discussed and will continue to raise ethical questions as long as we keep score.

Coach Tried to Keep Score Down

I remember Clemson's Tigers scoring on every series against an out-manned Wake Forest football team. I learned later that Clemson coach Danny Ford did everything possible to keep the score from escalating against the Deacons. A Wake Forest coach told me that Danny Ford's fourth string players were talented and better than Wake Forest's first string team. When the score kept rising, Ford sent a manager into the stands to get a player who had not dressed out that day. He had the surprised player go to the locker room and dress for the game. Reports have it that the player scored soon after he entered the game.

Officials Decide to Keep Score Down

I had the opportunity to watch the best football player I have *ever* seen. His name is Keenan Allen, a player who excelled at wide receiver, quarterback, halfback, punt returner, punter when needed and a great defensive back. Northern Guilford High School in Greensboro, North Carolina, was in its second year of football, but the team had a 60-year-old coach who had won a state championship in South Carolina and was a member of three sport halls of fame.

Allen scored 45 touchdowns and led his team to a quarter-final finish and a 10–1 record. During that year, he rushed, caught passes, returned kicks and scored on many pass interceptions. It was obvious to me that many of Allen's touchdowns were called back for penalties against his team. Block in the back and false starts were the favorite penalties against this high scoring football team. The penalties came one night after Allen had scored four touchdowns in a row, nullifying his great effort. I could not understand the frequent calls when Allen scored his many touchdowns, but that night the answer to my frustration was clear. After the game, the referees stopped the coach's wife and former athletics director for directions to a particular highway. She was helpful to them, but shocked when they said, "Aren't you ashamed of your coach, he runs up the score on every team he plays? We took care of that tonight. After Allen's touchdowns, we threw our flags when there no penalties and *we* kept the score down." Imagine their surprise when the coach's wife responded, "That coach is my husband and I am sure he will report your misconduct to the supervisor of officials." These officials were not permitted to officiate the high school's games again that year. One official contacted the coach and apologized for what they did that night. Keenan Allen now plays for the University of California at Berkeley and was on the 2010 NCAA Freshmen All-America Team.

Coach Fired Following 100-Point Victory

A Texas high school girls' basketball team beat an opponent by 100 points. The coach, Micah Grames, was fired the same day after he sent an e-mail to school officials saying he would not apologize for the lopsided score. He insisted that his team played with "honor and integrity." Administrators at Covenant School called the score against Dallas Academy "shameful and an embarrassment." A parent who attended the game said the Covenant girls played extremely well and that spectators and an assistant coach "were cheering wildly as their team edged closer to 100 points" (*The Oak Ridger*, 2009).

Substituting with a Large Lead

The high school basketball team I coached was playing a league game against a strong opponent at their campus. The school was a prep school that had outstanding players from all over the United States preparing to go on to Division I schools. The coach of the team was a close friend of mine for many years. His team got off to a blazing start and after 15 minutes led by 25 points. He knew his team had little to worry about after that great start, so he let our friendship alter his game plan. He took his starters out and put in his substitutes to keep from embarrassing our team.

Our team got hot and we closed the gap going ahead at halftime. When he put his starters back in they were ice cold and could not regain the big lead they had earlier. We won a very important league game and it took his team several games to recover. He vowed after the game to never take a big lead for granted until victory was completely in hand.

How many times have coaches substituted when their team appeared to be a sure winner? When Wake Forest University played Maryland in football, the Terrapins appeared to have the game won near halftime. Down on the five-yard line, they attempted a pass that was intercepted and returned for over 90 yards. This changed the momentum for both teams and Wake Forest played inspired football to tie Maryland and then go on to win the game in overtime. That game elevated the Deacons in the standings of the Atlantic Coast Conference and led to an Orange Bowl game against Louisville. Since that game, we have also witnessed a coach substituting with a large lead only to lose the game later. We often wonder how or what is the ethical thing to do in similar situations.

45–0 in Three Innings of Baseball

Three Lakes High School in Wisconsin had a 45–0 lead in three innings of a baseball game. One of its players, Ben Wales, had an unbelievable game when he went "6 for 6 while hitting for the cycle, drove in 12 runs and had a no-hitter in three innings." Jeff Liebscher, Three Lakes coach, said "he felt bad for Phelps High School after 22 runs, 23 hits, 21 walks and 11 steals in the first inning alone." Both coaches agreed to stop the game in the third inning before it became an official game. The Wisconsin Interscholastic Athletic Association ruled that "according to national rules, the game will be ruled a forfeit because it failed to reach the required number of innings" (*News & Record*, 2010).

Motivation or Abuse?

Coaches at all levels and for all sport-related activities can use teachable moments and encouragement to improve player performance. In many instances, coaches become frustrated when a shot is missed or a ball dropped, and they yell at, severely punish or physically abuse the player (*News & Record*, 2009). During the 2009 college football season, three coaches were accused of abuse to players on their teams.

University of Kansas football coach Mark Mangino had claims of verbal abuse brought against him by two players. Mangino allegedly scolded a player whose brother had been recently shot and killed by saying, "I'll send you back to St. Louis where you can get shot by your homies." In a second complaint, a player said that Mangino told him he was "going to be an alcoholic just like [his] Dad." Kansas officials investigated Mangino's alleged verbal abuse of the two players, causing him to resign and accept a buyout in his contract. Mangino joined Bobby Knight and Woody Hayes as coaches who used intimidation to make a point (*News & Record*, 2009).

South Florida's football coach, Jim Leavitt, came under investigation for allegedly grabbing "a player by the throat and slapp[ing] him in the face at halftime of the Bulls' game ... against Louisville" (Carey, 2009). Leavitt was fired, although he vigorously denied the charges against him and felt the investigation failed to give him due process. South Florida settled with Leavitt on the remainder of his contract (Carey, 2009).

Texas Tech fired head football coach Mike Leach following a claim by a wide receiver that Leach confined him to a dark room as a penalty following a concussion. Leach has filed a lawsuit against the university for wrongful termination.

High School Coach Suspended

Murrah High School in Mississippi's basketball coach Marlon Dorsey was suspended for "whipping players with a weightlifting belt" (Brown, 2010). In a letter to the *Clarion-Ledger*, Dorsey said he "paddled the players for various reasons" and that he "took it upon [himself] to save these young people from the destruction of self and what society has accepted and become silent to the issues our students are facing on a daily basis." Dorsey then added that he was "deeply remorseful of [his] actions." Many coaches try to help their students meet the challenges they face on a daily basis, but most avoid corporal punishment when they do so.

Youth Sport Players Drop Out of Organized Sport Before the Age of 13

Dave Helling and Diane Stafford reported in *The Kansas City Star* (2009) that three out of four youth sport players drop out of organized sports before the age of 13, citing overly aggressive coaching more than any other reason. Helling and Stafford believe the "win-at-all costs" mentality has filtered down from the professional and collegiate levels to high school and youth sports today. They refer to a survey by the Citizenship through Sports Alliance (CTSA) and note that "youth sport has lost its child-centered focus, meaning less emphasis on the child's experience on adult-centered motives such as winning." The CTSA "conducts training seminars for amateur youth sport coaches [and] has even published a code of ethics ... It requires adherence to place the emotional and physical well-being of players ahead of personal desire to win" (Helling & Stafford, 2009).

Football Coach with History of Player Abuse Back on the Field

Coaches motivate players in different ways and some successful coaches point to controversial methods as a positive approach to winning. Bernie Busken, fired from a Phoenix, Arizona high school for physical and verbal abuse, returned to coach at a school near the one he was fired from.

Busken was fired in 2004 from Mountain View High School for alleged incidents of physical and mental abuse by his players. Busken would not stop a hazing ritual known as "pinkbellies," in which a player "would be held down on the ground while another player slapped him in the stomach with an open hand" (*FOXNews.com*, 2010). He also allegedly slapped players on the head and pushed players to the ground. "Other hazing practices included a game in which players fought on their knees for a towel wrapped in tape, with the winner using the towel as a weapon against the loser" (*FOXNews.com*, 2010). One player said he was mocked after he sought mental health counseling because of verbal abuse from the coach.

Busken applied to coach at a high school in Chandler, Arizona because he still owns a home there and wanted to be near his daughter. He said he believed that for every complaint against him, 1,000 people were happy with him as a coach. Hank Nuwer, author of *High School Hazing*, said that "criticism of [Busken's] behavior has been well-deserved," but he feels that he deserves a second chance "provided he is sincere about changing his ways." Nuwer also commented that "the coach is setting himself up for a real challenge, because today's generation is a lot different. If he can do this, more power to him. But if he can't, he should take himself out of the game, literally" (*FOXNews.com*, 2010).

Ken James, Chandler's principal, acknowledged that the school had many applications for the coaching job and his first thought was, "'I don't want to go there,'... But we had him come in and talk to the [hiring] committee and he just soared to the top. I was expecting some big, brash egotistical person coming in and saying, 'this is how we do things,' but he was the most humble, gentle person" (*FOXNews.com*, 2010).

Bliss' Rocky Road to Redemption

Dave Bliss, former Baylor University head basketball coach, who seven years ago "resigned in disgrace ... is back in the public spotlight." Bliss was hired by Allen Academy, "a pre-kindergarten through 12 year private school" in Waco, Texas. He was hired as "dean of students, athletics director and boys varsity basketball coach." Jeff Miller, writing in *USA Today* (2010), said, "It's possible no second chance in American scholastic coaching has carried more baggage." Bliss himself said, "Everybody deserves a second chance; it's just part of life. But the second chance is to do what God plans for your life, to get back to doing what you were created to do. This is what I do" (Miller, 2010).

Bliss, 66, was entering his "28th season as an NCAA Division I head coach, his fourth at [Baylor]," when he paid tuition for two of his players, Patrick Dennehy and Corey Herring, violating NCAA rules. In June 2003, Dennehy was shot and killed by Carlton Dotson, his teammate. According to reports, Dennehy's absence for six weeks led to questions about his tuition payments. Bliss told his staff to lie and say that Dennehy financed "his schooling by selling drugs." Abar Rouse, a volunteer coach on Bliss' staff, exposed the plan through audio tapes he recorded. As a result of the tapes, Bliss was forced to resign in August 2003 (Miller, 2010).

Bliss incurred violations by the NCAA that led to Baylor's five-year probation. The NCAA's investigation found the following violations: (1) improp-
erly soliciting booster money, and (2) failure to report that several players had
failed drug tests. Any NCAA institution that wants to hire Bliss before 2015
will require special permission from the NCAA. However, Bliss said he will
not seek another college job. Dennehy's father criticized Allen Academy's hiring of Bliss, calling it ludicrous. He questioned why the private school's parents did not "rise up and stop it."

Bliss accepted an opportunity to make a gratis appearance for basketball
coaches before the Final Four at San Antonio, with the stipulation that "the
session couldn't be rehearsed and no subjects would be off limits." Turner
Sports' Ernie Johnson, Jr., who emceed the appearance, noted that "the room
was deadly quiet from the first question," and that Bliss' talk was "pretty powerful. And it was probably cathartic for him" (Miller, 2010).

John Rouse, hired at Allen Academy to increase enrollment, commented
that "Bliss quickly convinced him that he had the passion and commitment
for the job." Robert Sloan, Jr., then president of Baylor, now president of Houston Baptist University, said, "Speaking for [Bliss] was not hard to do. For years
now, David has turned his life over. He's definitely sorry for what he'd done.
It's not just a courthouse confession" (Miller, 2010).

Five years ago, Dotson began his 35-year prison term for Dennehy's murder. He won't be eligible for parole until 2021. Bliss hasn't spoken to Dotson
since the events in 2003, but plans to at an appropriate time. He commented,
"I'd sure like to do what we can to help."

Winning or Fun?

In 2004, Jeff Joyce, a graduate student at Appalachian State University, surveyed youth sport children and their parents in Watauga County in Western North
Carolina and Guilford County in North Carolina, and found that on a scale from
one to ten, parents placed winning as number one on their list of youth sport
values, while the youth surveyed ranked fun as number one (Joyce, 2004).

Parents believe in the goals and code of ethics of the National Alliance for Youth
Sports, but many, like those surveyed in Joyce's study, want their children to win,
particularly when they spend hundreds of dollars and hours to improve their children's athletic performance. What may be unacceptable in middle school and Little League sports is often acceptable in Division I-level NCAA football programs.

Gary Abram, a management consultant at HCap International in Kansas
City, Missouri, noted that "among the forces that have allowed the 'screamers

and punchers' to stay active in the sports world … are baby boomer parents. Some are fixated on their kids' athletic successes at all costs and on players who sense the attitude that coping with abuse is the price of admission" (Helling & Stafford, 2009).

Is the Right to Hire the Right to Fire?

It is very clear that universities nationwide will not tolerate losing seasons and are quick to fire athletics directors and/or coaches who do not meet their expectations. The newly appointed Chancellor at North Carolina State University had been on the job for four months when he said that he would evaluate his athletics director, Lee Fowler. One day later, he announced that Fowler, athletics director for 10 years, agreed to resign from his job that would have ended in 2013. Chancellor Woodson was unhappy with the accomplishments of both basketball and football and was willing to pay Fowler $280,000 per year until his contract expires. NC State won 13 ACC team titles during Fowler's administration, but failed to have winning seasons in football since 2006 or make the NCAA tournament in basketball since 2006.

Former NC State basketball coach Les Robinson, who did what he was asked to do by cleaning up the athletics program, was fired for not winning. Herb Sendek, who graduated all his players and went to five NCAA tournaments, was fired for his failure to keep up with Big Four rivals, Duke, UNC and Wake Forest. Ron Wellman, one of the nation's best athletics directors, shocked Wake Forest followers when he fired head basketball coach Dino Gaudio. Gaudio accepted the head job after the tragic death of Skip Prosser, and Wellman admitted that Gaudio did a remarkable job under difficult circumstances. His Wake Forest teams won 61 games during his three-year term as head coach and reached a No. 1 Division I team national ranking. Wellman explained his controversial decision to fire Gaudio as "his own decision, based on the team's poor performance at the end of the season each of the three years and the fact that a promising team won only one post-season game in the ACC Tournament and the NCAA playoffs during Gaudio's three years as head coach" (Appenzeller, 2003).

Coach's Record for Coaching Football and Basketball 6–109–3

Winning big, not operating a clean program and graduating student-athletes appear to be the goals and when they are not met, firings occur. It is evident that Division I schools are expected to win and achieve national prominence. Compare a college that emphasizes academic values. Charles "Block" Smith, a 1934 graduate of Guilford College, was hired to coach basketball and football at Guilford, and assumed the duties of athletics director at the same time. Although Smith's record of basketball and football combined was 6–109–3, he was beloved by his players and the student body. We often wonder how long he would have remained as coach and athletics director in today's world.

In 1971, unlike the time of "Block" Smith's tenure, Guilford College finally fired its football coach after 32 straight losses. The reason given for terminating the coach was not the losing record but his refusal to recruit football prospects when the college went to a non-scholarship program of athletics (Appenzeller, 1987).

Grade Changing

The Texas Education Agency ruled that a principal deliberately changed the math grade of a football player to keep him from failing and being declared academically ineligible to participate in the state playoffs. Dallas Carter High School officials appealed the ruling and a state district court issued a temporary restraining order that enabled the school's team to win the rest of their games and the state championship. A state district court judge later upheld the ruling, stating that "it should be up to the individual school district to determine the outcome of grade disputes" (*San Antonio Light*, 2009).

Teacher Harassed after Star Player Received Failing Grade

A tenured English teacher came under attack when she failed the basketball team's star forward, rendering him ineligible for the rest of the season. The student rarely attended class and refused to do his homework. The basketball coach circulated a petition calling for the teacher's dismissal and a copy was published in the local newspaper. As the teacher was driving to work, someone fired a shot into her car. Bumper stickers were sold at the concession stands during games that read: "I didn't shoot Anne McGhee—I tried and missed."

The teacher gave in to overwhelming community and school pressure and changed the grade to a D+. Upset by the situation, depressed and fearing for her safety, the teacher sought psychiatric care and missed two and a half days of teaching. She was fired by the school board for missing school.

The teacher filed suit against the school board, and the Tennessee Supreme Court reinstated her and awarded her back pay (*McGhee v. Miller*, 1988). By allowing the star forward to play, even though he did not earn his grade in English, the principal, local school board and Campbell County, Tennessee made a statement about their priorities. It is clear that the emphasis in this case was the athlete-student and not the student-athlete.

A Short Cut to Division I Success

Some athletes expect passing grades without going to class on a regular basis. Some coaches assign staff members to check up on attendance for its "blue chip" athletes. The staff members go to the athletes' rooms to make sure they are up in time to go to class.

Sally Dear, an adjunct professor of human development at the State University of New York (SUNY) at Binghamton found herself in a campus-wide controversy when the school was attempting to make the leap in basketball from Division III to Division I. Dear went public and reported that she was pressured "to change her grading and attendance polices for basketball players." Binghamton is known for its excellent academics and its affordability, not for its athletics.

In 2007, Binghamton built an events center at a cost of $33.1 million and hired Kevin Broadus to coach men's basketball "with a mandate to go the for the gusto" (Applebome, 2009). Broadus recruited players who had talent for the game, but not for off-campus activities. He succeeded in taking his team to the NCAA playoffs for the first time, which was described by many students as "the coolest thing that ever happened at Binghamton" (Applebome, 2009).

Dear described the pressure she received "to give a pass to basketball players who didn't show up for class, came late and left early when they did." The university said she did not follow proper procedures for raising concerns and that her attendance policy should have been more flexible. Dear was "given the cold shoulder by a few colleagues, supported by others, and received encouraging e-mail messages from across the country" (Applebome, 2009).

The pressure to win may have encouraged Kevin Broadus to recruit athletes who already had academic problems at other schools. John Thompson, a successful coach who had a winning record and national championship at Georgetown University, praised Broadus for recruiting disadvantaged players and giving them an opportunity to succeed in college (Wieberg, 2009).

"Keep Quiet or I'll Be Fired"

An outstanding athlete was a freshman sensation at a Division I school, noted for its academic rigor. We discussed ethical behavior in sport and he immediately said, "Let me tell you about my professor and what she did this semester." He recalled a class in which the baseball team's star pitcher attended only a few classes the entire semester. The player did not show up for the final examination, to nobody's surprise. Word got out that the professor gave him a separate exam at a later date. She then realized how this exception to school policy looked and called her class together and pleaded with them not to tell anyone about her action. She said, "If you tell anyone about the favorable treatment of this athlete, I'll be fired." I do not believe her plan was honored, as word spread all over campus about her leniency for the star athlete.

On a Personal Note

My college football coach was a demanding task master who had total control of our team. No one challenged him for anything and from a discipline standpoint things went very well, without many, if any, incidents regarding what he expected of us. However, we all were surprised when three outstanding football players, who were starters on the team, disappeared on Monday before our opening game against George Washington University. We learned that they had gone to Connecticut to a cabin owned by one of the three players' parents. We were certain that the three would be cut from the team with a loss of their athletic scholarships. To our surprise, the trio returned on Friday of that week, kept their full scholarships and started in the opening game, which our school won 20–0.

Good conduct rules for sports teams vary from coach to coach, institution to institution. The rules can be complex or as simple as the one legendary Georgia Tech football coach, Bobby Dodd, had for his team. Coach Dodd was revered by his players, who were highly successful during his tenure at Georgia Tech. His one and only rule was: "Be a gentleman and go to church." Dodd believed if this rule was followed, success would follow for players who adhered to the rule. Most coaches develop rules based on their interpretation of ethical behavior.

Coach Sets Wrong Example

I asked a former athlete who was a high school football and basketball player if he remembered any incidents of ethical or unethical behavior during his high school and college days. "Yes," he immediately replied, "and one I will never forget." His high school basketball coach believed in "tough-love" discipline, and he insisted to his basketball team that any violation of his good conduct rules would result in swift and immediate punishment with absolutely no exceptions, star player or not. During the season, his team looked invincible and expected to win the state championship. One night a dance was held in the school's gymnasium, when suddenly four starters on the basketball team who were drunk threw cherry bombs through the glass windows, disrupting the dance and destroying property. The four were arrested by local police and taken to jail. The following day, the coach called his team together to discuss the problem. He started crying uncontrollably and said he knew what he had said about his good conduct rules, but, he said, "the boys who broke the rules could only come back and play if everyone on the team voted to bring them back—one dissent could disqualify the four boys." He also said he believed the team with these players who violated the rules could make it to a state championship. The vote was unanimous and the four were allowed to rejoin the team. As expected, the team went undefeated and won the state championship. The player I interviewed commented, "We all knew the coach was wrong in what he did, but we also knew we wanted to win the state championship and gave our coach what he wanted us to do." Looking back, he said, "We really lost respect for our coach because he was wrong when he could have used the incident to teach not only the guilty boys, but also the rest of the team at a crucial time in our lives. Three of the boys got in trouble after high school and stayed in trouble when we believed punishment for violating rules could have changed their lives for good." The player also said, "The coach we looked up to really changed our attitudes toward what we considered fair play."

No Exceptions for Outstanding Players

As athletics director at our college, I asked each coach to write their good conduct rules, which I would then get our Faculty Athletic Committee to approve. Our football coach said he appointed a committee made up of freshmen, sophomores, juniors and seniors to meet and recommend rules they believed represented the best rules for the team. When the student committee recommended the limited use of alcohol following a game, the coach vetoed the proposed rules and set his own. So much for his desire to let his team devise rules.

Another football coach several years later was a disciple of "tough love." He was an exceptional coach, but I had to constantly remind him to turn in his proposed rules. Finally, I asked for his rules to send to the Faculty Athletic Committee. He told me he wanted to make exceptions for any player who was outstanding. "If a second string quarterback violates my rules, I will dismiss him from the team, but if the quarterback is outstanding, I want to treat him with a different standard because the team and I will need him." We agreed, nevertheless, to write one set of rules for everyone, and he agreed to comply with the good conduct rules for the entire team. He led our team to a 8–2 season and the second bowl game in school history.

Ethical Questions

1. Are there any coaches who have had an influence on your career, personal life, etc.?
2. Should athletes be held to letters of intent or free to change their minds about colleges of their choice?
3. What is your opinion about coaches who cut an athlete's scholarship? When is it legitimate?
4. What is your opinion about parents suing coaches?
5. What is your opinion about coaches' techniques of motivation?
6. What is your opinion about rewards for winning coaches in today's economy?
7. How would you address the crisis on many campuses over the cost of an athletics program?
8. Should college coaches be paid as much as entertainers?
9. Does football cost too much?
10. Comment on Pepper Rodgers' 1980 salary and perks.
11. Comment on Doug Elliot's view of coaches' salaries.
12. Running up the score raises ethical questions but differs between coaches. What is your opinion?
13. How would you motivate an athlete to increase performance?
14. Would you permit coaches who have been fired for abuse to return to coaching?
15. Is the right to hire the right to fire?
16. Discuss the practice of keeping athletes eligible, specifically how it involves admission policies and educational exploitation.
17. Should Little League ban physical advantage or the ability to throw fast baseballs?
18. Should coaches make exceptions for exceptionally talented athletes?

Chapter 3

Financial Issues

"College football's best trick play is its pretense that it has nothing to do with money."—Michael Lewis (New York Times *2009*)

I started my teaching and coaching career at a small rural school in Wake County, North Carolina. My teaching salary for the year was $1,800 and my supplement for coaching basketball and baseball for the year was $225.

Our basketball team won the Wake County Championship and our baseball team had an outstanding record. I was approached by a principal of a school 12 miles from the one at which I was teaching and coaching. The principal offered me a supplement of $1,000 to coach for the year. This was unheard of in our county and it was a very attractive offer, particularly since I would have the opportunity to coach football, the sport I felt I knew the most from my playing days in high school and college.

I turned the job opportunity down because I wanted to continue coaching the returning student-athletes. The present school offered to match the $1,000 supplement offered by the school I turned down. I asked how they could pay this high supplement, and the answer surprised me. I was told the parents of my athletes had agreed to pay the supplement. I envisioned many problems with the arrangement, such as if a particular player did not get much playing time, would non-contributing parents feel that their son was penalized because they failed to pay anything toward my supplement? Or vice versa, if a large contributor's son got generous playing time, would it be suspected because of his parents' generosity? It was obvious that this plan had too many potential problems, some that had ethical ramifications. Therefore, the offer was turned down and the $225 supplement remained.

The principal at the school I had turned down, who I admired, made the identical offer the following year and I accepted the new job. A different problem developed at that school that had not been anticipated. Each year, all teachers at the school had to spend several days in the fall working at the school carnival. To make the carnival a financial success, it required the teachers to man booths and spend large blocks of their time. The teachers resented the work and dreaded the carnival. Later, I asked a simple question: where does this money go? The answer was quick and angry: "It goes to pay your coaching supplement." No one on the faculty or staff got a supplement to supervise any co-curricular activity at the school but me.

This was, in my opinion, an ethical concern. I determined to support every activity that our teachers sponsored and supervised. I attended every teachers meeting, school play and band concert, and made sure the teachers could count on not only my presence at their events, but also my constant support of their programs. This was my habit wherever I taught on the high school and college levels.

Can Sports Exist in Today's Economy?

Today, many school districts in the United States are struggling to fund extracurricular activities, especially sports. Until the 1970s, high school sports emphasized three sports: football, basketball and baseball. In 1972, the United States Congress passed the Educational Amendments Act, referred to as Title IX. Title IX mandated equity in women's sports for institutions receiving federal support. Title IX created a need for more interscholastic and intercollegiate teams, which required coaches, uniforms, facilities, equipment, officials and travel budgets. These new costs came without additional budget increases. In addition, sports such as track and field, wrestling, soccer, lacrosse, swimming, diving, tennis and golf became part of many interscholastic and intercollegiate sports programs.

In the 1970s, our college added 10 sports to the three traditional sports we offered to the men. My philosophy was to not add a sport until our students requested it. At that point, I would add the sport as a club sport, funded by the students. If the sport continued, we would elevate it to varsity status funded by the college. The coaches of our three men's sports were very upset because they were certain the new sports would cut the amount of their already small budgets. They were right because we lacked funds to hire a coach, purchase equipment, find a place to practice and play, travel, add insurance and generally attempt to maintain a team. Somehow, however, we added new sports and today, the same college sponsors 20 intercollegiate sports with unusual success.

In 1980, Dr. William Rogers left an endowed professorship in philosophy at Harvard to become the president of Guilford College. As I expected, he called a meeting with me to ask that I add crew to the athletics programs. He was pressured by students who wanted to participate in the sport of crew, so I reluctantly agreed to try to make it happen. Duke University offered to provide three shells at no expense. A former crew coach at the U.S. Naval Academy lived in our community and volunteered to coach at no cost, and three lakes in Greensboro agreed to let us practice and compete at any one of the three excellent facilities for $200. Everything was set until the seniors who wanted the sport graduated and suddenly there was no interest in the sport. If a renewed interest develops, there is still a crew file for the athletics director to follow to initiate the sport.

The administration agreed to add a sport only when there was sufficient student interest, a facility available to practice and play, a qualified coach, equipment, and an adequate budget necessary to field a team. This was a sound policy and one that could help a new sport succeed.

In many districts, the school board considers a tax to support a realistic sports program. However, taxes have been voted down consistently in many communities. Proposition 13 in California and Proposition 2½ in Massachusetts failed miserably. Dr. Harold van der Zwagg, professor of sport management at the University of Massachusetts Amherst, has predicted that a tax revolt would eliminate sports as we know them. Dr. van der Zwagg has also predicted that in lieu of tax increases, outside organizations such as YMCAs and YWCAs, Boys and Girls Clubs, and city and county recreation programs would replace the public schools as sponsors of sport (Appenzeller, 2003).

Many schools are requiring fees to participate in sports on the high school level. Others seek funds from local booster clubs. Dr. Tom Appenzeller, a youth sport expert, raises the question in an unpublished paper, "Is it time to turn the operation of sport programs to [such] outside agencies." He adds, "At some point, will we return to [such] a classical approach of education championed by Dr. Charles W. Eliot of Harvard and Robert Hutchens of the University of Chicago?" It will be interesting to follow the situation that confronts school administrations across the United States as they try to find solutions to an overwhelming problem (Appenzeller & Appenzeller, 2008).

Termination of Football Programs

Murray Sperber, an English professor at Indiana University, writes about the dilemma coaches face in the recruiting process of big-time athletics. In *Onward to Victory: The Crisis That Shaped College Football* (1998), Sperber relates a problem that Georgetown University faced with its football program in 1951. Father Guthrie, Georgetown's president at the time, explained why he dropped the school's illustrious football program, listing his reasons as:

1. It's a big business, exploiting a small number of students for the benefit of paying customers.

2. It forms no part of an honest educational system.
3. It has as much reason to subsist on the campus of an educational institution as a night club or a macaroni factory.
4. The athletics program is the training business for the NFL and NBA.

Father Guthrie concluded, "History, recent experience and common sense seem to vote unanimously in the negative for continuing the football program." The university later restored the football program to a Division III program that did not award football scholarships and competed on a lower level.

About a week after Georgetown terminated their football program, the *Saturday Evening Post* reported that Blair Cherry, at the height of his success as a winning football coach at the University of Texas, resigned. Cherry explained why in an article for the *Post* (1951) entitled, "Why I Quit Coaching." Cherry "denounced the corruption and hypocrisy in big-time college football—centered on the ferocious recruiting game." He commented, "It has become as much a problem to land a star-athlete as to elect a Congressman." He also said, "You have to devote more time recruiting than coaching." Cherry's pessimistic article in the *Saturday Evening Post* signaled his reasons for resigning at the height of his career.

Balancing Academics and Athletics

In his book *Beer and Circus*, Murray Sperber discusses Florida State University's high ranking as a football power along with its high rank as a "party school" throughout the nineties. Sperber is critical of FSU's low academic rating and its quality of undergraduate education. He criticizes FSU when he says:

> As a university with research ambitions, FSU has poured millions into its research and graduate programs. This school is the current national championship in college football, and a prime example of an institution that provides its students with beer and circus, and not much undergraduate education. If a beer and circus poll existed, FSU would be the national champion. (Sperber, 2000)

Sperber goes on to describe the "phenomenon of universities striving for research fame, neglecting undergraduate education, and promoting their college sports franchises" (Sperber, 2000). Sperber names many institutions that emphasize research and sports.

When I started graduate school toward my doctorate, I witnessed graduate students teaching undergraduate courses while the full-time professors spent their time with research and teaching graduate classes on a limited basis.

The Knight Commission calls the ever-increasing rise in costs of college sports unsustainable and "hopes it will 'restore balance' between academic and athletics expenditures across the nation." The Commission conducted an 18-month study of athletic finances and hopes its report will result in more fiscal responsibility. The study involved 97 public colleges that have major football programs. It found that spending for athletics between 2005 and 2008 increased from four to eleven times more than spending for academics. The Commission predicted that realignment of conferences will lead to "further escalation of athletic spending and ever greater imbalances of fiscal priorities" (Carey, 2010).

At Guilford College, a small liberal arts college, our outstanding professors taught freshman classes and carried full teaching loads. I was a full professor from the time I started, along with my duties as coach and as athletics director. To me, this was a plus for our undergraduate students. The institution supported my research in sport law and sport management that led to 21 books. The school's philosophy of education was evident in the emphasis on strong and capable teaching for all students.

University of South Carolina Athletics to Assist Academics

Athletics Director Erick Hyman has announced that the University of South Carolina is committing $15 million in athletic funding over the next 15 years to the school's academic programs. Hyman attributed the move to the lucrative media deals the Southeastern Conference (SEC) schools have obtained. He reported that the university received $10.6 million from the SEC for its 2008–09 budget. In addition to arrangements with ESPN and CBS, the projected income to the university will be $16 million. The ESPN deal alone will result in over $2 billion in income to NCAA schools. The amount with CBS has not yet been disclosed (*News-Sentinel*, 2010).

Hyman said that the influx of money made the decision to help the academic programs an easy one. Sources say that the money will be used for programs such as the "Gamecock Guarantee," a need-based program which is designed to help students of families with incomes of $25,000 or less. In addition, the funds will help 3,000 graduate students with university assistantships who face economic problems when families lose jobs and can't afford the escalating costs of college (*News-Sentinel*, 2010).

Recruiting Weekend Cost $140,875.99

The media in Oregon, under the state public records law, reported that 25 high school football recruits cost Oregon University $140,875.99 ($6,635 per recruit) for a three-day recruiting trip. The report noted that the recruits would "stay at the Hilton Hotel, dine on made-to-order omelets, chat with professors, tour the campus, dine on steak, bear witness to all of the bells and whistles of Oregon's high tech athletic machine, dine on more steak and lobster, play paint ball and get a glimpse at Phil Knight's Autzen Stadium's toilet." Four jets were used that weekend. When several prospects could not catch the charter planes they flew commercial jets at a cost of $10,009.72 each. Former football coach Mike Bellotti said, "The extravagance was intended to make them feel special" (White, 2004).

Georgia Signs $92.8 Million Media Rights Deal

ISP Sports and the University of Georgia agreed to an eight-year, $92.8 million marketing deal. This is one of the most lucrative guaranteed deals in college athletics. ISP Sports will be responsible for Georgia's radio broadcasts and coaches show, and TV and digital rights. University officials believe the Georgia contract with ISP is comparable to the one Ohio State University has with IMG for at least $110 million over 10 years. It is also comparable to the University of Florida's deal with Sun Sports and IMG for $100 million over ten years (*From the Gym to the Jury*, 1999).

Memphis University Taps Beer Revenue

The University of Memphis has started selling beer at its home football games. The City of Memphis spent $5 million to upgrade the stadium, but expected a loss of $261,000 in general operating costs. City officials believe the sale of beer will net the city $200,000, helping to reduce the deficit. University of Memphis athletics director R.C. Johnson said he understands why city officials have decided to sell beer at football games, but is not sure the $200,000 estimate of net profit is realistic. "Football is built so much around tailgating, and getting there early. In fact, our problem is getting the tailgaters to come in ... I guess we'll see how it goes. I think if it was a cure-all for everything, most schools would do it, and not all schools do it" (Morgan, 2009).

Are Athletic Scholarships Unethical?

In 1956, I received a telephone call from a local businessman who was on the board of trustees at Guilford College. His message was direct and emphatic: "It's time for you to come to Guilford College." I was flattered and interested in Guilford College because the junior college where I was teaching and coaching had sent many of their students and student-athletes to Guilford, a school with high academic standards and Quaker values. However, I had just built a house because I planned to stay there indefinitely. We had four winning seasons in football and won four out of five post-season appearances. Our basketball teams were the best in school history, and our baseball and football teams had won Conference championships. Morale was high, our student-athletes happy with the college and our president and faculty supportive of the entire athletics program.

After I explained this to the trustee, Edwin P. Brown, who owned Georgia Pacific, he responded: "I'll buy your house." I was, for all intents and purposes, hired over the telephone with one condition—approval from the Guilford College president and his search committee. I agreed to visit Guilford College and interview with the group. After three trips of 400 miles from Murfreesboro to Greensboro, North Carolina, I still had not received approval for the position of athletics director and head football coach. I asked the president what they were looking for in the position. The president, Dr. Clyde Milner, was reluctant to tell me that the committee wanted someone with a name in a particular sport. My immediate reply was, "I'm glad you told me—I hold the record for the longest intercepted pass, 98 yards, in Gator Bowl history." I signed a contract that day.

Ten years later, a student writing for the school paper wrote a story about me. He wrote, "Let's clear up the interception that set a record." He continued, "Herb Appenzeller did not intercept the football and run for 98 yards and a touchdown, he threw the ball!" I had never told the whole story, just the part about the record. Today, 64 years later, the record still stands, even though some pass-oriented teams throw 39 and 49 passes in a game. I often question whether my early response to the search committee was unethical conduct on my part. I leave this to the reader to decide!

When I accepted the position of athletics director and head football coach at Guilford College, we had no athletic scholarships in a conference that permitted 45 full football scholarships, 10 full basketball scholarships and two for baseball. Guilford College had no athletic scholarships, instead 35 need-based grants for the three sports. I allocated 22 of the $300 need grants for football, eight for basketball and two for baseball. The need-based grants had the following requirements:

1. Absolute need, based on parents' income.
2. No automobile.
3. A "C" average each semester.

Any violation of the three requirements would remove the need grant.

Six years later, in 1962, the administration made a drastic decision: Guilford College would drop intercollegiate athletics after 74 years, during which the college sports teams had unusual success.

The Administrative Council called a meeting to issue to the media the new policy that there would be an intramural program replacing athletics. When I entered the room, I asked where our Faculty Athletic Chairman (FAC) E. Garness Purdom was, and I was told, "He's teaching his physics class and cannot be disturbed." I left the room and ran to King Hall, where our FAC was holding class. He immediately dismissed his class and literally ran to the president's office. He registered such a strong dissent that the Administrative Council very reluctantly decided to hold the media announcement and select a committee to study the entire athletics program.

The college accepted the recommendation of the Ad Hoc Committee and agreed to provide a limited number of athletic grants, which would be funded one-third by the college, one-third by three trustees, and one-third by the Quaker Club (the booster club of the college). Football, basketball and baseball would be the sports that would receive these scholarships, beginning in 1964.

College Booster Clubs

T. Boone Pickens, a retired oil man and investor, gave his *alma mater* Oklahoma State University (OSU) $165 million for its athletics program. For years, boosters have influenced the hiring and firing of coaches, athletics directors and even college presidents. Regarding the huge gift to OSU, Pickens said, "With a gift like that, … of course they're going to be respectful, and I'm going to be asked my opinion on things" (Brady, 2008).

Shelton Steinbach, former general counsel of the American Council on Education, said, "The idea donors get some deference should come as no surprise. Money buys influence in many spheres" (Brady, 2008). Pickens has repeatedly said that he wants OSU to be competitive in athletics and academics. His name is not only on the football stadium but also on the School of Geology.

Brit Kirwan, University of Maryland System Chancellor, is co-chairman of the Knight Commission, which urges reform in college athletics. Kirwan sees danger in boosters giving money for exorbitant salaries to attract top coaches. He thinks colleges are at risk of Congress stepping in and questioning tax-exempt status when coaches are paid multimillion-dollar contracts funded in large part by donors who get tax write-offs (Brady, 2008).

Big-Time College Football Coaches Sequester Teams at Hotels Before Home Games

Coaches at all levels prefer to monitor their teams when they have a home game the following day. They complain that life in the residence halls on campus is often hectic on weekends, with noise until early morning and parties that are loud and boisterous. Schools with big-time aspirations frequently sequester their football teams in first-class hotels that are quiet (unless they are by an airport) and have free HBO and few distractions. The practice, in all probability, came from professional football teams in the NFL, where money is not a major problem.

This expense seems excessive to many administrators at a time when universities are facing a financial crisis. The Raleigh *News & Observer* reported that during the 2008 football season, North Carolina State University spent $85,923.79 and UNC Chapel Hill spent $78.627.95 before their home games. (The figure includes the cost of transportation to and from the campus to the hotel.) Clemson University topped the list by spending $110,000 on hotel stays before home games.

One of the arguments made by coaches in favor of "Friday night sleep-outs" is that they are used to recruit prospective athletes. Former Florida State coach Bobby Bowden said the school participates in them even though he says "they're not a necessity." Bowden said that he would only give them up if everyone else did. Such is the power of recruiting. With universities laying off employees and cutting educational budgets drastically, such expenses for hotel rooms and chartered buses raise ethical questions for all concerned (Tysiac, 2009).

As a side observation about recruiting, many Division I schools with big-time athletics programs require the parents of their athletes to use their insurance policies to be the primary source of insurance. The parents pay whatever their policy covers and the schools pay the remainder of the bill up to the limits of their insurance coverage. Some coaches of various sports tell recruits that they do not require parental coverage as the primary source of insurance. They use this to get an edge when engaged in a recruiting battle with a school that requires parental coverage.

North Carolina Legislature Attempted to Save Booster Clubs $9.4 Million

North Carolina lawmakers faced a huge deficit in their 2009–10 budget. The $19 million budget needed painful but necessary cuts. Legislators raised taxes on alcohol and cigarettes to maintain education as a top priority. It also relied on a one-cent sales tax increase to raise revenue. School districts were forced to cut $225 million from their budgets, thereby increasing class size and eliminating many teaching jobs.

In light of the cost-cutting methods to try to balance the budget, "the biggest outrage of all may be the preservation of more than $10 million for a tuition break that allows all full-scholarship students from out of state to qualify for in-state tuition" (*News & Record*, 2010). This means that athletes from out of state will benefit from the exception, and booster clubs at N.C. State, UNC Chapel Hill and Appalachian State, as well as other schools that have football, will save money. With the number of out-of-state athletes at North Carolina's schools, booster clubs would save considerable money at the expense of worthwhile programs that are eliminated to save money. Many people questioned the action or inaction of the General Assembly for its shameful and indefensible policies.

Because of the outcry of citizens violently opposed to the legislature's ruling, the House of Representatives and the Senate reversed their previous decision in June 2010. Booster clubs will now be called on to make up the difference in cost for their out-of-state scholarship players (*News & Record*, 2010).

Sources of Revenue for Athletics

Today, marketing has become a large part of an urgent push to raise revenue in the athletics programs, as well as other areas of college. The first NCAA basketball tournament held at Northwestern University's Patten Gymnasium attracted 15,000 fans and lost money. In 2009, the NCAA tournament had a 70,000 seat venue at Ford Field in Detroit, Michigan, and now is a mega-event comparable to the NFL's Super Bowl. The late Myles Brand, former NCAA President, once said, "College athletics are not big business." He changed his opinion soon after he took over as NCAA President. Brand gave his blessing for many schools to utilize sponsors and advertisers. He even allowed schools to utilize advertising and promotions by casinos, a practice once frowned-on by the NCAA because of the threat of gambling (Wieberg & Berkowitz, 2009).

Naming rights for arenas and stadiums are for sale at many colleges. At Wake Forest University in Winston-Salem, North Carolina, the football field is now called BB&T field. Maryland's Comcast Center, Texas Tech's Jones AT&T Stadium and San Diego's Jenny Craig Pavilion are examples of corporate sponsors and methods to raise revenue for athletics programs. Comcast agreed to pay Maryland $20 million over 10 years to have its name on the basketball arena.

Athletics programs have turned to various ways to increase revenue because raising ticket prices is unpopular among alumni and fans. Instead, they opt for naming rights for arenas and stadiums, as well as signage, much like NASCAR. Trademark and licensing fees, and digital media rights and advertising are also popular ways to increase revenue.

Kansas University reviewed its contract with Nike and felt it was undervalued, so it switched to Adidas and more than doubled its revenue in a new eight-year, $26.7 million contract. In 2007, 35 schools had received a combined total of $117 billion by handling their media rights.

New Mexico University signed a five-year agreement for $2.5 million that makes the Route 66 Casino Hotel, operated by the Laguno Pueblo Native American tribe, its "exclusive gaming sponsor" (Wieberg & Berkowitz, 2009). Although the NCAA does not accept advertising from "organizations or companies primarily involved in gambling or gaming business activities," it allows colleges to do so (Wieberg & Berkowitz, 2009).

The Route 66 Casino Hotel "can post exclusive signs at The Pit, University Stadium and other campus sports venues, with advertising and promotional materials at football, men and women's basketball, soccer, baseball and volleyball events" (*The Associated Press*, 2008). When asked if having a casino as a business partner presents any problems for the university, University President David Schmidly replied, "They don't do any gambling on sports events or things of that nature, so I think it's a win-win." Athletics director Paul Krebs described the agreement as a "generous financial commitment … that will benefit hundreds of UNM student-athletes for many years" (*The Associated Press*, 2008).

Writer Deplores the Status of College Sports Today

Michael Lewis, writing in the *New York Times* (2007), deplores the status of college sports today. He believes that "college football's best trick play is its pretense that it has nothing to do with money, that it's simply an extension of the university's mission to educate its students" (Lewis, 2007).

Lewis asks, "why [are] these enterprises that have nothing to do with education and everything to do with profits exempt from paying taxes? Or why don't they pay their employees?" He notes that everyone involved in the operation of football is getting rich except the people who do the work. He observes that the National Collegiate Athletic Association (NCAA) sits between the buyer and the seller "to ensure that the universities it polices keep all the money for themselves—to make sure that the rich white folk do not slip as much as a free chicken sandwich under the table to the poor black kids" (Lewis, 2007). According to the NCAA, college sports should not be commercialized. However, they already are for everyone except those who play the game.

Lewis made an interesting comment when he said, "If the NCAA genuinely wanted to take the money out of college football it'd make the tickets free and broadcast the games on public television and set limits on how much universities could pay head coaches" (Lewis, 2007).

Vanderbilt Upgrades Sports Program by $60 Million

Vanderbilt University, well known for its academic excellence, has been criticized by other Southeastern Conference (SEC) schools for a lack of commitment to its athletics program. In an attempt to upgrade its athletics program, the university approved nearly $60 million to improve its facilities and other aspects of the program (Patton, 2008).

Recession Lingers, but SEC and Big Ten Prosper

The current economy in the United States is reminiscent of the Great Depression, and athletics programs face cutbacks in the budgets. However, the Southeastern Conference (SEC) and the Big Ten are leading all conferences in obtaining profitable media rights. The SEC has negotiated a deal for media rights of $206 million-plus over 15 years from ESPN. The Big Ten is looking at a similar package. According to Big 12 Commissioner Dan Beebe, "There's a concern and awareness of the possibility of being left behind to some degree" (McCarthy & Wieberg, 2009).

Unique Ways to Handle Budgets

When I was coaching college football, I once stopped by the athletics department of a rival school at the end of the school year and visited with the football coach, who was a good friend. He took me into his equipment room and to my surprise, there was a large wall with over 50 shelves filled with never used footballs. I asked why he had so many game balls. He told me that he had several thousand dollars left over in his budget, and the college had a fiscal policy that took money left over and put it in a general fund. Rather than give up the money, he purchased over 50 game footballs that were the brand used by our conference. He asked if I would buy 10 or 12 at a reduced price. He estimated that he would get enough "buyers" to give him a start on his next year's budget. It was certainly a unique way to get his upcoming budget off to a good start.

An athletics director at another nearby university once told me that he faced a dilemma with his coaches regarding their budgets. Almost everyone had little money left in their athletics budget and several exceeded their budgets by a large amount. This university also had a policy that any surplus money left in an individual sports budget would be turned in to a general fund. The athletics director was frustrated with coaches who exceeded their budgets, so he got permission from the business manager to implement a new policy for athletics: any coach who had money left over in his/her athletic budget could carry over the amount and start the following year with extra money. Also, any coach who exceeded his/her budget would have that amount taken away from the upcoming year's budget. The athletics director told me the following year that the new policy worked and he did not have any coaches exceeding their budgets.

New Alliances Changing College Sports

Speculation is growing over the reshaping of college conferences, which will dramatically change the face of sports as we know them. The decision by established conferences to add schools to their memberships is simply driven by money. The new alliances are "aimed largely at increasing television revenue from the schools' football programs" (Garcia, 2010). Nebraska, once a member of the Big 12, has decided to join the Big Ten. Colorado has left the Big 12 to join the Pac-10, a conference that had not added a school since 1978 (Garcia, 2010). Utah University also accepted an invitation to join the Pac-10, leaving the Mountain West Conference. Athletics Director Chris Hill said, "Today is an absolutely great day to be a Ute" (Smith, 2010).

For years, athletics advocates preached loyalty as a benefit and characteristic of sport. However, it is evident that loyalty to a conference is not a consideration today—instead "it's about who brings the most value to the table," according to Karen Weaver, athletics director at Penn State-Abington, who also wrote a doctoral thesis on the launch of the Big Ten Network. Joe Tiller, former Purdue football coach, echoes her sentiment when he says, "Who are we kidding? It's all about the money. It's not necessarily what's good for the sport; it's all about the money" (Garcia, 2010).

Jim Delaney, Big Ten Commissioner, acknowledges that the Big Ten Network is a reason to expand, but also has said that "academics are a top priority." Andrew Zimbalist, economics professor at Smith College, said of the Big Ten's repeated emphasis on academics, "Of course they're going to say that." He points to the Big Ten's acceptance of Nebraska, saying, "If the Big Ten truly valued academics, it would not pick Nebraska" since its academics are not "on par with those of Michigan, Illinois and other Big Ten schools." Zimbalist points out, "What's happened over the decades, more so in the last two, commercial value has trumped academic value, and that's decidedly wrong." While he understands that schools face financial pressure, Zimablist insists that "it doesn't mean that it's the right thing to do to subject yourself to the needs of TV and media" (Garcia, 2010).

Longhorn Network

The University of Texas athletics department has launched the Longhorn Network, a "24-hour cable channel devoted to coverage of University of Texas sports and educational programming" (Finger, 2011). A major investment, the network is meant to be a new source of revenue for the university. When it was announced that the network was being developed, Texas women's athletics director Chris Plonsky said, "In order to survive with college athletics well into this century, we have to be thinking not only how athletics looks, but how higher education will be teaching people in five, 10 years. Digital technology and media are taking us there" (Bohls & Rosner, 2010).

Superconference Chaos Postponed, for Now

The University of Texas declined an invitation to leave the Big 12 and join the Big Ten or Pac-10. Texas' decision to stay in the Big 12 prevented a domino effect that would have impacted not only the Big 12, but also the Big East, the

ACC, and probably the SEC. For the time being, at least, a forecast of a "football Armageddon" has been put on hold, due to the action of Texas (*From the Gym to the Jury*, 2010).

In a *USA Today* (2010), article, Michael Hiestand suggests that Texas's decision to stay in the Big 12 is only postponing the inevitable. Hiestand recommends that the top schools organize a long-awaited conference of football's powerhouse programs. He names big-market schools such as "Texas, Florida, Ohio State, Southern California" who have TV appeal and marketability, rather than "quaint 20th-century notions such as tradition, geography and even truth-in-labeling." Hiestand admits that schools excluded from a new power league might try to get the power schools out of the lucrative NCAA men's basketball tournament, but also suggests that the new league would eliminate the BCS controversy. He urges college football to form the power league today and avoid the inevitable (Hiestand, 2010).

Austin Murphy, writing in *Sports Illustrated* (2010), responded to the question of what happened to college football, in reference to conference realignment, when he concluded:

> Superconferences, though not here yet, are coming. Texas is college football's new kingmaker. Coveted by the SEC, Big Ten and Pac-10 alike, the Longhorns can call their own shot. In 2008, ... Texas led the nation in total athletic revenue, amassing a jaw-dropping $138.4 million—almost $20 million more than second-place Ohio State.

The Longhorns concluded that they've "got a pretty good thing going in this conference" (Murphy, 2010).

It will be interesting to follow the developments of existing conferences attempting to create a superconference of 16 schools. When the time arrives for superconferences to emerge, the roles of the NCAA and BCS Bowl recipients will possibly be diminished or restricted.

Michael Jordan and Charlotte Bobcats Fund Middle School Athletics

When Michael Jordan bought the Charlotte Bobcats of the National Basketball Association, he talked about contributing to the community in a positive way. Charlotte schools had to cut $1.25 million from their athletics program and are charging middle schoolers $50 and high schoolers $100 to play a sport. Jordan and the Bobcats donated $250,000 to subsidize the athletics programs in middle schools in Charlotte (*From the Gym to the Jury*, 2010). Jordan, a University of North Carolina alumnus, has always believed in athletics in middle schools. More states are eliminating middle school athletics due to the budget crunch and this is a tragic loss to many students who need the middle school athletics experience. I applaud Jordan for his generosity.

The University of North Carolina at Chapel Hill Signs Lucrative Pact with Nike

The University of North Carolina at Chapel Hill (UNC) signed a 10-year, $37 million contract with Nike. All 28 sports in the program will receive funding, with much of the money for apparel and equipment, and all 19 coaches in the athletics program will have individual deals with Nike The former UNC-Nike contract, signed in 2001, included separate contracts with seven coaches: football, men's and women's basketball, men's and women's soccer, track and field and baseball (*From the Gym to the Jury*, 2010).

Athletics director Dick Baddour said that he had been working on the Nike contract for over a year and considered it to be a priority. He noted that the new contract will be a bonus for Olympic sports such as field hockey and women's lacrosse that have experienced national success. Baddour pointed out that the funding amounts "are in balance with [coaches'] salaries," and broke the contract down as follows:

- $31.6 million—ranging from $2.8 million in the first year of the contract, to $3.4 million in the tenth—for uniforms, coaching gear, shoes, balls and other equipment for all teams. In past years, Baddour said, some teams had to pay for some of those items out of their operating budgets, but the increase in this contract should cover it all.
- $2 million for the Chancellor's Academic Enhancement Fund, an increase of $1.2 million over the last contract. Chancellor Holden Thorp will direct the funds to faculty support, according to the news release, which should help at a time when the university is facing serious budget cuts.
- $1.625 million for team travel and trips.
- $1 million for signing the contract; those funds will be used to overhaul the lighting and sound systems at the Smith Center.
- $1 million to fund bonus payments to the coaches based on achievements and excellence by their respective student-athletes in the classroom and on their fields of play.

- $450,000 for university-sponsored tournaments (*From the Gym to the Jury*, 2010).

High School Football Power Signs Uniform Deal with Nike

Since 1996, the Maryville, Tennessee High School football team had worn the same uniforms and their coach, George Quarles, thought it was time to change. In 2008, the Maryville City School Board gave its approval to a three-year deal with Nike. The team was the first high school in the state of Tennessee to sign such an agreement with Nike. Nike and Maryville agreed that the football team would wear Nike uniforms, and that its coaches would wear Nike gear on the sidelines during practice and at games. Coach Quarles said that all other teams at Maryville can use Nike clothing if they like, but to date, the basketball team is the only one that does so. Nike has encouraged Maryville to play other schools who wear Nike products. Other sporting goods companies tried to convince Maryville to join them in a separate deal, but Nike was the favorite, winning the contract (*News-Sentinel*, 2008).

Nike Deal: "Just Do It" Bigger

Nike and the Public High School Sports Association of Texas have agreed to sign a deal "to make Nike, Inc. its official brand." The arrangement will be a lucrative one in terms of revenue and discounts on equipment such as footwear, uniforms and apparel for 1,300 member schools. The schools are not required to use Nike products, but if Nike products are used, member schools will receive discounts on those items (*From the Gym to the Jury*, 2011).

Defections Called "Selfish" as Fresno State and Nevada Leave WAC

Karl Benson, Commissioner of the Western Athletic Conference (WAC), described the move of Nevada and Fresno State from the WAC to the Mountain West Conference as "selfish" (*USA Today* 2010). The departure of Nevada and Fresno State in August 2010, and of Boise State earlier that summer, has left the remaining WAC schools confused and worried about the future of the league. BYU has been thinking of going independent, which could leave the WAC with potentially only six schools, when eight are needed to continue as a major football conference. Benson said the remainder of the league "will begin immediately to target schools" from other conferences. It will be interesting to follow the various moves schools will make regarding conference affiliations, but, at this moment, the WAC is on the verge of failing to qualify as a major football conference (O'Toole, 2010).

A School in Delaware Under Scrutiny

Red Lion Christian Academy received national attention when one of its students, 13-year-old David Sills V, committed to play football at the University of Southern California. Red Lion's head football coach said in 2007 that they "want to be a nationally recognized program within the next four years," even though their football program was only started in 2004 (Tresolini, 2010). The Delaware Interscholastic Athletic Association (DIAA) has launched an investigation of the sports program. Kevin Charles, DIAA Executive Director, reported allegations of improper procedures in the Red Lion athletics program that include:

1. School officials pressuring teachers to keep a player eligible.
2. Recruiting students for the athletics program.
3. Providing scholarships and housing for incoming athletes.
4. Practicing out of season.
5. Using ineligible players.
6. Playing too many middle school games in a season.

If the allegations prove to be true, Red Lion "could face fines, game forfeitures, sanctions against players or coaches, prohibition from state tournaments and even the suspension of sports programs" (Tresolini, 2010). Red Lion superintendent Shannon Dare said the only legitimate allegation was "playing one too many middle school football games last season" (Tresolini, 2010).

Scholarships for students unable to pay the cost of attending Red Lion are available from a foundation co-founded by David Sills IV, the father of the 13-year-old quarterback. David Sills IV has a commercial contracting company that "built the Pusey Center gymnasium and upper school addition ... before [his son] became more actively involved in athletics. Since Sills V became involved in the school's athletics program, Sills IV's company "has built a wrestling building, Lions stadium and a football practice field," which he said were "personal donations" (Tresolini, 2010).

Atlantic Coast Conference Signs 12-Year Deal for $1.86 Billion

Under the leadership of Commissioner John Swofford, the Atlantic Coast Conference (ACC) signed a TV deal for 12 years with a payoff of $1.86 billion dollars. Gerald Witt wrote in an editorial for *News & Record* (2010) that the ACC "produces a very good product and deserves to be paid for it." Witt reported that the lucrative deal will double the average take for each school in the conference. He noted that "the contract involves all sports, but revolves around the familiar cash cows, football and basketball" (*From the Gym to the Jury*, 2010).

NC State's Director of Athletics, Dr. Deborah Yow, put the revenue in the right perspective when she said, "The athletics program will never have to come hat-in-hand to the university and say we need help" (*From the Gym to the Jury*, 2010). NC State will get an additional $13 million per year. This revenue will pay for the out-of-state athletes, who cost more to the universities, and was voted down in reversal by the NC Legislature in July 2010.

High Cost of College

At Pomona College, tuition is $38,394, not including room and board. This is 2.9 times what the top-flight liberal arts college charged in 1980. However, according to Andrew Hacker and Claudia Dreifus, writing in the *Los Angeles Times* (2010), this is the norm for the massive tuition increases colleges are charging today. Williams College in New England charges $41,434, or 3.2 times the cost in 1980. University of Southern California's cost of tuition is $41,022, a 3.6 multiple of the 1980 bill. Tuition at public universities has escalated even more as the "University of Illinois' current $13,658 is six times its 1980 rate after adjusting for inflation. San Jose State's $6,250 is a whopping 11 times more" (Hacker & Dreifus 2010).

Hacker and Dreifus point to athletics spending as one of the reasons for the high cost of education at many colleges. They refer to volleyball teams that travel extensively and have high coaches salaries and "customized uniforms." There are 132 more colleges that sponsor football than there were in 1980, for a total of 629 schools. All but 14 lose money. The average size of college football teams has also increased dramatically as specialization has become a trademark for today's squads. The cost of sports continues to rise, and "because there are no revenues for most sports, the deficits often have to be covered by tuition bills" (Hacker & Dreifus 2010).

Hacker and Dreifes, in their book, *Higher Education: How Colleges Are Wasting Our Money and Failing Our Kids—and What We Can Do About It?*, sum up the current problem when they write:

> The travesty of high tuition is that most of the extra charges aren't going for education. Administrators, athletics and amenities get funded, while history departments are denied new assistant professors. A whole generation of young Americans is being short changed largely by adults who have carved out good careers at places we call colleges.

Tennessee Gets Out of UNC Series by Paying $750,000

The University of Tennessee wanted to back out of a 2011–12 contract with the University of North Carolina at Chapel Hill. Tennessee Athletics Director Mike Hamilton said that Tennessee's 2011 football schedule "[had] Cincinnati before the Vols travel to Florida and UNC, home games against Georgia, LSU and a trip to Alabama." Hamilton explained the reason for dropping UNC in 2011 as follows: "Going into the season having two BCS non-conference opponents is problematic when you're trying to rebuild a team." Tennessee paid $750,000 for a buyout with UNC (*News & Record*, 2010).

Dropping an Opponent Breaks Contract

The University of Louisville was dropped by Duke University several years ago and a lawsuit for breach of contract was filed against Duke. A judge said the two programs were not compatible, citing losing records for several years, and held that Duke could therefore drop the University of Louisville without penalty.

As athletics director at Guilford College, I scheduled Furman University after they reportedly were dropping from Division I in football to a non-scholarship program. The game was set for several years later when Division III status would have time to take over. However, by the time we were scheduled to play Furman University, they had decided to go back to Division I in football, and had a large number of football scholarships. We decided to play them anyway and the game was one-sided in favor of Furman. I believe we honored our contract, as well we should, and I believe that Duke should have compensated Louisville for breaking the contract. Today, Duke's football program is getting stronger and could compete with the University of Louisville.

University of California at Berkeley Faces Budget Scrutiny, Cuts Sports

In November 2009, University of California Berkeley computer science professor Brian Barsky and seven other professors at the university asked Chancellor Robert J. Birgeneau to stop subsidizing the athletics department, and to create a plan that would pay off the department's debt and keep it permanently out of the red. The university's academic senate met to discuss the resolution. Athletics director Sandy Barbour issued a 22-page report on the state of athletics funding at the university and sent it to the academic senate. Her report revealed a $5.8 million deficit for 2008–09 and projected a $6.4 million shortfall for the 2009–10 budget year. At the time, Barbour said the department would begin repaying the debt that year (Carey & Wieberg, 2009).

In 2009, Berkeley saw budget reductions of almost $150 million, resulting in layoffs of faculty and staff, dropped courses and the institution of a furlough program. Professor Barsky contended that the multi-millions spent to prop up the athletics program, which in his opinion should be self-sustaining, represent a misplaced priority by the university. He argued that if athletics are being subsidized while academic programs are being cut, it upholds the message that athletics are more important than academics on campus (Carey & Wieberg, 2009).

As a result of the "drastic reductions in state higher-education funding in California," and its athletic budget increasing from $7.4 million in 2007–08 to $12.1 million in 2009–10, Berkeley decided to eliminate five of its varsity sports. Barbour called the decision to discontinue men's and women's gymnastics, women's lacrosse, baseball, and men's rugby "very painful." Chancellor Robert Birgeneau said, "The situation has raised heated debate about the size and cost of our Intercollegiate Athletics program" (Berkowitz, 2010).

The move by Cal shows that no athletics program on the national level is immune from severe budget cuts that may lead to the elimination of various sports. Washington, Arizona State and UCLA have previously dropped sports, but none eliminated more than three. When the Pac-10 conference expands to 12 schools in 2011–12, only Cal and Colorado will be the only schools without baseball (Berkowitz, 2010).

Keeping Up With the Joneses

Cal Athletics Director Sandy Barbour previously said that the subsidies to the athletics department were essential if the university was to keep up with its opponents. It is difficult to see how the athletics department will begin paying back loans advanced to them by the university. Keeping up with the Joneses has always been a problem for athletic departments. As long as an administrator tries to stay on a level financial field, the keeping up with others will continue to be a major problem.

When I was an athletics director without any athletic grants, our school finally became competitive when the conference schools agreed to reduce the number of football, basketball and baseball scholarships for each member school. This reduction by the conference schools allowed us to give a limited number of grants and become competitive.

Some years ago, the Big Ten schools decided to forego need-based athletic scholarships. This noble plan was praised by the conference faculty and administrators as the right thing to do. However, before it could work, Big Ten schools faced pressure to return to athletic grants so that they could compete with non-conference opponents who were not limited to need grants.

Student Fees Boost College Sports

A *USA Today* article (2010) reported that student fees are supporting ever-expanding athletics teams for schools in NCAA Division I. According to the article, "the amounts going to athletics are soaring, and account for as much as 23% of the required annual bill for in-state students" (Berkowitz et al., 2010). Student fees at 222 Division I public schools totaled $795 million for the 2008–09 school year. This amount represents an increase of 18% since 2005, adjusting for inflation, contributing to the increasing cost of higher education at public schools.

A parent of a student at Radford University in Virginia estimates that her daughter paid $5,000 for her athletic fees during her four years at the school. The parent said her daughter "is not a 'die-hard' follower of the Highlanders sports teams" (Berkowitz et al., 2010).

For years, some students at colleges and universities have objected to fees that are charged to them and used by the athletics programs. Jack Boyle, vice president for business affairs and finance at Cleveland State University, answered the question of why some schools don't reveal how much students pay toward athletics, to try to avoid controversy. Boyle was direct and to the point when he said, "Why would you? ... Whenever we spell something out, somebody decides they don't want that service. We don't spell out in tuition that 1.8% of it goes to run the religion department. 'I'm an atheist. Why should I pay for them I'd never go to any of their courses.'"

However, paying a fee for athletics is not always a problem for students. At James Madison University in Virginia, Andrew Reese, the president of the student body, said that "'it's not cause for much concern for (students)' because the school provides free admission to events, puts students in prime seating areas and 'athletics is a large part of the student culture.'" (Berkowitz et al., 2010). (When the James Madison football team upset heavily favored Virginia Tech in 2010, I am sure student fees for athletics were not mentioned by the students.)

For years, objection to student fees for athletics has been a source of concern to many university officials. In *Moye v. Board of Trustees of University of South Carolina* (1970), the University of South Carolina wanted to expand and improve the football stadium and sought a method to do so. In 1970, the General Assembly of South Carolina passed an Act that gave the Board of Trustees of the university the authorization to issue "special obligation bonds" that would provide five million dollars for Carolina Stadium. The Trustees decided to add a specific fee for all regular, full-time, degree-seeking students, excluding summer school students (Appenzeller, 1975).

University of South Carolina student Richard Moye and his father expressed dissatisfaction with the proposed fee and sued the University's Board of Trustees and the Attorney General of South Carolina. The Moyes claimed that enlarging the football stadium was certainly not an educational function. The plaintiffs then used the argument that still prevails today on many campuses, when they reasoned that they did not use the facility or attend the games, so why would they pay fees (Appenzeller, 1975). The Moyes also contended that Carolina Stadium was already large enough for the entire student body.

The Supreme Court of South Carolina very forcefully held that:

> A university, by its very nature, is a highly diversified institution whose aim is the highest development, mentally and physically, of those who repair there to pursue excellence in their chosen fields. Indeed one of widely recognized criteria for judging the quality of a university is the breadth of activities, academic, social and athletic which it is able to offer both its students and the state of which it is an integral and vital part. The modern university is a monument to the ideas that the greatest benefit will be derived when men are free to choose among a variety of possible pursuits, to follow those which they find appealing, and to test themselves and their ideas in an atmosphere of tolerance and cooperation. (*Moye v. Board of Trustees of University of South Carolina*, 1970)

The South Carolina Court then referred to a Texas case, *Ramirez v. Malone* (1940), in which students objected to, but were overruled for challenging, the payment of fees to the student union. The South Carolina Court then quoted an Iowa court that rejected a similar play by students against fees. The Iowa court made its position on student fees very clear when it asserted vigorously that "the fact that a student may not participate or take advantage of every facility does not mean that he is or should be relieved from paying student fees allocated to various projects" (*Iowa Hotel Assn. v. State Bd. of Regents*, 1962).

The South Carolina Supreme Court concluded that the question of student fees should be left to those in authority. It held the charges of denial of equal protection and violation of the South Carolina Constitution to be out of order. Finally, it answered the argument, set forth by the plaintiff, that the stadium was adequate for the student body by determining that:

> Students are not the only people to whom seating may properly be made available. Parents and family of students, their friends, alumni and their families and friends, faculty and staff, supporters, and opponents have an interest in attending games. And they too help finance the stadium out of their admission fee. (*Moye v. Board of Trustees of University of South Carolina*, 1970)

The Court supported the verdict of the lower court by reaffirming the authority of the legislature Board of Trustees to improve and enlarge Carolina Stadium (Appenzeller, 1975).

For years, court cases supporting the schools' right to charge fees for athletics and other student extracurricular activities have used the South Carolina case to support the practices of colleges and universities. However, through the years until the present, students still challenge the legality of certain fees that are required of them. Students who have little or no interest in athletics argue that only those who attend athletic contests should pay an athletics fee. Still others claim that they do not read the school newspaper and should not be charged a fee to support the paper. The argument goes on and on to varying degrees of intensity on most campuses. The reader should decide on the legality and, to a degree, ethical behavior relating to the issue.

Pay for Play Debated

Referring to student-athletes getting paid to play, Mark Emmert, NCAA president, says, "It's grossly unacceptable and inappropriate to pay players ... converting them from students to employees." Emmert believes it is time to discuss the topic and determine "whether and how to spread a little more of the largesse to those doing the playing and sweating." He suggests, "maybe bump up the value of players' scholarships by a few thousand dollars to take care of travel, laundry and other typical college expenses that aren't covered now" (Wieberg, 2011).

Legal analysts predict that "if change doesn't come voluntarily ... the courts eventually may require it." Hall of Fame basketball coach Roy Williams of the University of North Carolina at Chapel Hill "questions why athletic scholarships can't measure up to top academic awards, such as UNC's Morehead-Cain scholarship, that take care of a recipient's travel, computers and other incidental extras." Williams advocates changes for revenue-producing sports such as football and basketball (Wieberg, 2011).

USA Today (2011) estimated "the full value of a Division I men's basketball scholarship," and calculated a worth of at least $120,000 a year. "Athletic scholarships cover a median $27,923 in costs each year at the 120 schools in the top football-playing Football Bowl Subdivision" (Wieberg, 2011). Beyond the basic cost of an athletic scholarship, which includes room, board, tuition and fees, an athletic scholarship also includes the following perks: elite coaching, academic counseling, strength and conditioning consulting, media relations assistance, medical insurance and treatment, free game tickets and future earning power (Wieberg, 2011).

For years, educators and college administrators have taken the position that paying the athletes would present financial problems, such as: if you pay revenue sport athletes, how would you avoid lawsuits from the non-revenue athletes? They believe it would open a Pandora's box that would be unmanageable. This will continue to be a topic for debate, and one that Emmett wants to discuss at NCAA meetings.

Spurrier's Unusual Proposal

Steve Spurrier, head football coach at the University of South Carolina, stirred up some controversy at a recent Southeastern Conference football coaches meeting. Spurrier suggested that a football squad of 70 players get checks for $300 per game from the coach's salary. Several SEC coaches make over $2 million. The suggestions may not get very far among the football coaches, but according to ACC Commissioner John Swofford, it is a starting point that merits discussion (*News & Record*, 2011). Some years ago when our athletics program was a Division III non-athletic scholarship program, our alumni and booster club recommended a full scholarship golf program. As athletics director, I believed we could compete with Division 1A schools in golf, but such a program would not be fair to the rest of our sport programs.

Why single out one sport for full grants when no others were given scholarships? The idea was dropped, although the golf program prospered under a Division III non-scholarship program.

Payment Under the Table

As far back as 1944, some high profile athletes were paid by coaches willing to take a chance. An outstanding fullback at a Division I school showed me a letter he received from another Division I college that offered him a full athletic grant, including room board, tuition, fees and laundry. In addition, the football coach offered him $75 a month. In 1944, $75 per month would be equivalent to $750 today. At a coaching clinic in South Carolina, a Division I coach told me that he could have offered Herschel Walker a better car if he had known that the school he attended provided him with a new car. He said, "Heck, we would have given him a bigger and better car." Auburn came under NCAA scrutiny when it was reported that Cam Newton's father wanted $180,000 from Mississippi State but elected to go to Auburn. Appearing on Bryant Gumbel's television show *Real Sports* on March 30, Auburn football players said they received money. Stanley McClover, Troy Reddick, Chaz Ramsey and Raven Gray said they received thousands of dollars in "bookbags, envelopes and handshakes." McClover, who left Auburn for the NFL after two years, received money from LSU, Michigan State and several others when he was recruited.

2010–11: A Year for Scandal

Christine Brennan, writing in *USA Today* (2011), asks, "Has there ever been an academic ... year with more lying, cheating, poor leadership and all-around misbehaving in football and men's basketball than the 2010–11 school year?" Brennan deplores the unethical behavior of the four former Auburn players who received money during their recruitment and playing days. The foursome cited illegal payments during recruitment at LSU, Ohio State and Michigan State. One player said he also received sexual favors at Ohio State (Brennan, 2011).

Two of the executives of the Fiesta Bowl "funneled campaign contributions to local political officials, then tried to cover them up." Bowl money was spent extravagantly by the executives. *The Arizona Republic* reported the following: $1,200 bill at a strip club; $65,000 to fly legislators and their families to a college game in Boston; and $30,000 on a birthday party for John Junker, chief executive of the Fiesta Bowl (Brennan, 2011).

Other recent violations were subjected to punishment by the NCAA: Reggie Bush and USC football, Jim Tressel's coverup of his violation of NCAA rules, Bruce Pearl's firing for breaking NCAA rules, Notre Dame football, Cecil Newton's asking price for Mississippi State to sign his son, Cam Newton.

Fiesta Bowl's BCS Penalized

Fiesta Bowl President and CEO John Junker was fired for an alleged scheme to reimburse employees for political contributions and an apparent conspiracy to cover it up. A report conducted by Fiesta Bowl board members "showed $4.85 million in reimbursements for travel, political contributions and a trip to a strip club, among other things." The three-day Fiesta Frolic "cost the nonprofit bowl more than $300,000 a year and was listed among other dubious expenses" in the report (Witt, 2011).

The Bowl Championship Series recently announced that the scandal-plagued Fiesta Bowl would "remain part of the system that decides college football's national championship" (Wieberg, 2011). However, BCS officials imposed the Fiesta with a $1 million fine and other sanctions, among them the order "to set up more stringent audits and tighter oversight of its board of its directors" (Wieberg, 2011). In a later decision, the NCAA Postseason Bowl Licensing Subcommittee also agreed to reaffirm the licenses for the Fiesta Bowl and the Insight Bowl, but the Fiesta Bowl organization will be placed on a one-year probation (Smith, 2011).

The book *Death to the BCS: The Definitive Case Against the Bowl Championship Series* (2010) by Dan Wetzel, Josh Peter and Jeff Passan depicts how many bowls have frivolous spending and excessive salaries for their CEOs. It will be interesting to follow the BCS investigations of bowls like the Fiesta Bowl.

Ethical Questions

1. Are salaries of football and basketball coaches reasonable or unreasonable?
2. Is the "keep up with the Joneses mentality" necessary?
3. Is the cost of recruiting out of hand?
4. Should beer revenue be used to balance a school budget?
5. Discuss Michael Lewis's observation that "college football's best trick play is its pretense that it has nothing to do with money and its mission is to educate students." How would the writer change the present system? Do you agree or disagree with his recommendations for change?

6. Should NCAA athletes be treated like regular students?
7. The Knight Foundation deplores the fact that Booster Clubs can lead to the firing of athletic personnel. What is your opinion on the matter?
8. Are colleges and universities eligible for being considered for non-profit status and exempt from taxes? And should they be?
9. Should football teams be sequestered the night before a home game in hotels at the cost of thousands of dollars?
10. Legislature votes to pay in-state fees for out-of-state athletes to save Booster Club expenses. Is this fair to the state?
11. Is the cost of moving from Division III to Division I reasonable?
12. Should media rights be given to allow TV the right to dictate the time of games?
13. NCAA conferences are in chaos. What should happen?
14. Has commercial value trumped academic value of athletics?
15. Will "pay to play" eliminate middle school activities?
16. Can sports exist in today's economy?
17. Should high schools join with Nike to meet budget crises?
18. Is it ethical for Division I power teams to schedule teams that are in a lower division and clearly out-manned?
19. Should athletes be paid or should their scholarships be raised to the level of academic scholarships?

Chapter 4

Disability and Discrimination in Sport

"Toleration of individual differences is basic to our democracy, whether these differences be in religion, politics, or life-style." — Bishop v. Colaw *(1971)*

Athletes with Disabilities

In the 1970s, a new day dawned for individuals with disabilities, impairments and handicapping conditions, and new opportunities in physical activities and sports were a big part of the progress. These exceptional people are climbing mountains, participating in grueling marathons and competing in practically every sports activity. Participation in sports can increase a sense of self-worth for the disabled individual.

Success came through the media, Congress and the courts. The media created a new awareness both of problems and potential solutions in this area by highlighting the accomplishments of exceptional disabled individuals. Congress enacted a new political and administrative climate with statutes mandating that new opportunities be available to all who can benefit from them. Public Law 94-142, now I.D.E.A., and Section 504 of the Rehabilitation Act have given more people the right to participate in physical education, intramurals, club and organized sports programs, no matter what or how severe their disability. The courts are increasingly positive concerning the benefits of sports participation and the right of individuals to obtain them. The attitude of many Americans toward these changes, however, too often remains negative.

The late Eunice Kennedy Shriver, Director of the Kennedy Foundation, referred to the disabled as the "bypassed millions in our nation … and urged the nation's leaders to use their best efforts to benefit the cause of the people" (Appenzeller, 1983). Shriver lived to see her dream of sports participation for the mentally challenged as sports for individuals with disabilities drew millions of participants worldwide. Progress has been made from a time when individuals with disabilities had little opportunities to engage in competitive sports. Steven Roberts wrote in *The New York Times* (1978) that for disabled people, "the main obstacles they must overcome are in people's minds," and that "they want to rely on themselves" (Roberts, 1978). Roberts wrote that many individuals with disabilities often have a negative feeling about the way society views them. He quoted an anonymous writer:

> The wheelchair I sit in is not made of steel. It's made of stares and whispers, closed classroom doors, inaccessible public buildings. And the wheelchair seems to get larger every time I'm unable to enter a restaurant or movie theater; every time people curse me in public or try to do their good deed.

The anonymous writer concluded:

> Sitting in a wheelchair isn't bad. It is the mental wheelchair that makes me believe I'm different, ugly. Not to be touched or loved. In the mental wheelchair that isolates, confines and limits me. It's the mental wheelchair that makes me believe that I'm defeated before I begin. The wheelchair I sit in is not made of steel. It's made of misunderstandings, ignorance, fear of the unfamiliar prejudices.

In the 1970s, people with disabilities were making tremendous progress in their efforts to overcome discrimination. The Department of Health, Education and Welfare (HEW) received 377 claims in the first four months of 1978, more claims than for race and sex combined (Appenzeller, 1983).

In 1973, HEW mandated that federally assisted programs may not prohibit sports participation. The regulation is referred to as the Rehabilitation Act of 1973, 29 U.S.C.A. 794. The law protects the right of the disabled in sports as never before and signaled the beginning of a new era in sports. Since 1978, when society may have had negative feelings toward individuals with disabilities and sports competition, attitudes and expectations have improved as never before.

Roses in December

In 1950, well before Eunice Kennedy Shriver persisted to gain national recognition of the benefits of sports participation for the disabled, I had an experience with a disabled student that influenced my teaching and coaching of sports forever.

Coaches more times than not use their hearts instead of their heads to make tough decisions. Unfortunately, this wasn't the case when I realized we had a baseball conference game scheduled when our seniors would be in Washington, D.C., for the annual senior field trip. We were a team dominated by seniors, and for the first time in many years, we were in the conference race for first place. I knew we couldn't win without our seniors, so I called the rival coach and asked to reschedule the game when everyone was available to play. "No way," he replied. The seniors were crushed and offered to skip the much-awaited traditional trip. I assured them they needed to go on the trip as part of their educational experience, though I really wanted to accept their offer and win and go on to the conference championship.

But I did not, and on that fateful Tuesday, I wished they were there to play. I had nine underclass players eager and excited that they finally had a chance to play. The most excited player was a young mentally challenged boy we will call Billy. Billy was, I believe, over age, but because he loved sports so much, an understanding principal had given him permission to be on the football and baseball teams. Billy lived and breathed sports and now he would finally get his chance to play. I think his happiness captured the imagination of the eight other substitute players. Billy was very small in size, but he had a big heart and had earned the respect of his teammates with his effort and enthusiasm. He was a left-handed hitter and had good baseball skills. His favorite pastime, except for playing sports, was to sit with the men at a local rural store talking about sports. On this day, I began to feel that a loss might even be worth Billy's chance to play.

Our opponents jumped off to a four-run lead early in the game, just as expected. Somehow we came back to within one run, and that was when we went to bat in the bottom of the ninth. I was pleased with our team's effort and the constant grin on Billy's face. *If only we could win,* I thought, *but that's asking too much. If we lose by one run, it will be a victory in itself.*

The weakest part of our lineup was scheduled to hit, and the opposing coach put his ace pitcher in to seal the victory. To our surprise, with two outs, a batter walked, and the tying run was on first base. Our next hitter was Billy. The crowd cheered as if this were the final inning of the conference championship, and Billy waved jubilantly. I knew he would be unable to hit this pitcher, but what a day it had been for all of us. Strike one. Strike two. A fastball. Billy hit it down the middle over the right fielder's head for a triple to tie the score. Billy was beside himself, and the crowd went wild.

Our next hitter, however, hadn't hit the ball even once in batting practice or intra-squad games. I knew there was absolutely no way for the impossible dream to continue. Besides, our opponents had the top of their lineup if we went into extra innings. It was a crazy situation and one that needed reckless strategy. I called a time-out, and everyone seemed confused when I walked to third base and whispered something to Billy. As expected, Ben swung on the first two pitches, not coming close to either. When the catcher threw the ball back to the pitcher, Billy broke from third base sprinting as hard as he could. The pitcher didn't see him break, and when he did, he whirled around wildly and fired the ball home. Billy dove in head first, beat the throw, and scored the winning run.

This was not the World Series, but don't tell that to anyone present that day. Tears were shed as Billy, the hero, was lifted on the shoulders of all eight team members. If you went through town today, 42 years later, you would likely see Billy at that same country store relating to an admiring group the story of the day he won the game that no one expected to win. Of all the spectacular events in my sports career, this memory is the highlight. It exemplified what sports can do for people, and Billy's great day proved that to everyone who saw the game. J. M. Barrie, the playwright, may have said it best when he wrote, "God gave us memories so that we might have roses in December." Billy gave all of us a rose garden (Appenzeller, 2002).

Harold James, the Kangaroo Kid

Harold James was a victim of polio while an infant and the aftereffect left him with a small, withered left leg which was the size of an average person's arm. As a young boy, he refused to accept the advice of doctors to give up his desire to compete in athletics. Instead, he grew more determined than ever to participate like his friends. He limped home night after night, exhausted from trying to keep pace with his friends who could run faster, climb higher and play games better than he. The harder he tried to keep up with his friends, the more his small leg hurt. But one thing he refused to do was to accept defeat. Sympathetic teachers and friends merely spurred him on with a fierce determination to excel, and this carried him through grammar school.

Soon the challenge of high school confronted him and the way was not easy. Again, Harold had to convince his parents, coaches, and doctors that he could, and, in fact, had to play high school athletics. His coach, a former college classmate of mine, had a reputation as an excellent coach but one who was demanding of his athletes. He would not pity this struggling athlete, but would expect the same from him as any boy with normal legs. The price Harold would be called upon to pay would be high if he were to play.

Harold James played the game the only way he knew how, giving no quarter to anyone and in turn expecting none from anyone. His high school record was known all over the Tidewater Area of Virginia where he led his football, basketball and track teams to many great victories. To climax his high school career, he was honored by being named the outstanding athlete at Virginia Beach High School.

The future looked dark to Harold after high school graduation. He was only an average academic student, having spent more time and interest in athletics than in scholastic achievement. He decided to try to apply for an athletic scholarship on the basis of his high school sports record, but the college coaches lost interest when they saw his left leg. Today, college athletics require speed, size, and agility; the risk was too great.

I first met Harold when one of our Guilford College athletes, who had been a teammate of his in high school, asked me to give him a tryout. I still remember the shock I experienced when he took off his sweat pants and began to jump over the bar at the high jump pit. A crowd of curious students quickly gathered as he continued to clear the bar at regular intervals until he had defeated all of our varsity jumpers. When he talked to me about college football, I was confident that he would be given a chance, but certain he would be discouraged if he attempted to play. I felt, however, that he would be an asset to us in track.

Harold's application to Guilford College was rejected and a letter was sent expressing regret that his grades were not acceptable. We soon discovered that he was not ready to give up. His mother called and told us he was almost completely demoralized by our letter because he knew he could do the work if we gave him a chance. "Don't turn him down," she pleaded. "He needs a chance, and he'll prove to you that he can do it, if you just try him for a semester." After a brief, hurried consultation, our Admissions Director reviewed his case and agreed to give him a chance for a semester on probation.

Misfortune plagued Harold throughout his first three years at Guilford. He dislocated his shoulder and broke his finger in football, injured his knee in track, and even became scholastically ineligible for a semester as a sophomore. His determination to make the varsity team in football never wavered, however, and he put all his energy toward reaching this goal.

During his four years at Guilford, Harold broke many existing records of both the school and the district. He scored more points in a dual meet and for an entire season than anyone before him at Guilford. In one meet when the squad was limited in numbers, he ran the high hurdles, high jumped, broad jumped, pole vaulted, and threw the javelin and discus. In a meet with an archrival, Guilford needed a second place in the javelin to win the meet. Harold did not appear to have a chance as his first two throws fell pitifully short, but as he lined up for the final throw, he smiled at me and said, "Don't worry, coach. We'll win." He helped us do just that as he found some reserve strength and threw the javelin far enough to capture second place and a victory for the team.

In the conference track meet, Harold came back after two narrow misses to try for the final high jump. The tension was terrific as he walked to the bar time and time again to get ready for the most important jump of his career. I prayed that he could make the height and win in his last meet of the year. I visualized the hours of work, the sacrifice and self-denial that this young athlete had put in and decided that win or lose, he had been truly great. I could barely see as the crowd closed in on the pit for the last jump. Suddenly a tremendous roar was heard, and I knew he made the jump and was the new conference champion. People left the track in disbelief at this young man with the withered leg who refused to believe he could lose.

Harold entered his senior year and starred as a defensive halfback. He had the knack for sensing plays and hit like a ton of bricks. In our opening game upset of our heavily favored rival, he played as we had never seen him play. It was in this game that he hurdled over an opposing blocker to make a vicious tackle. The surprised blocker looked up in bewilderment and shouted, "Hey you, are you some kind of a kangaroo?" The name stuck and from then on his teammates affectionately referred to him as the "kangaroo kid."

In the next game against a powerful opponent, our out-manned team entered the game as a five-touchdown underdog. It was here that I felt Harold finally earned his starting spot at quarterback. We did not win, but he put on one of the greatest offensive shows to bring us within a one-touchdown loss. Later during the season, he scored against the nation's number-one small college team and again made plays that were fantastic.

During one game, an overly aggressive lineman twisted Harold's little leg during a pileup, and as he limped off the field, I saw a grin on his face. "Coach, don't get upset," he said. "I'm flattered that anyone would think that much of my ability." He climaxed a great personal year by being named to the all-conference team as a quarterback.

In his senior year, Harold entered the conference track meet undefeated in the regular season in the high jump. He had won a tremendous following of both Guilford students and admiring opponents. To him, the conference championship was the biggest and most important event. When I arrived at the jumping pit, I found that he was visibly upset by the new hard-surfaced approach area. "Coach," he pleaded, "do something about this pit. I can't get traction on it." I knew his entire season and hopes were wrapped up in the event, but I was helpless to change things. He tried desperately to clear a height he could usually clear in warm-up and was defeated early in the competition. I still remember the deep hurt in his eyes and body as he limped pathetically from the track, disappointed and humiliated because he felt that he had let his friends and school down.

This temporary defeat was forgotten at the end of the year, however, when he was chosen as Sportsman of the Year in Virginia, an honor awarded to the truly great in Virginia. Later, a writer interviewed him and asked him to tell of his greatest thrill in sports. Was it the day you scored against the national champions in football? Was it the day you broke the district high jump record, won the conference high jump championship or the all-conference football selection, or received the honor of being chosen as Virginia's Sportsman of the Year? He was quick to answer and his answer surprised me. He said, "None of these. It was the time we played East Carolina when my coach put his arm around me before the game and told me he had decided that I was his number-one quarterback. For you see," he told the surprised writer, "I knew that in America, a handicapped boy could reach his goal if he wanted to badly enough." Harold James was named to the Guilford College Sports Hall of Fame. The two young men I coached, one in high school, the other in college, are now typical of athletes today who have disabilities and compete in sport.

The Number of Disabled Athletes Competing in College Sports Today Is Growing

In 2008, 76 deaf and hard-of-hearing athletes, both male and female, participated in NCAA and NAIA sports, and 39 played in Division I. The numbers are increasing each year, and might be even greater because many individuals prefer not to be identified (Klemko, 2009).

AMA Guidelines Prevent Participation in Sports

In 1976, the American Medical Association (AMA) set guidelines for disqualification from certain sports for conditions that included uncontrolled diabetes, jaundice, active tuberculosis, enlarged liver and the absence of a paired organ.

The AMA guidelines were merely recommendations, but many school officials accepted and enforced them as mandatory requirements. Countless numbers of student-athletes were denied participation in contact sports such as football, hockey, lacrosse, baseball, soccer, basketball and wrestling because of the AMA guidelines.

The majority of student-athletes with conditions specified in the AMA guidelines reluctantly accepted the decision prohibiting them from sports competition without seeking redress in the courts through litigation. Today, however, student-athletes with physical impairments often refuse such prohibition and seek relief in the courts, insisting that federal laws guarantee them the opportunity to participate in sports on the club, interscholastic, intramural and intercollegiate levels (Appenzeller, 1980).

Many athletes from junior high school, high school and intercollegiate athletics have sought relief from decisions by school physicians and officials denying them the opportunity to participate in sports. The courts noted that physicians and school administrators felt that disqualification was necessary to protect the individual from serious injury. However, because of the passage of 94-142, now I.D.E.A., and the Rehabilitation Act of 1973, courts now rule, in almost every case, that the plaintiff (athlete) has the right to participate.

Two names come to mind immediately in relation to this issue: Jay Cutler, quarterback for the NFL's Chicago Bears, and Scott Verplank, a member of the PGA Tour. Both athletes have diabetes and are on an insulin pump. Both are outstanding athletes who have profitable careers in professional sports.

As a former coach of basketball, baseball, football and track and field, and an athletics director for 40 years, I understand the reasoning of school officials and team physicians. There is a sincere desire to protect the student-athlete on all levels from potential injuries that could be life-threatening. However, through Congress and courts, individuals today are protected by legislation and litigation, and have the opportunity to decide whether to play or not play sports.

Athlete with Blind Eye Disqualified

In 1975, I was invited to speak by the sport administration department at Ohio University. When I arrived on campus, I realized that everyone was in an uproar. Michael Borden, a two-time high school MVP, had tried out for the junior varsity basketball team at the university and made the team. However, the following day Borden was examined by the school physician and dismissed from the team because he was blind in one eye.

Borden's dismissal got the attention of the Ohio campus and the state of Ohio, and gained Borden national support. While I was there, Morris "Moe" Udall, a Senator from Arizona, arrived on campus to help Borden's cause. Udall himself has a blind eye but played college basketball and had a stint in the National Basketball Association. He played one-on-one basketball with Mike Borden to illustrate that Borden could and should play. He declared that people had encouraged Borden all his life because he had only one seeing eye and now it was being held against him. Borden maintained that he was not materially handicapped since being blind in one eye had not prevented him from being successful both in school and in sports. He remarked, "I didn't know what it was like to have two eyes, that would be a dream—but I know I can compete with anyone." Borden sought and received an injunction from the court, enabling him to rejoin the team. Ohio University complied with the court order and reinstated Borden. In his first game, he scored 22 points and pulled down eight rebounds.

The following year, although the court order was not in effect, the university officials refused to pursue the issue any further. John Burns, Legal Affairs Officer, stated that, "It's still spiritually intact. It would be silly to go to court each year" (*The Columbus Dispatch* 1977).

Two Student-Athletes Go to Court to Play Football

In a similar case to Borden's, Kinney Redding and Keith Evans, both outstanding athletes at Missouri Western State College, were told by the team physician that they could not play football because each one was blind in the left eye (*Evans and Redding v. Looney*, 1977). Both players were granted permission to play for Missouri Western as soon as each signed a waiver releasing the college from liability. The federal judge who granted them the injunction believed that failure to play would cause serious damage for them and that it would represent a violation of their constitutional rights.

Physicians Often Are the Problem

A continuing problem is that well-meaning physicians advise school officials, in many instances, to exclude athletes with certain conditions from participation in sports. Part of the problem was that the disqualification was encouraged by the American Medical Association. Athletes with disabilities who are denied the opportunity to participate in sports file lawsuits claiming they are protected by the Fourteenth Amendment of the Federal Amendment of the Federal Constitution. As a result, many athletes with one eye, one kidney or impaired hearing are filing lawsuits, even in the 21st Century, and getting approval to participate in varsity sports, physical education, club sports and intramurals.

The examples of athletes with physical impairments go on and on. They are convincing and compelling, but they represent only one side if the coin. Today, we still have many athletic trainers, team physicians and coaches who do not approve of athletes with disabilities participating in sports. One such physician, Dr. James Brewer, Guilford College's team physician, did not believe the legislation was in the best interest of our young people. "After all," he said, "how can you legislate morality, ethical conduct or safety for our people?" This was said in 1978, and today, when many individuals are participating in sport, there is still a belief that such participation is not safe.

Our Protocol for Participation

As a football and track coach and athletics director for over 30 years at Guilford College, I respected the federal legislation and decisions of courts nationally who granted permission to athletes with disabilities to go out for a collision or contact sport. I followed this protocol when faced with the situation where a student with a disability wanted to participate in sports:

> I had a conference with all the people involved, including the athlete, the parents and/or spouse, the physician and the coach of the team in question. We discussed the consequences of participation and possible injury, and considered alternatives such as non-contact sports or an association with the sport, such as a manager or athletic trainer. (Appenzeller, 1980)

If the athlete and the parents were in agreement with the opinion of the physician, and it was determined that the athlete could benefit from participation in sport, we provided a waiver form for all to sign to that effect. We kept the notes of the meeting on file, stating that such a meeting was held and that all parties were aware of the situation or possible consequences resulting from injury and still chose to participate. We then had all those present sign the statement and kept the record on file for future reference.

During my tenure as athletics director, we had many instances where an athlete with a disability and his parents or spouse chose for him or her to play. On very few occasions did anyone decide not to play.

An Unexpected Disability Later in Life Calls Attention to the Importance of ADA Guidelines

Ironically, I experienced a physical disability later in life. As a result of a back injury, my legs were affected and I was forced to wear metal braces on both legs and walk with two canes. During that time, I observed first-hand many of the things people with disabilities experience every day. My wife and I attended a football game in Florida at a major conference school. We asked at the gate when a golf cart would be available to take us the long distance to our section and seat. We were told emphatically that "this university does not provide such transportation for people with disabilities." It was evident that I could not walk the distance required to reach my seat. We were surprised because my *alma mater*, Wake Forest University, makes golf cart volunteers available to help accommodate individuals with disabilities such as mine. My wife, in a kind manner, told the ticket taker that the university was violating the Americans with Disability Act (ADA), and like magic, a golf cart appeared and allowed me to get to my seat and see the game.

Athletic officials, as well as teachers, coaches and administrators, should become familiar with ADA guidelines before there is a need for litigation. The Americans with Disabilities Act provides helpful information regarding mandates and guidelines for compliance with the law. One of the most misunderstood guidelines is the statute regarding participation in sports, physical education and intramurals by individuals with disabilities. There is a presumption that most educators are familiar with the basic processes of law, recent legislation and the judicial decisions affecting their profession, but this appears to be the exception, in too many instances, rather than the rule.

The Right to Play Baseball

In 2007, Jesse DeSanto's heart stopped as he crossed home plate during a high school baseball game. The 16-year-old was a sophomore at Manteo High School in Manteo, North Carolina. DeSanto survived the cardiac arrest and planned to play college baseball for Guilford College. Now 19 years old, DeSanto was disqualified from playing after his previous cardiac arrest was made known during his pre-participation physical examination. DeSanto and his father continued to practice baseball on the weekends, and both tried to convince Guilford's team physician that they would do whatever it took for Jesse DeSanto to play on the collegiate level. The 165-pound athlete was cleared to play high school baseball after he had a defibrillator cardioverter implanted in his chest that acts like a pacemaker. He was named MVP on his high school team, won the team batting title and played in the 2008 State Games of North Carolina. He was also selected All-Conference twice in the Class 1-A Four Rivers League.

DeSanto and his father retained the services of a lawyer in an attempt to overturn Guilford College's decision to not let him participate in the baseball program. Guilford officials spent countless hours researching the situation so that they could make a decision that would protect both DeSanto and the college. DeSanto's father said that he waived any liability on the part of the college should his son sustain a cardiac problem. He said, "The next guy who comes along with an ICD, they won't brush it off … we fought it because it was the right thing to do." Finally, on February 9, 2010, DeSanto was approved to play. He has since played in junior varsity games and said that "the opportunity to play is the one thing that brings him peace." He added, "Baseball is my rehabilitation from the whole experience … I was fighting for this" (Witt, 2010).

Players Denied Sports Participation
Transfer to Other Schools

Stephen Larkin, brother of Cincinnati Reds short stop Barry Larkin, suffered from a heart condition while a student at University of Texas. Baseball coach Cliff Gustafson said that school officials told him not to play Larkin, who was batting .338 after seven games. Larkin's mother stated that university officials should not have been afraid of liability if problems arose from her son's condition. The Larkins offered to sign a waiver releasing the school from liability and threatened to transfer to a school that agreed to let him play (McNabb, 1992).

Emmanuel Negedu transferred from the University of Tennessee after school officials refused to let him play basketball because of a cardiac condition. Negedu, a highly recruited player, sustained a cardiac event after practice on September 28, 2009. Negedu did not play during the 2009–2010 season. Vols Athletics Director Mike Hamilton denied Negedu's request to return to varsity basketball for the 2010 season. Coach Bruce Pearl said he wished Negedu well, but agreed with and supported the university's position. Negedu was offered the opportunity to stay on scholarship at Tennessee, but chose to transfer to New Mexico University. He said "he felt like he was dead" when he was told he could not play. The New Mexico Lobos are reportedly doing everything to protect their new recruit. (Katz, 2010).

Athletic officials at Tennessee made the decision not to clear Negedu for basketball after they conferred with medical experts and received medical studies about his condition. Many other schools, nationwide, take the same position on student-athletes with disabilities about their participation in sports. We applaud Tennessee's policy to keep Negedu on scholarship if he remained at the university. Negedu became a New Mexico Lobo, however, because of his desire to play basketball.

Arkansas Player with Cerebral Palsy
Scores Touchdown in Wheelchair

Dylan Galloway, a senior at Manila High School in Arkansas, was born with cerebral palsy, but never gave up his dream to score a touchdown in football. Galloway's football team was trailing Rivercrest High 47–0, and the Mercy Rule was in effect. The coaches from both teams got together with five minutes remaining in the game to set up a play so Galloway could score. They placed the ball on the four-yard line, where he could get the ball in his wheelchair. They put a football helmet on the boy and told him to get in the game and score a touchdown.

Galloway's mother said the touchdown her son scored was one of her happiest moments. She thanked all who made it possible, saying, "Thank you and God bless you, and thank you for giving him a chance to be a part of something." Rivercrest players signed the football prior to Galloway's touchdown and presented it to him after he crossed into the end zone. Rivercrest's Coach Chandler said he and his players "took away memories of the moment that won't fade any time soon." Galloway's Coach Doke said, "All of [Galloway's] teammates went to celebrate with him … It was pretty special" (Smith, 2010).

Blind Golfer Sets Records

One of the best examples of how participation in sports changes lives of injured veterans is that of Charlie Boswell. He was an All-American football player at the University of Alabama in the mid-1930s with a future in professional baseball. He commanded a tank battalion in North Africa during World War II and was blinded when his tank took a direct hit. At Valley Forge Rehabilitation Hospital in Pennsylvania, Boswell exhibited a belligerent and negative attitude, feeling sorry for himself with a "what's the use of living" philosophy. He refused to take part in the sports program at the hospital until a staff member told him he was going to play golf the next day. Boswell, who had never played a game of golf, replied, "What in the hell can a blind man do on a golf course?" The staff member told him, "Shut up, we're going."

Someone put a golf club in Boswell's hands the next day and guided him through some preliminary swings. Finally, after some practice swings on his own, he hit his first tee shot ever. According to Boswell, he "hit the ball right between the screws and could feel it going 250 yards right down the middle." Golf gave him a thrill he had never experienced, and it became his rehabilitation and his road back to an active life. He often questions what would have happened to him if he had missed his first swing.

Charlie Boswell holds a record for a score of eighty-one for eighteen holes of golf in national competition. His record came in a tournament sponsored by the United States Blind Golfers Association. Boswell won twelve national titles in twenty years and scored a hole-in-one on a par three, 147-yard hold in Birmingham, Alabama. In 2009, ESPN reported that a legally blind teenager on a high school team ran for a touchdown. Could it be that the young player was motivated by Charlie Boswell's example? (Appenzeller, 1983).

Football Coach Not Stopped by Paralysis

Marc Strohmaier was paralyzed in a car crash when he was a 16-year-old linebacker for his high school team in Clovis, California. As an assistant football coach at Hamilton High School in Chandler, Arizona, he has been a part of two state championships. He must be careful when the weather is extremely hot because his body does not sweat. The temperature during his second pre-season practice reached 111 degrees and his players were constantly putting water on him to cool him off.

Strohmaier is classified as a quadriplegic, but he is independent and rides his motorized wheelchair home from practice each day. His brother gets frustrated because Strohmaier refuses help, willing to struggle rather than seek help. His brother is Hamilton's strength coach and was an NFL player from 1997 to 2001.

After Strohmaier received his bachelor's degree in marketing from Arizona State University, he worked for five years in marketing. He decided that he wanted to teach and get his master's degree. However, to graduate and teach, Strohmaier needed to work as a student teacher. He was unable to find a school that would give him an opportunity to teach because he was wheelchair-dependent.

His brother told him to call the football coach at Hamilton High School and offer to help coach. The coach agreed and after a short period of time he was given the chance to student teach. Initially, Strohmaier was intimidated by some of the other coaches, who had played and coached in college, and some had played in the NFL. He felt inadequate because he was a junior high school player when he was injured and had no college experience in football as a player or coach. His first year, he kept asking himself, "Am I a glorified cheerleader? What am I doing here?" (Halley, 2009).

Late that season, a junior at Hamilton broke his neck while making a tackle during a scrimmage and was paralyzed from the chest down. Strohmaier said, "Suddenly I went ... to where everybody was looking at me for advice or support, to explain the same thing that I went through when I was 16 and he was 16 ... I think maybe that was why I was put here—to get philosophical about it" (Halley, 2009).

Today, Strohmaier can't think about doing anything else but coaching and simply says, "I love it." When people tell him that he is an inspiration to others, he replies, "I look up to people who go through difficult things in life whether they're handicapped or they've suffered some other type of loss. So, if someone can use me as an inspiration, it doesn't frustrate me. But in the overall picture, you have to do more than be in a wheelchair to be inspirational" (Halley, 2009).

Player without Hand Lands Spot on College Basketball Team

Kevin Laue, a 6'11", 230-pound center for Manhattan College's basketball team, is an inspiration to many athletes with disabilities. Laue "has been missing his left hand and arm below the elbow since birth." A freshman, Lane wants to succeed both on and off the basketball court as he seeks a place on the team. He says, "Maybe me playing with one hand inspires others to try to work harder toward their goals. Or their dreams." In high school, he maintained a 3.6 average and a 4.0 in prep school. Laue wants to run for president of the freshman class and be involved in campus life. His basketball coach, Barry Rohrssen, says, "The Good Lord doesn't give everyone everything. What Kevin's missing in one part of his body he makes up for with his heart. Because that's twice as big as everyone else's" (McCarthy, 2009).

Laue, much like Michael Jordan, failed to make his seventh grade basketball team. However, he worked all summer to improve and made the eighth grade team. At Fork Union Military Academy in Virginia, he averaged ten points and five rebounds per game. With his determination to succeed, Laue will make a mark and inspire and motivate others.

Funding for Injured Veterans Approved by USOC

The U.S. Olympic Committee (USOC) committed $10 million "to provide training, equipment and other sports-related assistance to injured veterans." The USOC has pledged $10 million annually, including $2 million for veterans who work toward becoming Paralympians. USOC is partnering with the Department of Veterans Affairs in this effort. Paralympians will mentor injured veterans in the partnership. The USOC will attempt to expand its Paralympic program to 250 committees by 2012 (*USA Today*, 2009). We applaud the USOC and the Department of Veterans Affairs for their funding of a much-needed program. People with disabilities had little hope for a quality life until World War II. Because World War II accomplished many medical breakthroughs that enabled injured veterans to profit from sports participation, the quality of life for injured veterans improved dramatically.

Blind Hikers Know No Limits

Thirteen blind hikers embarked on a 24.3-mile trek around the rim of the Grand Canyon, a difficult challenge even for those who can see. The hikers were determined to prove that "those who can't see can achieve and appreciate one of the planet's Seven Natural Wonders without viewing it." Marc Ashton, chief executive officer of the Foundation for Blind Children, said, "Our goal was to prove to the world that blind people can do anything ... Our climbers proved they could" (Wagner, 2010).

The hikers, seven men, four women and two boys, "trained for months with volunteers, practicing on urban peaks." During the trek, each visually impaired person "work[ed] with at least one sighted guide who provid[ed] step-by-step instructions." With the exception of one hiker who fell and cut his leg and was flown by helicopter for medical treatment, all completed the trek. Ten from the group made the difficult adventure by the day's end. Two others remained on the canyon floor with their two guides, exiting the next day (Wagner, 2010).

Three Paralympians File Suit against the U.S. Olympic Committee for Alleged Discrimination

Three elite paralympians claimed that the United States Olympic Committee discriminated against them in violation of Section 504 of the Rehabilitation Act of 1973, which forbids discrimination on the basis of a disability under any program or activity receiving federal financial assistance. The plaintiffs contended that benefits provided for Olympic, Pan-American athletes were different than those provided for the Paralympics athletes. Disputed benefits by the plaintiffs included the following:

1. Access to athlete support programs
2. Specific basic grants programs
3. Basic grants and payments
4. USOC Tuition Assistance Programs (scholarships)
5. Health insurance
6. Access to training facilities
7. Operation Gold by which paralympic athletes received about one-tenth of the awards given Olympic athletes
8. Wheelchair participation in the opening ceremonies of 1992, 1996 and 2000, although other countries allowed wheelchair participants to be part of their teams

Although the claim of discrimination appeared to be valid, the U.S. Supreme Court refused to grant the paralympic athletes *certiorari* and review the case (*Hollonbeck v. USOC*, 2008).

The adverse decision by the U.S. Supreme Court to not review the case led many proponents of the implementation of Section 504 of the Rehabilitation Act to conclude that this denial would prevent not only those persons with disabilities experiencing discrimination from being heard, but also those experiencing discrimination of race, creed, national origin, age and gender (*STL-Today.com*, 2008).

Disabled Students Want to Join School Teams

Students in wheelchairs want to participate with regular students in track and field. Rachel Voss, a wheelchair athlete, has won medals in track and field across the nation and in South Africa. Finally, after two years of fighting to join her Collinsville High School Catholic team, she is allowed to join her team in the shot put and discus. Nevertheless, the Illinois High School Association said that her wheelchair is a danger to others and also an advantage against her competitors.

Progress has been made for athletes in wheelchairs in Washington, Louisiana, Oregon and New Jersey, where athletes in wheelchairs are permitted to compete against able-bodied athletes. These state associations believe that students with disabilities should have the opportunity to compete with everyone else and that their points should count in the overall team score. The ethical dilemmas that may arise should be considered if all students are given the opportunity to participate in sport.

Man with Cerebral Palsy Is a Consultant for NFL Teams

Doug Blevins dreamed as a boy of making it in the National Football League, but everyone told him he could never make it. Blevins, who had cerebral palsy, became a kicking coach for the Miami Dolphins and did his coaching from a wheelchair. Jimmy Johnson, Miami's head coach at that time, heard glowing reports from sources close to the New England Patriots, where Blevins analyzed films of the Patriots' kickers. Johnson's reservation was whether Blevins could operate the wheelchair safely on the field. Miami's place kicker, Joe Nedney, welcomed the help from Blevins, who made changes in his steps and his entire routine. Blevins has been a kicking consultant for the New York Jets and the New England Patriots, and in the World League of Professional Football. Blevins speaks to people with disabilities during the offseason and urges them to "follow your heart and do what you are capable of doing" (*USA Today*, 2009).

Competition between Athletes with Disabilities and Able-Bodied Athletes

Tommie Storms, Director of Operations and co-founder of the American Association of Adapted Sports Programs, writes in *Palaestra* (2007) about how litigation in Alabama and Maryland and plans to formulate programs in Georgia and New Jersey to set standards for students with disabilities to compete against able-bodied athletes are signs of progress. Storms notes that this is not the first time those with disabilities have sought the right to be included in school athletics. She concludes:

> As news of each student appeal spreads, others hoping to add momentum to this growing grass-roots movement have followed with their own actions or petitions. As we observe this new groundswell of advocacy, the decisions of the Court provide important direction, that, if heeded, will allow advocates, educators, and programmers to act more effectively, and in needed concert for change. (Storms, 2007)

It is obvious that progress has been made for individuals with disabilities to participate in sports, and the future will place importance on ethical behavior for coaches, athletics directors, disabled athletes and state associations.

Ethical Questions

1. Do you agree that the main obstacle facing individuals with disabilities is in their minds, and not concrete?
2. Do you have a story to tell about a person you know with disability?
3. Discuss I.D.E.A. and the Rehabilitation Act of 1973. Do you agree with this legislation?
4. Do you know any individual with a disability who achieves success in sports?
5. Should paralympics receive the same USOC benefits as those provided Olympians, Pan American Athletes?
6. Should students in wheelchairs compete in track and field with non-disabled student-athletes?

Religious Discrimination

Prayer in the Locker Room

Brad Fisher, an assistant athletics director at Reynolds High School in Winston-Salem, North Carolina, wrote in *Managing Sport and Risk Management Strategies* (2003) that religion "has caused feuds between neighbors, countrymen and whole nations." Fisher observes that our Founding Fathers decided that the "government could not force religious views on its citizens, yet, not stop them from expressing their own views." The debate has continued and the separation of church and state has found its way into athletic contests.

Establishment Clause vs. Free Exercise Clause: Prayer in Public Schools

In the United States, there is a conflict between the Establishment Clause and the Free Exercise Clause. The courts have held that the Establishment Clause means that "the government or any of its entities may not promote a specific religion." At the same time, the interpretation of the Free Exercise Clause means that the government should not inhibit anyone who desires to practice his/her religion (Appenzeller, 2003). In a public school setting, prayer is acceptable when it is nonsectarian, non-proselytizing and student-initiated. The key is student-initiated. Fisher predicts the possibility of litigation if "any teacher, coach, administrator or government official participates, encourages or has any control over the situation."

Balancing the Establishment Clause and the Free Exercise Clause

Paul Batista, a professor of sport management at Texas A&M, wrote about balancing the First Amendment Establishment Clause and the Free Exercise Clause in the *Journal of Legal Aspects of Sport* (2002). He lists various situations in which "participants seek[] to perform religious activities on public school property" and indicates whether they are permissible under free exercise:

1. Prayers in "a team huddle prior to the game in the locker room or on the playing field." If it is student initiated and led, this is clearly free exercise; however, if a coach or school employee initiates or leads the prayer, or encourages or requires team members to join in the prayer, then it is school sponsored and impermissible.
2. "Prayers conducted over the loud speakers with spectators and players being asked to pray together." This is ... unconstitutional school sponsorship of religion.
3. "Ministers use 'bull horns' to lead the crowd in prayer prior to athletic events." This is free exercise by private individuals and allowed, unless the school promotes, sponsors or endorses such activity.

4. "Ministers sat throughout the grandstands of local football games and led spectators in the Lord's Prayer." This is permissible as free exercise by private individuals, unless endorsed, sponsored or promoted by school officials.

5. "Fans used personal radios to broadcast a local radio station's pre-game invocation." Again, this is free exercise by private individuals, unless endorsed, sponsored or promoted by school officials.

6. "Prayers led by students at football games," and "student-led prayer at school sponsored athletic events." The decisive factor will be the source of the student-led prayer. If it is sponsored, endorsed or promoted by the school, and broadcast over the school public address system, then it is not lawful. If it is initiated by the students, without intervention of the school authorities, then it is free expression and lawful.

7. Athletes from the competing schools voluntarily meeting at center court for prayer after the game is free exercise, unless endorsed, sponsored or promoted by school officials.

8. A football player kneeling to pray after scoring a touchdown is free exercise.

9. An individual athlete voluntarily silently reading a religious book in the locker room before the game is free exercise.

10. An individual athlete voluntarily reading aloud from the same source is also free exercise.

11. A fan praying loudly in the stands during an athletic contest is free exercise.

12. A public school team involved in an athletic contest with a private school, on the campus of the private school, cannot require the host school to forego its pre-game invocation.

13. A pastor begins reciting "The Lord's Prayer" at five minutes before game time, pursuant to an advertisement in the local newspaper inviting fans to join in the prayer. This is free exercise, unless endorsed, sponsored or promoted by school officials.

14. A coach calls a team meeting and begins with a moment of silence. The Supreme Court has not decisively answered this question, until the court renders an opinion clarifying the application of *Wallace*. Although this may pass constitutional scrutiny, it will probably be unlawful if the coach encourages or expects prayer.

15. A public school on-campus Fellowship of Christian Athletes ("FCA") huddle group, sponsored by a coach who actively participates, is not allowed under the Equal Access Act, and constitutes unlawful Establishment. Conversely, an off-campus voluntary FCA huddle group sponsored by parents of players, or a community religious group led by a private citizen, is free

exercise. However, if a coach attends and participates in the off-campus FCA activities, the situation becomes more complicated. If attending athletes receive any benefit from the coach attending, or non-attending athletes receive any detriment, then it is arguably coercive and probably unlawful. However, if the coach merely attends and is not a leadership or sponsoring position, it is probably free exercise and association. The determining factor will likely be whether each athlete participates voluntarily and without actual or perceived coercion. (Batista, 2007)

Brad Fisher adds to Batista's comments. As applied to the sport manager, where the line is drawn is difficult to determine. The courts have viewed that prayer before a game over an intercom is unconstitutional. The fans receiving the invocation, by majority, seem not to mind since the practice has been carried out as long as football has been around. But when the crowd is not unanimous in its views, a majority vote is not enough. When the prayer is truly student-initiated or when spectators join to recite a prayer, there is nothing the school has done wrong, but they cannot promote the invocation. If school systems still feel that there should be a prayer before a game, a moment of silence is the best route to take. Those who wish to pray may do so, and those who wish not to pray do not have to participate.

Of all the quotes and citations used in sports-related prayer, the one I feel is most significant is the one that was said by the man to whom most pray. Jesus said, "When you pray, you must not be like the hypocrites; for they love to stand and pray in the synagogues and at the street corners, that they may be seen by men ... But when you pray, go into your room and shut the door and pray to your Father who is in secret" (Matthew 6:5–6, quoted in Appenzeller, 2003).

Running through Scripture Banners on Football Friday

Catoosa County, in northwest Georgia, became involved "in the war over religion in public schools." For six years, cheerleaders at Lakeview-Fort Oglethorpe High School had painted banners with Bible verses, which the football players would run through at the start of the game. One such verse was Philippians 3:14: "I press on toward the goal to win the prize for which God has called me in Christ Jesus." After complaints were made regarding the banner, the Catoosa County school system took action. The school system said the practice of using Bible verses on the banners was a "violation of the First Amendment of the Constitution" (Galloway, 2009).

Hundreds protested the school system's action banning the banners, and a state representative urged the protesters to challenge the school system by bringing religious signs and displaying them in a special area outside the football stadium. The representative from Lafayette said, "Our Founding Fathers had one thing in mind when they founded this country, and it was a Christian nation built upon the principles of Jesus Christ" (Galloway, 2009).

Denia Reese, school superintendent, commented that she appreciated the protesters' Christian values, but she had an obligation to "protect[] the school district from legal action by groups who do not support their beliefs." Bill Nigut, southeast regional director of the Anti-Defamation League, supported the superintendent and commended her for making the tough decision to uphold the First Amendment of the Constitution by banning the banners at football games. He recognized the controversy her decision had created in the community, but applauded her for doing the right thing. He concluded in his letter to Reese, "It is essential that high school sports programs keep in mind that the children entrusted to [their] care likely have widely divergent religious points of view. [Reece's] decision shows respect for this diversity" (Galloway, 2009).

Fired Wrestling Coach Sues High School

In 2005, Gerry Marszalek was fired by Dearborn Fordson High School in Michigan after allegations were made that one of his volunteer assistant coaches had "converted one of the team members to Christianity and baptized him" (Brayton, 2009). Marszalek filed a wrongful termination suit against the high school and the principal, Imad Fadlallah.

The volunteer assistant coach, Trey Hancock, was the father of one of the wrestlers on the team. Hancock was a Pentecostal minister who said that the boy in question was one of his son's best friends. The school's principal fired Hancock after the boy, who attended his wrestling camp in the summer, converted to Christianity and was baptized by Hancock. At the time of the conversion, the boy was not a student at the school. The principal told Marszalek to keep Hancock out of Fordson High School, even though his son was a student there and an All-State wrestler on the school's team. The principal then banned the entire Hancock family from helping out at the school's concession stands during events (Brayton, 2009).

After the 2007–08 school year, Marszalek was fired as wrestling coach, even though he was one of the most successful wrestling coaches in the nation. He was also in the state and national wrestling coaches Hall of Fame. Marszalek claimed that his constitutional rights had been violated, as well as his "First Amendment rights to free exercise of religion and freedom of association, as well as religious discrimination under Michigan state law" (Brayton, 2009).

NFL Oakland Raider Cornerback Penalized

When Chris Johnson of the Oakland Raiders picked off a pass, he celebrated by "dropping to his knees and raising his arms in triumph." An official immediately threw a flag for an excessive celebration penalty. Johnson complained that he was merely thanking God and did not understand why the official penalized him. The official explained that in 2006 the NFL passed a rule that had nothing to do with religion. The rule penalizes anyone who celebrates in the end zone by "going to the ground to celebrate a touchdown or using the ball as a prop." The controversy was over the fact that the rule is not enforced on a consistent basis. Mike Pereira, NFL vice president for officiating said that "there would be an exception to the 'going to the ground' rule for players who did so to 'praise the Lord.'" (Chase, 2009).

Going against the Law to Pray

Many high schools continue to pray prior to their football games, going against the Supreme Court's decision to uphold the separation of church and state. They ignore the law of the land until they are challenged in court and lose their case.

In East Tennesee, a police officer escorted a group of people to assemble in front of stadium stands just behind the goal posts before a Soddy-Daisy High School football game. They were not allowed to hold a prayer on the football field. In the group were the town's mayor, the commissioner, people from the stands and others, both for the home team and visiting Cleveland High School fans. A student led the prayer. The school superintendent had "ordered a halt to prayers over the loudspeaker at football games and other school events." Some students had complained to the Freedom from Religion Foundation. The town commissioner said, "I'm ready to defy Washington and the Supreme Court. I don't have a problem with it at all" (Belk, 2010).

This brings to mind Governor Terry Sanford of North Carolina, when he said after the Supreme Court's decision to uphold the U.S. Constitution's ban on prayer in the public schools that "we in North Carolina will defy the law of the land and continue to pray."

Ethical Questions

1. Should athletes be allowed to pray in locker rooms and on the field prior to the start of games?

2. What is the difference between the Establishment Clause and the Free Exercise Clause?
3. Discuss the various ways that prayer is legal and what practices are not legal.

Gender Discrimination

In 1971, I was interviewed for the athletics director's job at a prestigious NCAA Division IAA school. A female coach on the Search Committee started the interview by posing a tough question. She said, "Our women pay athletic fees of over $500,000 toward the department's million-dollar budget and the men pay the same amount." "However," she said, "the men's football team travels on chartered jets and eats lobster and steak for their postgame meals. The women's teams travel on trips of over 1500 miles, in crowded, uncomfortable station wagons, and eat postgame meals at fast food restaurants." "Is that fair?" she asked. "Of course it isn't fair," I responded, "and something must be done to correct such a situation."

Schools nationwide were doing the same thing in their athletics programs, as they favored men's football and basketball because they were the so-called revenue sports. Administrators still thought of women's sports in terms of play days, extramural, intramural and club sports.

One year later, it seemed that the situation would be corrected when the Education Amendments Act of 1972 was passed by Congress. Title IX of the Act received national attention because of the implication for women in sport. Advocates of Title IX realized that the inequities that existed would not be corrected overnight and the Act would raise many questions that would take months or years to answer. It was obvious to Title IX supporters that some issues such as scholarships might be so complex that they would only be resolved by local court action. The experts proved to be right and many female participants, encouraged by Title IX, sought equity in sport by filing lawsuits. As a result, a variety of lawsuits followed the 1972 legislation.

Girls Playing on Boys' Teams

One of the major issues following the 1972 statute was the prohibition of girls on boys' teams in high school. A number of cases involving this issue were brought to the court, with some ruling for the girls and others for the schools that prohibited girls on boys' teams. In 1978, Judge Carl Rubin, in a highly publicized case (*Yellow Springs v. Ohio High School Athletic Association*, 1981), supported the effort of two girls who had made the boys' basketball team. The school board, however, refused to let the girls play on the boys' team and created a girls' basketball team for them to play on. Rubin and the U.S. District Court S.D., Ohio reasoned that the rule that prohibits girls from competing on male teams was unfair. Rubin, in an unusual decision, commented, "It has always been traditional that boys play football and girls are cheerleaders. Why so? Where is it written that girls may not, if suitably qualified, play football? There may be a multitude of reasons why a girl may elect not to do so. Because of stature or weight or reasons of temperament, motivation or interest. This is a matter of personal choice. But a prohibition without exception based on sex is not."

Judge Rubin continued in the 1978 case by prophesying that things could change if women were given the opportunity to participate on men's teams. He boldly predicted, "It may well be that there is a female student today in an Ohio high school who lacks only the proper coaching and training to become the greatest quarterback in professional football history. Of course the odds are astronomical against her, but isn't she entitled to a fair chance to try." (*Yellow Springs v. OHSAA*, 1981).

This case signaled a new attitude on the part of the courts and undoubtedly opened the door for females to go out for football and other sports, such as wrestling. For example, Michaela Hutchison won the 103-pound wrestling championship title during Alaska's big school wrestling championships. She entered the state tournament ranked No. 1 in the 103-pound class. She ended the season with a 45–4 record, which included 33 pins, "one shy of the state single-season record." Hutchison became the first girl in the United States to win a state high school wrestling title competition against boys (*Sports Illustrated*, 2006).

Female Hired to Coach Football in D.C. High School

Natalie Randolph, 29 years of age, a biology and environmental science teacher, was hired to coach football at Calvin Coolidge High School in Washington, D.C. Randolph, reportedly "the nation's only female head coach of a high school varsity football team," said her desire to coach has less to do with being the first female to coach varsity football than with her love for the sport and coaching. She said, "While I'm proud to be a part of what all this means, being female has nothing to do with it. I love football. I love football, I love teaching, I love these kids." Randolph was a track star at the University of Virginia and played football for six years for the D.C. Divas of the National Women's Football Association. She helped the Divas win the title in 2006 (White, 2010).

There are those who claim that the hiring of Randolph is a mistake. They argue that football is exclusively for men. Randolph realizes the challenges she faces, but is sure that the administration, as well as the students who play on her team, support her.

Guilford's Female Athletics Staff

When I served as athletics director at Guilford College, our women's tennis and volleyball coach had more winning seasons than any women's coach in North Carolina. A NAIA Hall of Fame recipient, she won numerous conference and district titles, and a national title in tennis. Everyone on our staff knew that I believed she could be a successful football coach if she was given the opportunity. However, we needed her to continue as a highly successful volleyball and tennis coach for our women.

Guilford College was the first to hire a female athletic trainer in the state of North Carolina. Mary Broos was named the North Carolina Athletic Trainer of the Year and the elected into the Guilford College Sports Hall of Fame. She opened the door for women athletic trainers in the state of North Carolina.

Equal Access for Female Sports Reporters

Greg Aiello, spokesperson for the NFL, sent a memo to all 32 teams about equal access to women reporters in locker rooms. The memo read as follows:

> Women are a common part of the sports media. By law, women must be granted the same rights to perform their jobs as men. Please remember that women reporters are professionals and should be treated as such. (*Charlotte Observer*, 2010)

Obviously, from the many collegiate and NFL games that appear on TV, it is commonplace to watch women reporters on the sidelines interview coaches prior to, during and after games. Recently, Ines Sainz, a female reporter, was interviewing the New York Jets quarterback after a game and felt that she was treated crudely by the New York Jets players. The alleged mistreatment drew national attention to the status of female reporters, and led to the NFL sending the memo reminding all 32 teams of its equal access and conduct policy toward the media.

In North Carolina, Mary Garber, a female reporter for the *Winston-Salem Journal*, could be seen waiting to talk with athletes following games on every level. Garber was well-received by players, due to her acceptance in locker rooms as early as the 1960s. The members of sports teams treated Garber with respect and goodwill until her death. Mary Garber was recognized for her work by her selection in the NC Sports Hall of Fame.

Female Kicker Awarded Two Million Dollars by Court, Later Reversed

In 2000, Heather Sue Mercer was awarded $2 million by a federal jury for discrimination by Duke University for cutting her from the men's football team because of her gender. Duke was ordered to pay Mercer $2 million in punitive damages and $1 in compensatory damages. Mercer said that she wanted the court to tell Duke that it was wrong and they did. Duke University argued that Mercer was not qualified to play on a Division I-A school's team. Mercer, like many other females on the high school and collegiate level of football, was a place kicker (*The News & Observer*, 2000).

The federal court reasoned that the university failed to listen to Mercer's complaints. Punitive damages were awarded by jurors who felt that the university "acted with malice and reckless indifference." Mercer's lawyers said that the $2 million wasn't too much for the university to pay for discriminating against the female place kicker. The lawyers contended that in the four years in which Mercer was a Duke student, the university received $800 million in federal money. A $2 million dollar fine is only a fraction of one percent of that—a modest sanction for Duke's conduct (*The News & Observer*, 2000).

Mercer said she planned to use the award to create a scholarship fund for young female athletes. However, a three-judge panel ruled that "punitive damages are not available in private actions brought to enforce Title IX." The federal appeals court dismissed the jury's $2 million award in November 2002 (*The News & Observer*, 2002).

Gender Discrimination Corrected

After Slippery Rock University cut its women's swimming and water polo teams, 12 female students filed a Title IX lawsuit claiming discrimination on the part of the athletics department. In April 2007, the case was settled, but in June of that year, the women athletes asked that the case be reopened, alleging that the university failed to comply with the requirements of the settlement, which included making improvements to the softball field and providing equitable coaching for the women's track team.

Under a new settlement, the university agreed to upgrade the women's softball field and provide $300,000 to improve women's athletics. Part of the $300,000 will be used to "improve the soccer field, buy weights to be used by women's teams and install nets around the field hockey and lacrosse fields." The new settlement also requires "Slippery Rock's athletic department, varsity coaches and athletes to undergo a mandatory two-hour Title IX training session next year" (Ward, 2009).

It is apparent that Slippery Rock University is attempting to meet Title IX guidelines. For example, in addition to the changes agreed to by the new settlement, the school's president, Dr. Robert Smith, points out that the university complies with the proportionality requirement—for the past two years, women have made up 56 percent of the school, and 56 percent of the varsity sporting spots have been for women.

We wonder if one two-hour Title IX session can possibly be adequate to cover Title IX issues. We believe a one-day session will be needed to cover the many questions and issues of the targeted group. One of the best ways to prevent Title IX litigation is to learn from past Title IX cases, and understand why institutions were sued and why cases were lost or won. Another suggestion is, when in doubt over a situation involving Title IX, call the Office of Civil Rights in your area. They can be extremely helpful and can be contacted anonymously.

Florida High School Athletic Association Agrees to Title IX Settlement

The *Miami Herald* (2009) reported that the Florida High School Athletic Association (FHSAA) reached a settlement with parents in Jacksonville, who sued over alleged Title IX violations. The agreement includes the following:

- Require FHSAA to pay $41,200 in legal fees.
- Notify the parents in writing two weeks before any proposed changes in an amendment that involves sports scheduling cuts.
- Provide Title IX training at its representative assembly meetings and in its compliance seminars. (*Miami Herald*, 2009)

The parents sued because FHSAA had voted to reduce scheduling of all varsity sports by 20 percent, except football and competitive cheering. Roger Dearing, Executive Director of the FHSAA, in an email to the *Sun-Sentinel*, said:

It is our understanding that all schools have returned to the same number of contests they had in the 2008–2009 school year. It is unfortunate that the situation occurred while trying to help our member schools with the financial crises they are facing, which inadvertently created an unintentional disparity to our student-athletes. It seems that a lack of communication between the FHSAA and parents probably led to a Title IX lawsuit. It is important and essential that both parties communicate so that expensive litigation can be avoided and issues explained amicably.

Title IX Compliance Still Needed

As discussed in an article by Paul Steinbach in *Athletic Business* (2010), Ellen Staurowsky spoke at the NCAA Gender Equity and Issues Forum in April 2010. Staurowsky asked her audience of athletic administrators, compliance officers and legal councilors the following question: "How many of you have run a Title IX workshop for your athletic department?" Not one hand went up. She repeated the question and got the same response: no one.

Staurowsky, a professor of sport management in the graduate program at Ithaca College, commented that "from 1972 to the present, administrators haven't gotten the job done." She supports her opinion with the number of compliance problems that have continued to go to court over the 38-year period since the passing of Title IX. Along with Erianne Wright, of Bowling Green State University, Staurowsky found the following in a survey of over 1,100 male and female coaches in Division I and III: "82 percent indicated that they had never been expressly taught about Title IX, and more than 65 percent identified the mainstream media as their primary source of Title IX information" (Steinbach, 2010). Staurowsky estimates that about 40 percent of the respondents do not understand how the law works. For example, she explains that fewer than 40 percent knew that booster money is covered under Title IX.

Almost 40 years after Title IX was passed, too many sport programs are still being litigated. One of the biggest challenges as to ethical behavior still exists, and this is the commitment of sport programs to provide programs for men and women that are equity-based and that represent equity not only for boys and men, but also for girls and women. With the number of multi-million dollar awards to plaintiffs who file lawsuits, a program that educates everyone associated with sports is imperative and long overdue.

Title IX Is the Law, but It Still Must Be Fully Implemented

Since the passage of Title IX, my colleagues and I have conducted a large number of risk assessments (safety reviews) of athletics programs at high schools, colleges and other educational facilities across America. One of the most frequent issues that we have uncovered during our risk assessments concern the lack of Title IX compliance in the girls' and women's softball programs. In most cases, school officials try to comply with Title IX guidelines, but unfortunately fall short of required equity when baseball programs are compared with softball programs. Almost all baseball programs were well-established before softball came on the scene. As a result, baseball has developed a number of assistant coaches, adequate playing fields with stadium seating, lights on the field for night practice and play, dugouts, individual locker rooms, press boxes, separate practice fields and other amenities such as concession stands. Sadly, women's softball programs often lack many of these facilities.

In Rockingham County, NC, school officials plan to spend three years upgrading the county's softball programs. Officials want to correct inequities federal officials discovered in the system's athletics programs. The goal is to do the following for softball to be in parity with baseball: provide equal locker rooms; provide equal and separate fields for softball; add lighting, bleachers and other features.

As part of its investigation, federal officials determined that the Rockingham school system provided adequate medical facilities and equitable pay for coaches for both men's and women's sports. To further the school system's goal to insure equitable programs at the county's four high schools, booster clubs at all four schools that have traditionally supported men's athletics are expected to help fund the improvements for women's athletics as well (*News & Record* 2010).

When new facilities are in the planning stages, it is important that Title IX guidelines be taken into consideration and followed from the start. Title IX equity is a good and worthy goal for all who administer and participate in athletics.

Women in Intercollegiate Sports—
Drs. Carpenter and Acosta

Drs. Linda Carpenter and Vivian Acosta, Brooklyn College professors, have been leading researchers of Title IX for 33 years. Their February 2010 report, "Women in Intercollegiate Sport," showed only modest gains in the areas of "head coaching, athletic training and sports information, where women have long remained underrepresented." In an article titled "Are We There Yet?", Carpenter and Acosta answer, "No." Carpenter says, "We've gotten closer ... We've crossed a lot of milestones, made a lot of correct turns. But we're not there yet. And we're not going to get there unless the role of athletics is altered some" (Steinbach, 2010).

"Title IX in a Nutshell" by Vivian Acosta
and Linda Carpenter

- Title IX became law on June 23, 1972. Its language was patterned after Title VI.
- Title IX jurisdiction requires the presence of three elements:
  - education program,
  - Federal financial aid,
  - allegations of sex discrimination

- Title IX does NOT require that the education program be public, nor even a school *per se*. Among the non-school entities which have been drawn within the reach of Title IX are athletic leagues and city recreation programs.
- The one sentence above represents the "Law". Its details were spelled out in Regulations (the goals) which gained the force of law on July 21, 1975. In effect, the Regulations spelled out the goals of what it means to act in nondiscriminatory ways within the scope of Title IX. The Regulations were NOT specific about Title IX's requirements in sport. Remember, Title IX affects all education programs, not just athletics.
- In 1979 an additional document joined the Title IX package. It is known as the Policy Interpretations. The Policy Interpretations, in effect, becomes the yardstick with which to measure the attainment in sport programs of the goals found in the Regulations. The Policy Interpretations do NOT have the force of law but must be given great deference by the courts. It is within the Policy Interpretations that the "Three Pronged Test" is found. The "Three Pronged Test" has been the subject of considerable debate over the years but its validity has been upheld by the courts and by the Department of Education and its Office for Civil Rights (charged with the administrative enforcement of Title IX).
  - The Law   (Mission Statement)
  - Regulations   (Goals)
  - Policy Interpretations   (Yardstick for measuring attainment of goals)

Where to Look for Problems

There are many ways to organize Title IX's requirements but the most common way is to look at 13 areas. The 13 are: accommodating the interests and abilities of members of both sexes, equipment and supplies, scheduling of games and practices, travel and per diem allowance, opportunity to receive coaching and academic tutoring, assignment and compensation of coaches and tutors, provision of locker rooms and practice and competitive facilities, medical and training facilities and services, housing and dining facilities and services, publicity, recruitment, support services, and financial assistance.

Enforcement Avenues

- In house complaint
- Office for Civil Rights complaint
- Lawsuit

There are three avenues of enforcement and their selection is totally within the inclination of the complainant. In house complaints, tendered to the institution's required 'Title IX designated employee' may be made by anyone. OCR complaints similarly may be made by anyone. Both carry only the potential for a promise from the school to go forth and sin no more; the OCR complaint also carries the never-yet-used possibility of the removal of federal $$. A lawsuit may only be filed by a plaintiff who has legal standing (ex: coach or athlete) but carries with it the potential for money damages (compensatory AND punitive).

Significant Lawsuits and Legislation Having an Impact on Title IX

Grove City v. Bell, 1984: This case grew out of the 1978 requirement that all schools sign a statement saying they were in compliance with Title IX. Almost all schools did so, even though few were actually in compliance. Grove City College refused to do so based on its long standing rejection of any federal intrusion on its campus. There was no allegation of sex discrimination on campus but Grove City's refusal to sign the letter triggered a move to withdraw the only federal money anywhere near campus (BEOG grants given to its students directly who then, indirectly, used the money to pay Grove City's tuition). Grove City College sued the federal government to block the withdrawal. Two points of significance were the result of the Grove City decision. 1). The US Supreme Court ruled that even indirect funding was sufficient to trigger Title IX jurisdiction and 2) Title IX's jurisdiction extended only to the sub unit of the institution which actually received federal money. The impact of the first point maintained Title IX's broad jurisdiction of education programs but the second, in effect removed its jurisdiction over physical education and athletics programs. Physical education and athletics programs almost never enjoy federal dollars and thus were NOT institutional sub units which would fall within Title IX's reach. Almost instantly after the Grove City decision was handed down, many colleges withdrew scholarship aid for their female athletes and some terminated women's teams. High school programs were not impacted by the Grove City decision because their federal money is mixed into the entire operating budget.

Civil Rights Restoration Act of 1987 (enacted over presidential veto in 1988). The CRRA, in effect, corrected the second part of the Grove City decision; basically it said that Congress had indeed intended Title IX's jurisdiction to be triggered for the ENTIRE institution whenever one dollar of federal money appeared anywhere on campus. Thus, in 1988 college athletics and physical education programs were again within the sweep of Title IX.

Franklin v. Gwinnett Public Schools, 1992. Prior to this case, the best that a complainant to OCR or the plaintiff in a Title IX lawsuit could hope for was the withdrawal of all federal money from the campus of a non-complying education program. OCR has never withdrawn any federal money for a Title IX violation; Title IX's teeth were dull prior to Franklin. The Franklin unanimous Supreme Court decision found that both compensatory and punitive damages were available to the successful plaintiff who proved intentional discrimination under Title IX. The court further indicated that any school which had an athletics program which violated Title IX was most likely doing so intentionally because Title IX was, at the time twenty years old. The Franklin decision provided very sharp teeth for those seeking to enforce Title IX via the courts and many schools decided that it was fiscally sound to move to compliance rather than to spend their money on attorneys defending the indefensible.

Jackson v Birmingham, 2005. The 5–4 decision in this Supreme Court case was handed down in March, 2005. If decided differently it would have had a significant negative impact on Title IX enforcement. Jackson is a high school coach of a girls team. He discussed potential Title IX violations with his superiors and was fired in retaliation. Title IX includes a prohibition against retaliation. Title IX covers employees as well as students (although for most issues, employees find better help from Title VII or the Equal Pay Act). The issue in the case was whether Coach Jackson's remedies are limited to filing a complaint with OCR which has no meaningful value to an employee who was fired or if Coach Jackson (who was later rehired) has access to a 'private right of action' (the right to use a lawsuit, not just a complaint) which would carry the potential of money damages (both compensatory and punitive). The decision means that when an employee is fired in retaliation for talking about Title IX, the employee has a remedy available which has significance. If Jackson had lost (which he didn't), coaches and teachers who value their continuing employment would likely be have been silenced on Title IX topics.

Court Cases Involving Title IX

Former Coach Wins Title IX Suit

Lorri Sulpizio, former women's basketball coach at Mesa College in San Diego, was awarded $28,000 in damages by a San Diego Superior Court "after finding she had been retaliated against by the school for complaining about unequal treatment she perceived in its athletic facilities for women" (Schrotenboer, 2009).

Sulpizio was fired in 2007, without any reason given by the college, after she made her complaints public. The former women's basketball coach expressed her concern about the locker room for her female athletes. Her team was moved out when visiting football teams were on campus for games. Sulpizio allegedly reported her concerns to Athletics Director Dave Evans in 2006. She filed a Title IX gender discrimination suit in 2007 and Mesa agreed to correct disparities in the women's program in an agreement with the Office of Civil Rights (OCR). The OCR evidence was not admissible during the trial.

The college had offered to settle the lawsuit for $35,000, but Sulpizio chose to accept her annual salary of $28,000. Her attorney said the $28,000 was hers alone. If she had settled for $35,000, attorney fees and other legal costs would have left her between $10,000 and $20,000 (Schrotenboer, 2009).

In her lawsuit, Sulpizio alleged gender and sexual orientation violations. The jury did not find either in their verdict. However, Helen Carroll of the National Center for Lesbian Rights called the verdict a landmark "because it helped establish protection for two-year college coaches and athletes, instead of just the bigger four-year colleges that get all the headlines" (Schrotenboer, 2009).

Fresno State Awards Three Former Athletics Employees in Lawsuits

After three years of litigation, Stacy Johnson-Klein's sexual discrimination and gender harassment lawsuit against Fresno State University was settled. The California State University (CSU) System announced that it had agreed to a $9 million settlement that will be paid over a 23-year period. Former women's basketball coach Johnson-Klein was one of three women suing Fresno State in Title IX cases. In October 2007, former associate athletics director Diane Milutinvoch settled for $3.5 million, and in July 2007, former volleyball coach Lindy Vivas was awarded $5.8 million. Vivas' award was later reduced to $4.52 million, plus attorney's fees. CSU is appealing the cases against them by Milutinvoch and Vivas (Lieber-Steeg, 2008).

These three awards are a wake-up call for all college administrators. The costs of violating Title IX can be tremendous and are a waste of much-needed funds that should be used to operate athletics programs. Attention must be paid to Title IX guidelines so that money can be used for the operation of athletics programs, not Title IX awards. Hopefully, the California University System will correct the Title IX violations that the courts judged Fresno State to have violated.

Title IX Case Settled

Officials at Torrance High School in California settled a case that had approximately 21 Title IX violations. The case centered around the lack of adequate facilities for the girls' softball team. The lawsuit claimed the outfield used by the junior varsity softball team was also used by the boys' sports team for practice. The field lacked infield dirt, making base running dangerous.

The complaint cited that the "softball teams didn't receive the same fundraising opportunities as the baseball squads," that they experienced a lack of field maintenance and that "scheduling conflicts favored boys sports program, leaving the girls little time to use locker rooms, weight training equipment and batting cages" (Morino, 2009).

The school district settled the case before it went to court. It covered the plaintiff's attorney fees of $40,000 and an additional $40,000 for improvements to the facilities. The plaintiff said that once the issue was resolved, "the support from parents and other athletes was overwhelming. Once girls teams began getting recognized more, the boys teams started supporting [the girls softball team]" (Morino, 2009).

Ethical Questions

1. Should girls and boys play together in:
   a. physical education classes?
   b. intramurals?
   c. recreation programs?
   d. interscholastic contests?
   e. intercollegiate contests?
2. If your answer is yes for any category, would you eliminate any particular sport activity?
3. Discuss the Heather Mercer case. Should the court have awarded her damages? If yes, why? If not, why not?
4. Are coaches and staff aware of Title IX in high schools? Colleges? Recreation programs?
5. Should women reporters be granted access to men's locker rooms at every level?
6. Discuss Acosta and Carpenter's "Title IX in a Nutshell."
7. Discuss the three-pronged test of Title IX.

Racial Discrimination

A Touching Experience

I was at the Amateur Athletic Union (AAU) headquarters in New York waiting for the seventh and final athlete to report for our scheduled eight-week tour of the Far East. The AAU and the U.S. State Department were hoping that our seven track stars and two coaches would compete in friendly competition and exchange ideas in a spirit of friendship and cooperation with athletes in Malaysia, Thailand, Philippines, Korea and Hong Kong. Our mission was to create goodwill between the United States and the nations of the Far East.

All of our men had reported except Ray Saddler, a talented 400-meter runner, who earlier that year had broken the indoor 400-meter mark during a 1600-meter relay in Madison Square Garden. Ray had recently married and was a day late in reporting for the upcoming trip. When I saw Ray, all the stereotypes I ever had about African Americans went into action. Ray had on dark shades, a bright pink coat and pointed alligator shoes, and was humming and swinging his arms to the beat of a popular rock tune.

AAU and U.S. State Department officials had warned our other coach Rod Richards, a former University of California at Los Angeles sprinter, to send anyone who caused a problem home immediately. I thought that I had found the man, who in all probability would cause trouble on the trip, and I was ready to make sure I handled the potential problems Ray would bring swiftly and firmly. Just how wrong can our stereotypes and prejudices be? Ray was unbelievable, and a joy to work with in every country in the Far East. One particular memory about Ray still stands out from the rest.

Our team had worked extremely hard in competition and in assisting our friends in training techniques in Singapore, Malaysia and Bangkok. When we arrived in Hong Kong, we were told that because of the extreme heat and our demanding schedule in the previous two countries, we were only required to work in Kowloon in the morning. The rest of the time we could sightsee and have a good time. This was great news for everyone.

A request came in from the South China Track Club for a member of our nine-man team to go back to Kowloon after lunch each day and work with 100 Chinese boys and girls. I told the team I would go until Ray Saddler insisted that he be sent. "Coach," he said, "you know I'm homesick for my wife and I need to stay busy. I really love kids and want to go and help the South China group." After our grueling morning workouts, we would see Ray eager to return to Kowloon. At night, he would literally bounce into our quarters excited over the afternoon's workouts and experiences. Neither the heat nor the extra hours seemed to bother him, and reports came back about his ability to relate to the group of young Chinese boys and girls.

On our final night in Hong Kong, I was sitting in the lobby of the hotel when Ray came in. He had a different expression on his face and Coach Richards noticed it and questioned him about the day's activities. I can never forget his story. He got to the stadium as he had everyday, on time and ready to coach. When he entered the stadium, all 100 members of the South China group had already assembled and stood at attention awaiting his arrival. To Ray's surprise, the group roared approval and showered him with gifts and mementos for his help. "What did you do, Ray?" I asked, and he replied, "Coach, I just stood there and cried. After all, I'm black and I live in the South. I never expected this to happen to me and it has touched me like nothing that has happened before."

Ray Saddler later told me that he was considering joining the Peace Corps so he could continue to help people of other cultures. He contributed more to our Far East Asian Tour than I ever imagined possible. A victim at times of racial prejudice, he became a role model for all Far Eastern athletes and proved to me the folly of stereotyping people.

LA Clippers Owner Fined $2.73 Million for Discrimination

Donald Sterling, owner of the NBA Los Angeles Clippers, agreed to pay a $2.73 million settlement for "refusing to rent apartments to Hispanics, Blacks and families with children" (*From the Gym to the Jury*, 2009). Sterling, a real estate mogul, and his wife were sued by the Justice Department for allegations of housing discrimination in Los Angeles's Koreatown. "It was reported that the defendants allegedly made statements to their employees that African Americans and Hispanics were not desirable tenants" (*From the Gym to the Jury* 2009). In light of the $2.73 million settlement, we can only speculate on the attitude of the African American basketball players on the Los Angeles Clippers toward Sterling and his wife.

Racial Discrimination Suit Filed Against Historically Black School

Robby Wells was hired to coach football at historically black college Savannah State in 2008. Wells claims that he was forced to resign his position as head football coach in January 2010 because he is white. Similarly, four white players contended that their football scholarships were taken away because they are white. They filed suit against the university when Wells was forced to resign and their scholarship offers were withdrawn. In 2004, baseball coach Jamie Rigdon, who is white, settled a lawsuit for $265,000 after he was fired.

Interim athletics director, Marilyn Stacey-Suggs, pointed to several alleged violations as the reason Wells was forced to resign. These were listed as: undocumented campus visits by prospective student-athletes; failure to follow athletics department guidelines and procedures; less-than-professional behavior at practice and road games; and misuse of resources (Glier, 2010).

Savannah State President Earl G. Yarbrough said that his faculty is one of the most diverse in the country. He pointed to a 2001 statistic: "about 49% of the faculty was black, 30% white and 21% Asian, Hispanic, Pacific Islander or mixed race." In 2009, "about 42% of the faculty was black, 24% white and 33% Asian, Hispanic, Pacific Islander or mixed race." Savannah State's white golf coach, Art Gelow, said that his "integrity was insulted by [Wells]," whose losing records were "grounds to lose [his] job," in Gelow's opinion. He noted that 40 college coaches lost their jobs in 2009 due to losing records (Glier, 2010).

Coach Charged with Racial Discrimination

Bruce Smith has been a successful basketball coach at Whitmer High School in Toledo, Ohio, for 19 years. However, several players and their parents have accused the successful coach of making "racially insensitive remarks to his players" and being "verbally abusive" (*Toledo Blade* 2010). According to several complaints, Smith "referred to some black players as 'monkeys' and racially segregated the team on several occasions for practice drills, telling multiracial students they'd have to choose which side to play on" (Kirkpatrick, 2010).

The coach insisted that he is not a racist and said he never made racially charged remarks. "He called the complaints by some parents and the resulting media coverage 'character assassination' and a 'witch hunt,' and referred to the parents as 'a lynch mob'" (Kirkpatrick, 2010). Several players said they "fully supported the coach and didn't believe any of the allegations." Some former students who played for Smith, both black and white, defended the coach, calling him a "father figure to them and an important role model." One former player said that when he played on the team, the black and white players chose to separate themselves by race for competition and fun (Kirkpatrick, 2010).

During the investigation, it was clear that some parents who were too involved with the basketball team would attend practice to closely watch the behavior of the coaches and report their concerns to the administrators. Other parents did not want to be identified because they felt that the coach would retaliate against their sons. Coach Smith denied this complaint and offered to meet with the parents "to discuss their unspecified concerns, but only in individual sessions and not in a 'town hall-style' format." A letter to the school board president, signed by more than 20 parents, "stressed confidentiality for those who signed their names for fear of reprisals from coaches and school administrators against their children" (Kirkpatrick, 2010).

Minority Football Coaches Scarce in FBS

According to a 2009 report by *The Tennessean*, only 7.5 percent of head coaches in the Football Bowl Subdivision schools are black. "That means only nine of the 120 head football coaches positions are held by minorities" (Mullen, 2009). University of Tennessee Athletics Director Mike Hamilton said, "Someone needs to take a chance [on hiring minority coaches]. When that happens, maybe the glass ceiling will be broken." Sylvester Croom, who became the first minority head football coach in the SEC when he was hired in 2003, said "the biggest problem right now" is "a feeder system that fails to put minorities in positions to become head coaches" (Mullen, 2009).

A Hollow Victory

I was a part of blatant racism and the memory of the event still haunts me. In late August 1951, I accepted the positions of athletics director and head coach in football, basketball and baseball at a small junior college in eastern North Carolina. I had never visited the school, but I knew that it had been a prestigious institution for women until it become coeducational. Chowan College had closed its doors in the early 1940s for lack of financial support and in 1949 an intense fundraising drive enabled it to reopen. The president, a renowned Baptist minister, was a controversial figure in Baptist circles for his strong opposition to the use of tobacco money to move Wake Forest College to Winston-Salem. His vigorous stand attracted supporters, but also earned him defiant enemies who felt that Wake Forest could grow to university status and serve its constituency more effectively if it moved to Winston-Salem. At any rate, Chowan's trustees saw his notoriety as a plus for the struggling school.

In 1951, blacks outnumbered whites eight to one in the college town and racial tension in that area as well as other parts of North Carolina was evident. President Mixon informed me that it was crucial for the institution to field a football team. When I informed him that only ten men reported for the first practice, he refused to accept my suggestion that I actively recruit and field a team the following year. "Somehow, someway," he said, "find a way to get a team together." I implored each of the ten men to recruit one other player so we could field a team. I had little hope that we could pull it off, but I agreed to try because of the president's insistence that we field a team for public relations purposes. What followed was a mini-miracle, a once in a lifetime experience. The following day, 19 men reported for practice and we were on our way.

Stories of the recruitment by the original ten were fascinating. A 6'2", 185-pound tight end with a talent for football but not academics had dropped out of school and worked for a candy company, delivering candy to stores in the area. A former teammate spotted him in town and convinced him to lock the van up and report for practice. He did just that and brought a large supply of candy for post-practice snacks. Our quarterback, an exceptional, talented athlete, drove home to persuade his cousin, a commercial fisherman, to reel in his nets on the Chowan River and join us as a linebacker. One man who played six-man football and his closest friend who had never played football appeared on campus without any money but a desire for an education. The president told them to go back to their farms and sell a pig each and come on! The stories went on and on, but "somehow, someway" they came. The president believed in the power of prayer and miracles, and frankly I became a believer, too! As the years pass, I find that the 19-man squad was an amazing feat.

Now the problem: we had only five games scheduled and needed two games desperately. You can only practice for so long—you need to play to keep the team interested and motivated. I received a call from Captain John Stanley, a football coach at Camp Lejeune, North Carolina, who wanted to play a game as much as we did. We agreed instantly on an early September game and our men were excited. Now, an unexpected problem developed that really disturbed me. President Mixon was elated over the upcoming game but immediately asked if Camp Lejeune had any black players on its squad. My response was, "So what? I expect they do, after all they are Marines." He was deeply troubled over the possibility that people who opposed the mixing of races would cause trouble for the college because we were both in our first year at the college. He felt that we could create a situation that would threaten the existence of the college. I quickly responded that I would cancel the game, preferring that to asking a coach to play without his full team, specifically two outstanding halfbacks.

Captain Stanley said we had to play and that his two men would understand because they were, like me, from the South. We pulled an upset of major proportions before an overflow crowd at the game. The 12–7 victory enabled me to get off to a strong start. But to me it was a hollow victory because of those two missing players.

I wrote a letter of apology to Captain Stanley, but the letter returned unopened. Stanley, a great spokesman and leader of men, had been killed the week after the game when his aircraft crashed on a routine training mission over the Albemarle Sound. He was without a doubt one of the finest men I had known, even though our association was brief. I took a pledge that I would never again let prejudice play such a role in my coaching.

Our Game Made a Statement

Two years later, and one year before the 1954 *Brown v. Topeka Board of Education* case that ended segregation, our team was undefeated and attracting state and national attention. Our crowds were growing and support was increased. Our opponent was the Portsmouth Marines from Virginia. I knew that a large number of blacks were on the team and many were key players. I never mentioned to President Mixon or anyone else that we would be playing a racially mixed football team. We had a tough, hard-hitting game and won a hard fought victory 28–14. This time we won with honor. No one criticized me or the president following the game. It was the start of a new era and I am still proud of the part we played in the tension-filled days that followed the *Brown* decision. Our game made a statement that Chowan College and its athletics program would no longer be a part of racial injustice.

Chowan College's sports history is well-documented, as its sports teams have been integrated without incident and at times its rosters are dominated by black athletes. Many have gone on to four-year colleges after graduation and others to the professional ranks, such as Nate McMillan, former player for the Seattle Supersonics of the National Basketball Association, and others in professional football who played at Chowan College. Chowan College is now a member of the historically black athletic conference: the Central Intercollegiate Athletic Association (CIAA). Chowan College's relationship with the predominantly black conference schools has been a success and its teams are supported by the community. (Chowan is now a university.)

Ethical Questions

1. Discuss the case involving the owner of the Los Angeles Clippers.
2. Discuss Whitmer High School's parents' action toward the school's basketball coach. Discuss his coaching style.
3. Discuss any situation you experienced or observed involving racial discrimination that was negative. Discuss one that had a positive impact or result.

Chapter 5

Medical Issues

"The most effective way to deal with an emergency catastrophic accident is to plan in advance." —*Michael Clopton*

The Importance of Planning

Michael Clopton is a former administrative assistant to the head football coach at University of Oklahoma and someone who assumed many duties during his time with the university's athletics department. Safety was one of them. He wrote about having "a catastrophic injury plan" and stressed that "proper planning and training will reduce confusion and eliminate unnecessary errors when an emergency occurs" (Appenzeller, 2005). He emphasized the importance of having policies and procedures for risk management strategies when dealing with medical emergencies.

The Pre-Participation Physical Examination

I never had a pre-participation physical examination in high school or college in the 1940s for football or track. I participated two years in varsity track in high school and four years in college, and two years in varsity high school football and two years and three spring practices in varsity college football. When I attempted to join the armed forces during World War II, I found that I had a physical defect that had gone undetected during the years I participated in sports and was rejected from service as 4F.

In 1976, I was invited to speak at a campus in the Midwest. I discovered that the school had 145 walk-on athletes trying out for the various teams that fall. No one was given a pre-participation physical examination; according to the school's policy, only those who made the team were required to receive a physical exam by the university medical staff. In my opinion, the school was extremely vulnerable to a lawsuit if a walk-on sustained an injury due to a disabling condition. This was in 1976, and 34 years later, many schools still have outdated policies that require walk-ons to provide medical exams from their personal physicians before they try out for teams. They then get a physical check-up by a university doctor or medical staff if they make the team.

For years, our coaches have scheduled physical examinations for their athletes in the fall when all sports are represented. This causes doctors to look at as many as 1,000 athletes at a time, and they cannot devote the time needed to properly ensure a complete and satisfactory examination. A helpful suggestion is to schedule various teams early in the summer to lessen the number of athletes doctors have to examine. Since many athletes work out in the summer heat on a voluntary basis, they could have their physical examinations completed during that time.

Janie Crowley, a sports trainer for the Springdale School District and Trinity Sports Medicine in Springdale, Arkansas, has a novel plan. Crowley spends hours, with the help of local doctors, providing free physical examinations that include checking blood pressure, heart rates, body weight, hernias and body strength. Crowley and her medical associates believe that more tests are required because we are "dealing with matters of life and death." The National Center for Catastrophic Sport Injury Research reports that there are 20–25 deaths every year due to cardiac deaths among high school and college athletics. Dr. Frank Cetta of the Mayo Clinic in Rochester, Minnesota, said, "sport physicals need to include an electrocardiogram (EKG) and echocardiogram so that athletes with unknown heart issues can be treated" (*The Morning News*, 2010).

The Need for Physical Examinations During Try-Outs

Colleges have many different policies for participation in sports. One college I visited did not allow a walk-on athlete to receive a physical examination by a school physician until the person made the team. At this college, 145 athletes were trying out for a particular team without physical examinations. This could lead to a lawsuit if a person sustained a serious injury because no one knew of a potential medical problem.

Players with Sickle Cell Trait Die, Parents Sue Schools

The family of Aaron O'Neal agreed to a $2 million settlement over the death of their son. O'Neal, a linebacker for the University of Missouri, collapsed on the field after a preseason workout and died. The parents complained that the school's employees failed to take medical precautions required by O'Neal's sickle cell trait. The hereditary condition has been linked to heatstroke and exercise-induced collapse. The family sued 14 employees named as defendants that included football coach Gary Pinkel, Athletics Director Mike Alden, Medical Director Rex Sharp and 11 athletic trainers and strength coaches. The settlement included a scholarship fund of $250,000 in O'Neal's name (*The Associated Press*, 2009).

The parents of Ereck Plancher, a redshirt freshman wide receiver at the University of Central Florida who died during off-season conditioning drills, filed a lawsuit against Central Florida officials. An autopsy revealed that Flancher had the sickle cell trait. In 2007, the National Athletic Trainers Association (NATA) recommended that college teams screen their players for the sickle cell trait. NATA noted that many athletic trainers "mistake the ailment for heat exhaustion, muscle cramps or heart problems." NATA reports that 10 athletes have died in the last eight years from complications related to the sickle cell trait. Their ages ranged from 12 to 19 years (*The Associated Press*, 2009).

"I'll Make the Team or Die Trying"

Jospin "Andre" Milandu wanted to make the track team at NC A&T State University. He told his sister Ferline that he would make the team or die trying. Athletics Director Wheeler Brown said Milandu was a walk-on who ran the 300-meter hurdle. As such, A&T's policy was that to participate in track, he had to have a complete physical on file and a signed waiver.

The team was running laps, when Milandu collapsed and died. His family said that he had no known heart problems. Wheeler Brown said the school would investigate whether Milandu had met the requirements of a complete physical examination and a signed waiver before he began practice. The University required that an athletic trainer be present at track practice. On the day Milandu died, no athletic trainer was present.

Only if Milandu had made the team would a university doctor have given him a physical examination. All reports point to a dedicated athlete who was passionate about track. University officials attribute his death to "complications from an elevated heart rate, the sickle cell trait and the lack of a physical examination" (*News & Record*, 2010).

A&T Chancellor Harold Martin said, "Had our processes been followed, trainers would have been scheduled and in place, proof of physical examinations would have been obtained, and signed release waivers would have been on file." The specific violation of rules included:

1. NCAA policy requires a physical for athletes at tryouts, practices and events, which was broken along with A&T's own similar policy.

2. Milandu had not signed a required release waiver for the A&T athletic department, a violation of school policy.
3. No trainer attended the practice, which is required by A&T for tryouts, practices and events.
4. The practice was not officially scheduled with the athletics department. The practice was held on August 19, but athletic trainers at A&T were under the impression that practice would begin on August 26
5. According to Chancellor Martin, 29 athletes participated in the August 19 tryout (*News & Record*, 2010).

Jospin "Andre" Milandu did not have a physical examination before he tried out with the track team. If he had known that he had sickle cell trait, and the NC A&T athletic trainers had been aware of his condition, they could have treated him and he could have lived. "Instead, he collapsed and died in an unofficial tryout with no trainers present" (*News & Record* 2010).

Milandu became the eleventh student from a U.S. college who died during athletic training because of the sickle cell trait. The other 10 were playing football. In 2008, Chad Wiley, a football player also at A&T, died from complications from a heat stroke. He had the sickle cell trait as well. University policies were violated because the tryout did not appear on the school's scheduled athletic events (*News & Record*, 2010).

Since 2000, 10 of 16 deaths during football conditioning drills were caused by the sickle cell trait. Sport medicine specialists have been following sickle cell trait since 1970, when the first death from the trait took place. However, the lawsuit against Rice University after a football player died in 2006, and others that followed, led to the NCAA requiring mandatory testing "for all athletes at Division I schools." Dr. Bert Fields, head of the Sports Medicine Center at Moses Cone Hospital in Greensboro, North Carolina, "has studied the condition for 30 years." Fields has worked with several colleges to develop a response plan to stop sickle cell episodes before they happen.

After Milandu's death, "it was found in the autopsy" that Milandu did not know he had the trait. He did not have a physical that was an NCAA requirement before he tried out for the track team. A&T officials investigated the situation and "found that physicals for Milandu and six others in the tryout weren't on file at the athletics office." A&T filed a violation of rules with the NCAA and "fired its athletic director and compliance director." The longtime track coach announced his retirement (*News & Record*, 2010).

Awareness of Sickle Cell Trait Saves Athlete

A female student on a track and field team in California lived after a sickle cell episode, two months after Milandu's death, because her athletic trainers knew she had the condition and had a treatment plan in place. A sports physician at her school said the student participated at a high level and that the coaches and athletic trainers were briefed about her condition. In an October practice, the student was participating in interval training, "when she began to feel leg cramping, abdominal pain and weakness" (*News & Record*, 2010).

The sports physician reported, "Because we went through education regarding sickle cell trait, the trainer brought the athlete into the training room and cooled the athlete down and hydrated the athlete and was able to alleviate the symptoms before the athlete deteriorated into a worse situation." He continued, "A whirlpool and electrolyte drink in time helped save the student from greater danger" (*News & Record*, 2010).

Since the deaths of Wiley and Milandu, an awareness of sickle cell trait has increased. The test for the trait in all newborns is conducted in all 50 states. Scott Anderson, head athletic trainer at the University of Oklahoma, said, "Teaching people about what to do and how to treat the athlete is the key." Anderson notes that many athletes in the NFL have the trait under control and are playing well. Dr. Fields commented, "The problem you get into in a lot of schools is training staff and coaches change, year to year, and the training staffs and reaction plans are not followed. He concluded that "still more needs to be understood about the condition … There will probably be more research to know what to do better" (*News & Record*, 2010).

There is often a lack of communication between the athletics department and the athletic trainers over the starting date of tryouts. As an athletics director for over 40 years, I always worried about our coaches failing to help check the eligibility of their athletes, making sure all our policies and rules were followed. It was my watch and I felt responsible when policies were violated and rules not followed. It is unfortunate that tragedies such as these cause many to have "righteous indignation" over the situation and look for someone to blame. However, the fact is that we are reporting this situation not to assess blame on anyone, but to help others make sure this unfortunate incident does not happen to them.

No Physical Exam for Cross Country Runner

A college cross country runner complained of chest pains. His coach took him to a CVS Pharmacy Minute Clinic instead of his certified athletic trainer, who later discovered that he had not been given a pre-participation physical before he started his strenuous running. In a time when there has been tremendous emphasis on the importance of a physical examination, we still let our student-athletes at every level participate in sports without physical exams. Once again, this is, in my opinion, medical malfeasance.

"Concussion in Sports" by Adam Kendall

Catastrophic events lead medical providers to be extremely cautious in concussion cases. Other clinical *sequelae* associated with concussion include post-concussion syndrome, depression, memory deficits, and *dementia pugilistica*. Post-concussion syndrome involves ongoing symptoms of concussion that can last weeks, months, and even years. Rarely the symptoms will become permanent. *Dementia pugilistica* is a chronic brain injury which can lead to symptoms similar to Parkinson's disease, slowed mental processing, memory and speech problems, tremors, and inappropriate behavior. This most often occurs in boxers who have suffered multiple concussions from repetitive blows to the head.

How do we recognize when an athlete is suffering from a concussion? Well, there is often a dazed or slightly disoriented look that appears on the face of the athlete. They also typically have other signs including a headache, confusion, dizziness, vision disturbance, event-related amnesia, nausea and vomiting, and inability to follow directions. Loss of consciousness may occur with a concussion as well but is not necessary for a diagnosis.

The management of a concussion is also a highly debated topic. However, a few common themes are present in the literature. First, a concussion needs to be managed by medical personnel familiar with the diagnosis, treatment options, and complications associated with a concussion. Additionally, an athlete will need to be cleared by a physician prior to returning to play. Finally, a step-wise, monitored return to play protocol is the most commonly used method to safely return an athlete to competition.

Testimony on the Impact of Concussions on High School Athletes

James Schmutz, Executive Director of the American Sport Education Program, testified before the US House of Representatives Committee on Education and Labor on "The Impact of Concussions on High School Athletes":

Over the years we have seen dramatic and positive impact of … educational efforts. Take for example the salt tablet and water deprivation. This was common practice in the 1970s. But [once] scientists (nutritionists) and sports medicine specialists decried this accepted training tactic and studies pointed to the serious health risks involved, thinking on this slowly turned. And not until coaching education services hammered this message home and taught alternate, safe hydration and heat illness prevention guidelines did this practice, with exceptions, stop altogether. We should be mindful of those exceptions so that we sustain a relentless approach to educating every coach. (Schmutz, 2010)

House Panel Sets Concussion Guidelines

A House panel approved legislation "to increase the government role in protecting young athletes from sports-related concussions." The Department of Health and Human Services (HHS) will convene a conference of experts to develop concussion management guidelines for student-athletes. The measure passed by the House Energy and Commerce subcommittee gives the HHS authority to give grants to states to implement concussion guidelines and buy equipment that will protect young people (*The Associated Press*, 2010).

New Technology for Researching Concussions

It has been said that the football field is "an impact-rich environment." Eight colleges, including three Big Ten schools, are using Riddell's high-tech helmets "which wirelessly relay real-time data—gleaned from the same sensors found in car air bags—to a sideline computer that can send a pager alert if a player receives a hit or a series of hits that exceed a certain magnitude" (*TIME Magazine* 2007). Kevin Guskiewicz, director of the University of North Carolina's Sports Medicine Research Laboratory, commented, "We don't pull people out of a game or a practice simply because they registered some high-value hit." Guskiewicz planned to "publish five semesters' worth of helmet data from UNC players showing the wide range of force that led to concussions" (Rawe, 2007).

The National Institute of Health funded a five-year study for Brown, Dartmouth and Virginia Tech to use the sensor-laden helmets. The cost of the helmet may be in the $1,000 range. A Riddell official said, "If people buy $1,000 [golf] drivers and $500 baseball bats, we hope they'll spend that kind of money on head protection" (Rawe, 2007).

The University of North Carolina Tar Heels are part of a concussion study that required the players who are tested to swallow a $40 pill. Eighteen football players gulped the vitamin-sized thermometer and radio transmitter that will be in the intestine for several days to measure core body heat. The goal is to determine whether higher body temperature can increase the possibility of concussions. UNC coaches plan to use the data to "better regulate drills during practice and during games in heat that often reaches the high 90s through the early stretch of fall games." Symptoms of concussions and heat-related illnesses overlap, and "there's long been a theory that dehydration could make concussions more likely," so the thermometer pill will help determine whether that theory is valid (Pickeral, 2009).

A study conducted by Waukesha Memorial Hospital and its ProHealth Care Neuroscience Center & Research Institute involved 396 male athletes from eight Milwaukee-area high schools, Concordia University in Wisconsin and Carthage College in Kenosha. The study was funded by BrainScope Co., a medical neurotechnology firm that is "developing hand-held devices that help doctors assess brain function. BrainScope hopes to market a device, currently under development, that would act as a marker of recovery from a sports-related concussion." The findings of the study suggest that "the time it takes for the brain to fully recover after a sport-related concussion may linger even after the symptoms disappear" (Walker, 2010).

National Football League Encourages Concussion Research

The study of concussions, their treatment and their long term effects is not confined to the high school and college level. The National Football League has been studying concussion-related injuries for years amid concerns that some retired players who had concussive episodes in their playing days now suffer dementia (Walker, 2010). The NFL's concern about brain injuries has been boosted by a $1 million research grant to Dr. Bob Cantu and his Center for the Study of Traumatic Encephalopathy at Boston University School of Medicine. This is another example of the current national attention given to concussions at all levels of sport.

New NFL Rules Designed to Limit Head Injuries

Under the leadership of NFL Commissioner Roger Goodell, referees now "take on more responsibility ... to protect players from helmet-first hits to their heads and necks" (*The Associated Press*, 2010). The NFL expanded its rules to "prevent 'defenseless' players from taking shots above their shoulders." The new rules also "prohibit a player from launching himself off the ground and using his helmet to strike a player in a defenseless posture in the head or neck"; this rule applies to all players, not just receivers. In addition to the rules about helmet-to-head contact, the NFL referee now whistles a play dead whenever a player loses his helmet (*The Associated Press*, 2010). The emphasis on safety to protect a player from concussions should extend to all leagues, from Little League and youth sports to the professional level.

USA Football Tweaks Rules on Hits

In an attempt to make the game safer, USA Football, the official youth football development partner of the NFL, recently amended its rules with an emphasis on deterring illegal hits to the head and neck. The wording of the rules now includes "that the helmet, shoulder or forearm being used on an opposing player above the shoulder will be assessed a 15-yard personal foul penalty" (Alic, 2010). Another change made all horse collar tackles illegal. The group also adopted language that gives game officials the responsibility of removing a player from a game because of concussion symptoms (Alic, 2010).

NFL and Players Union Approve Experts in Neurology

For years, some NFL players who were injured complained that team physicians at times cleared them to return to play when they were not fully recovered from an injury. These players wanted outside physicians to approve the return to play instead of team physicians who had special interest in getting players back on the field.

The NFL and its players union have approved "independent doctors to evaluate head injuries ... as part of a new program" (*The Associated Press*, 2009). Dr. Thom Mayer, the medical director for the NFL Players Association, said, "The quality of people brought forward has been first rate." The NFL is requiring teams "to find outside experts in neurology to aid their medical staffs when players get concussions" (*The Associated Press*, 2009). This new program approved by the NFL is a good move for all concerned.

Emergency Room Visits for Concussions Have Increased Among Young Athletes

According to a study published in the journal *Pedatrics*, "the number of children in the U.S. seeking emergency medical care for concussions incurred playing competitive sports more than doubled" between 2001 and 2005 (Healy, 2010). The report noted that the increase came not from high school athletes, but "middle-schoolers and even elementary school students who have flocked to play on elite travel teams and in competitive youth leagues across the country" (Healy, 2010).

The study found that 40 percent of the sport-related pediatric concussions that led to visits to emergency rooms occurred among student-athletes between the ages of eight to thirteen. The study used injury reports provided by hospitals of 502,000 cases of children and teens visiting emergency rooms for concussions over a five-year period; one half of those visits were related to concussions in sports and other recreational activities. The findings provide "growing evidence that younger children's brains are not only more susceptible to injury, but those injuries may take longer to heal and can be more damaging than concussions in adolescents or adults" (Healy, 2010).

Christopher Giza, pediatric neurologist at the University of California, Los Angeles, who was not involved with the study, said the results "will help forge consensus among coaches, parents and physicians about what to do when a child is dazed after a rough tackle" and will help coaches take "a more conservative approach" when dealing with potential concussions.

The research team who conducted the study added that "parents, coaches and physicians need better guidelines for recognizing brain trauma in younger kids, determining when and how long to sideline them and finding ways to protect them from long-term harm" (Healy, 2010). In 2009, the state of Washington "was the first to require that any student-athlete suspected of having a concussion be removed from the game and return until cleared by a licensed medical professional" (Healy, 2010).

High School Football Player Dies from Concussion

Andrew Swank, a 17-year-old football player from Spokane, Washington, "took a hard hit during a game, walked to the sideline and collapsed." The blow to his head led to his death two days later (*The Associated Press*, 2009).

The state of Washington has the toughest sports-related concussion law in the country. The legislature passed the "Zackery Lystedt Law," which requires all athletes under the age of 18 who may be injured and suspected of a concussion to "get written consent from a licensed medical provider trained in evaluating concussions before returning to play" (*The Associated Press*, 2009). Second Impact Syndrome has been the cause of many fatalities because many players return to action too soon after suffering a concussion.

The Brain Injury Association of Washington and the US Centers for Disease Control and Prevention reported that 3.5 million sports-related concussions occur each year in the United States (*The Associated Press*, 2009). We agree with the importance of sports-related concussion legislation, such as the one in the state of Washington, and hope more states will consider such a law.

Researchers Find Damage in Late NFL Player's Brain

Dr. Julian Bailes, Director of the Brain Injury Research Institute, a research center affiliated with West Virginia University, informed ESPN that the late Cincinnati Bengals receiver Chris Henry had chronic traumatic encephalopathy (CTE), "a form of degenerative brain damage caused by multiple hits to the head" (Keating, 2010). Henry, 26, died a day after "he either jumped or fell from the back of a moving pickup truck being driven by his fiancée." When he hit the ground, Henry suffered a fractured skull and massive head injuries. After Henry's death, his mother "gave BIRI permission to examine his brain in detail." Bailes wants to make football safer and emphasized "tak[ing] the head impacts out of the sport as much as possible" (Keating, 2010).

LaSalle University to Pay Brain-Injured Football Player $7.5 Million

Preston Plevretes, former linebacker for the LaSalle University football team, was severely injured in a game against Duquesne University as the result of a punt return collision. Plevretes had suffered a concussion during a practice a month before getting injured in the game. A lawsuit was filed against LaSalle University that claimed "LaSalle prematurely cleared him to return, without having him undergo proper testing or be seen by a doctor." As a result, Plevretes' lawyers argued that their client became a victim of "second-impact syndrome," in which "the brain swells rapidly after a person suffers a second concussion before symptoms from an earlier concussion have cleared up" (Fitzpatrick & Wood, 2009).

Plevretes, 23, originally from Marlboro, New Jersey, fell into a coma after the collision during the game, and has since undergone several operations and treatments in facilities from Pittsburgh to Cologne, Germany. Plevretes now has difficulty walking and talking, and requires around-the-clock care. The Plevretes family filed the lawsuit on November 2, 2007, just 17 days before LaSalle University dropped its football program. Joe Donovan, assistant vice president for marketing and communication at LaSalle, issued a statement on behalf of the university that said, "LaSalle University confirms that the lawsuit brought by Preston Plevretes and his family has been amicably resolved without the need for a trial, sparing both sides further burdens and expense and allowing all concerned to put the litigation behind them" (Fitzpatrick & Wood, 2009).

The university's insurance carrier will reportedly pay the cost of the settlement, but the short and long term medical costs for Plevretes will be equally staggering. Memory loss, throbbing headaches, depression are only some of the more serious medical problems that victims of sports injury like Plevretes will face in the future.

Insurance Costly

In my experience as a former athletics director at a small liberal arts college, one of the issues that dominated our administration was the cost of insurance, which can be staggering, as insurance companies, out of necessity (and the pursuit of greater profits), continue to raise their rates for supplementary and liability insurance. The NCAA sometimes provides coverage for severely injured athletes, although that policy carries a $75,000 deductible, which will soon increase to $90,000.

Creating Awareness about Concussions in Youth Sports: 69 Years Ago and Today

The Weequahic High School football team I was on played South Side High School, our big rival, on Armistice Day, November 11, 1941. Two things happened that day before 8,000 spectators at City Stadium in Newark, New Jersey. South Side came on the field, to the surprise of everyone, with new and never before seen plastic helmets. Our team was shocked at the sight of the new helmets, which looked to us like something from outer space. Every other team we played at that time wore leather helmets. The most important thing that happened that day was not the shiny new headgear, but the fatal injury to one of my closest friends, Walter Eisele.

Walter was the epitome of the scholar-athlete. A great football player, Walter played both as a defensive back and as a fullback for the offense. Walter made a tough tackle on a ball carrier and suffered a concussion. Later in the fourth quarter, he reentered the game and made another hard tackle, rendering him unconscious. Walter was taken to the hospital and after several surgeries, died three days later.

The *Newark Star-Ledger* reported the injury and after Eisele's death, conducted a survey of New Jersey schools that played football to determine the medical coverage that was available at games. The findings by the *Star-Ledger's* survey provided needed awareness of the problem of concussion injuries in football, and the need for athletic trainers and physicians at all football games.

In 2010, 69 years later, the *Newark Star-Ledger* published three excellent articles on concussions in youth sports. The series points out a number of concussion-related injuries in sports other than football. New Jersey has approximately 258,000 high school athletes, and 85% of the high schools have athletic trainers on staff, compared with a national average of 42%. Even with athletic trainers present, however, concussions are a major problem. Micky Collins, one of the nation's leading concussion doctors, reports, "We sometimes see that the mild injuries become severe and the severe injuries become mild. The kids who have a few symptoms, they continue to play and that's when they get hit again. Those are the kids that end up taking the longest to recover." Dr. Collins urges unequivocally that after a concussion, "the athlete be removed from play immediately until he can be intricately evaluated by medical personnel. The recovery process then necessitates a 'constellation' of efforts to ensure effective recovery for young athletes. Those efforts must be prevalent in the schools—both academically and athletically" (Stanmyre & Friedman, 2010). The article concludes with several suggestions for the recovery process:

1. Notifying the athlete's school of the injury so teachers and administrators recognize the need for reduced cognitive stress.
2. Encouraging the athlete to reduce cognitive stress at home by eliminating text-messaging, video game play and other brain stimulators.
3. Eliminating physical exertion until the symptoms of concussion dissipate (Stanmyre & Friedman, 2010).

The *Star-Ledger* has done a service to all sport participants by creating renewed awareness of the concussion problems still present in contact sports.

Heat-Related Problems

A Terrifying Experience

High school coaches in the 1940s seldom had athletic trainers responsible for injuries to athletes. Instead, the coach was the one given the duties of an athletic trainer, even though they lacked medical competence.

In 1948, I was hired to coach football, basketball and baseball at a union (part rural and part urban) school in Zebulon, North Carolina. The day my hiring was publicized in the local paper, I received a telephone call from the athletic trainer at Wake Forest College, and was elated and surprised when he offered to be our athletic trainer whenever the Wake Forest football team was not on the road. It was unheard of for a 1-A high school to have an athletic trainer, and not only that, he wanted to do it at no cost to us! I always believed our 8–2 record that year was due to the outstanding service and help our volunteer athletic trainer gave us.

Several years later, I accepted the position of athletics director and football coach at Guilford College. No school in our conference had a certified athletic trainer and, once again, the responsibility for medical care was left to the coach.

Our football team was preparing for our opening game against our traditional rival. I realized that the two quarterbacks I was grooming would not be ready for the game. I took a freshman quarterback with outstanding credentials and had him work with all three teams so he could get prepared to start the game, which was five days away. I did not consider the hot and humid day, where temperatures soared to the 100-degree mark.

Suddenly, at the end of practice, the freshman quarterback collapsed and was on the verge of a heat stroke. Our plan was to have our veteran line coach, who was certified in first aid, to administer first aid to the overheated player. My responsibility was to get him to the hospital, since we did not have EMS at that time. I remember putting him on my shoulder and running to my car. I stopped at the nearest hospital, which was not the best one, but the closest to our campus.

After an hour of waiting, the medical staff came to the waiting room and told me that my player would have died if I had brought him five minutes later. What a terrifying experience and one I never forgot. As a result, I was able to convince our administrators to hire a part-time athletic trainer for one year, and then put her on a full-time basis the following year. Every school in our conference soon hired a certified athletic trainer and sport safety prospered.

Heat Stress and Athletic Participation: There Are No Excuses for Heatstroke Deaths

Fall football practice and games are played in hot and humid weather in many parts of the United States. Other sports like cross country and soccer also play in the fall, but due to the bulky equipment and uniforms, football has been associated with most of the heat-related problems.

The first heatstroke death in football was in 1955, and since then, there have been a total of 119 heatstroke deaths involving football players. The year with the greatest number was 1970 with eight. There have been a number of years with zero heatstroke deaths, but recent years have been more troubling. From 1995 through 2007, there were 33 heatstroke deaths in football, with high schools accounting for 25.

These numbers are too high, and most heatstroke deaths are preventable if the proper precautions are taken. Following is a list of preventive measures, as recommended by Dr. Fred Mueller and originally published in *From the Gym to the Jury* (2008), that will help reduce the number of heat stroke deaths in football:

1. Every athlete should have a physical examination with a health history. A history of previous heat illnesses and types of training activities before organized practices should be included.
2. Lack of physical fitness impairs the performance of an athlete participating in the heat. Coaches should know the physical condition of their athletes and set practice schedules accordingly.
3. Along with physical conditioning the factor of acclimatization to heat is important. Acclimatization is the process of becoming adjusted to heat and it is essential to provide for GRADUAL ACCLIMATIZATION TO HOT WEATHER. It is necessary for an athlete to exercise in the heat if he/she is to become acclimatized to it. It is suggested that a graduated physical conditioning program be used and that 80 percent acclimatization can be expected to occur after the first seven to ten days. Final stages of acclimatization to heat are marked by increased sweating and reduced salt concentration in the sweat.
4. The old idea that water should be withheld from athletes during workouts has NO SCIENTIFIC FOUNDATION. The most important safeguard to the health of the athlete is the replacement of water. Cold water must be on the field and readily available to the athletes at all times. It is recommended that a minimum ten-minute water break be scheduled for every twenty minutes of heavy exercise in the heat. Athletes should rest in a shaded area during the break. Fluid replacement should take place before, during, and after activity. COLD WATER OR OTHER LIQUIDS SHOULD BE AVAILABLE IN UNLIMITED QUANTITIES.
5. Check and be sure athletes are drinking the water. Replacement by thirst alone is inadequate. Test the air prior to practice or game using a wet bulb, globe, temperature index (WBGT index) which is based on the combined effects of air temperature, relative humidity, radiant heat and air movement. The following precautions are recommended when using the WBGT Index:
    *   Below 65   Low risk
    *   65–73   Moderate risk
    *   730–82   High risk
    *   82 plus   Very high risk

6. An alternative method for assessing heat and humidity is the weather guide or heat index. Refer to the NFHS Sports Medicine Handbook section on heat related illness published by the NFHS.

7. Cooling by evaporation is proportional to the area of the skin exposed. In extremely hot and humid weather reduce the amount of clothing covering the body as much as possible. NEVER USE RUBBERIZED CLOTHING.

8. Athletes should weigh each day before and after practice and WEIGHT CHARTS CHECKED. Generally, a three to five percent weight loss is in the danger zone. Over a three percent weight loss, the athlete should not be allowed to practice in hot and humid conditions. Observe the athletes closely under all conditions. Do not allow athletes to practice until they have adequately replaced their weight.

9. Observe athletes carefully for signs of trouble, particularly athletes who lose significant weight and the eager athlete who constantly competes at his/her capacity. Some trouble signs are nausea, incoherence, fatigue, weakness, vomiting, cramps, weak rapid pulse, visual disturbance and unsteadiness.

10. Teams that encounter hot weather during the season through travel or following an unseasonably cool period may be physically fit, but will not be environmentally fit. Coaches in this situation should follow the above recommendations and substitute more frequently during games.

11. Know what to do in case of an emergency and have your emergency plans written, with copies to all your staff. Be familiar with immediate first aid practices and pre-arranged procedures for obtaining medical care, including ambulance service.

HEAT STROKE—THIS IS A MEDICAL EMERGENCY—DELAY COULD BE FATAL. Immediately cool body while waiting for transfer to a hospital. Remove clothing and immerse torso in ice-cold water. Immersion therapy has the best cooling rates. If not available, rapidly rotate ice water towels combined with ice packs. Continue cooling efforts until EMS arrives.

HEAT EXHAUSTION—OBTAIN MEDICAL CARE AT ONCE. Cool body as you would for heat stroke while waiting for transfer to hospital. Give fluids if athlete is able to swallow and is conscious.

SUMMARY—The main problem associated with exercising in the hot weather is water loss through sweating. Water loss is best replaced by allowing the athlete unrestricted access to water. Water breaks two or three times every hour are better than one break an hour. The best method is to have water available at all times and to allow the athlete to drink water whenever he/she needs it. Never restrict the amount of water an athlete drinks, and be sure the athletes are drinking the water. The small amount of salt lost in sweat is adequately replaced by salting food at meals. Talk to your medical personnel concerning emergency treatment plans (Mueller, 2008).

NATA Recommendations for Pre-Season Heat

Due to the heat stroke deaths of 39 football players (twenty-nine high school, seven college, two professional and one sandlot) from 1995 through 2008, the National Athletic Trainers Association (NATA) released a statement on pre-season heat acclimatization guidelines for secondary school athletes. The statement appeared in the June 2009 issue of the *Journal of Athletic Training*, and its recommendations are as follows:

1. During the first five days of the heat acclimatization period, athletes may not participate in more than one practice a day.
2. Total practice time should not exceed three hours per day.
3. A one-hour maximum walk-through is permitted during the first five days of the acclimatization period, but there must be a three-hour recovery period between the practice and walk-through (or vice versa).
4. During the first two days of practice, only helmets are allowed. During days three to five, only helmets and shoulder pads worn.
5. On day six, all protective equipment may be worn and full contact allowed. During days six through day fourteen of practice, double practice sessions must be followed by a single practice day.
6. On double practice days, neither practice should exceed three hours, and both practices combined should not be more than five hours in duration. The two practices should be separated by at least three hours in a cool environment.
7. Due to the risk of heat illness in pre-season practice, the consensus statement recommends that an athletic trainer be on-site before, during and after all practices. (NATA, 2009)

Importance of Fluids During Practices

Coaches need to stress the need for regular water breaks during sports practices. The players need to have access to fluids during the workouts. In the 1940s and 1950s, coaches believed not drinking water could benefit their players' conditioning. The belief was that they were better prepared for the upcoming season by not drinking water during practice. Today, we know that the body needs fluids during hot weather. However, some coaches still withhold water during preseason practice, many coaching like they were coached in high school or college. There is absolutely no reason to withhold water or other fluids. It is important that 100% of all coaches who coach sports activities provide fluids for their players.

I Discovered "Dr. Death"

One day during football preseason at Guilford College, our athletic trainer reported to me that I needed to attend practice that day. She wanted me to observe a situation that troubled her. I agreed to go to practice and what I saw really troubled me. On a day when the heat was excessive, one coach refused to let his offensive lineman take a break when every other group took time to rest and drink fluids. Instead, this coach had his lineman continue to spend the time others took for water hitting the blocking sled with full gear. I learned that the players called the coach "Dr. Death" because of his training methods. I called "Dr. Death" to my office and he immediately agreed to change his tactics and give his men water breaks on a regular basis. This particular coach was very cooperative and talented, and eventually moved on to Division I coaching, where he and his university have experienced success.

Family Suing Riddell over Korey Stringer's Death

Korey Stringer died ten years ago of heatstroke during a Minnesota Vikings practice. Stringer's family said that his equipment was a major problem and contributed to the NFL player's untimely death. They insist that the "Riddell equipment [worn by Stringer] should have had a heatstroke warning label." Stringer's former agent, who represents the family, said, "We have waited eight years for this moment, for the Stringer family (his widow) and his son to go to court for a jury trial." On the day he died, Stringer's temperature rose to 108 degrees and the Riddell equipment he was wearing at the time failed to warn him of his high temperature. The family hopes that the trial will "force manufacturers to take a closer look at products and use heatstroke warning labels" (*USA Today*, 2009).

Stringer's wife founded the Korey Stringer Institute in April 2010. The Institute has the backing of NFL and Gatorade, and "it focuses on heat illness and other causes of sudden death in sport. Its efforts include education, research and safety measures" (Mihoces, 2010). The nationwide attention given to heat illness has reduced the number of heat-related deaths. Doug Casa, Director of the Korey Stringer Institute, reported that there were no heat-related fatalities in football at all levels in August 2010.

Coach Defends Heat Training in a Different Way

During one summer, a Guilford County High School football coach had his players "wear wool caps as a training technique during conditioning drills." Medical professionals are critical of the attempt to acclimatize the players by wearing winter caps. Stephanie Helbert, a certified athletic trainer and sports medicine coordinator at Greensboro Orthopaedics "disagreed with the technique." Helbert said that this practice has no scientific basis and is dangerous. Bill Griffin, an athletic trainer who is on the executive board of the NC Athletic Trainers Association, also disagreed with the technique. Griffin commented that the use of winter caps during summer workouts was "not evidence-based" (*News & Record*, 2010).

The first-year football coach defended his practice and pointed out that no one had a heat-related problem when they used the winter caps. He said he observed the drill when he was a graduate assistant at The Citadel. He also said that his athletics director and the players' parents were aware of the technique and did not object (*News & Record*, 2010). With the nationwide attention placed on heat-related deaths in athletics, the use of winter caps during conditioning drills will certainly receive greater attention from experts in the medical field.

Insurers Pay $1.75 Million to Settle Heat-Related Death

In a highly publicized court case involving a 15-year-old football player, Max Gilpin, and his heat-related death during a football practice, insurers for the Jefferson County (Kentucky) Public Schools and its employees settled for $1.75 million. Gilpin's parents filed a civil suit against the football coach and school district for negligent conduct. A court ruled that the coach, who had been charged with criminal negligence, was acquitted (*The Associated Press*, 2010).

Athlete's Case Goes to Trial

Jermaine Lattimore, a former student at Ashford University, Iowa, collapsed during a basketball drill on September 5, 2007. Lattimore alleged that "he was denied a drink of water twice by Ashford coaches…, once during a position exercise and once during a five-mile training run" (Smith, 2010). Lattimore collapsed from heatstroke and was rushed to the hospital with a temperature of at least 106.7 degrees. He was then flown to University Hospitals and Clinics in Iowa City "with heat stroke and sepsis, a serious medical condition that causes inflammation throughout the body" (Smith, 2010).

Lattimore alleged that the heatstroke forced him to drop out of school and caused him to endure permanent health problems. Attorneys representing the school stated that the plaintiff refused water and any harm he experienced was from "his voluntary participation in strenuous physical activities." Lattimore is seeking monetary damages against the coaches and university (Smith, 2010).

AEDs and CPR by Kenny Morgan

AEDs Save Lives—Including Mine

I was preparing to meet with a travel agent to schedule a trip to Scotland, where a student of mine had planned a golf outing at the world famous St. Andrews golf course. I experienced chest pains early that morning, but decided that the pains were merely indigestion and nothing more. A friend whom I was planning to marry came by so we could work on the upcoming trip and immediately realized my condition was serious. She convinced me to go to the emergency room of a local hospital where my heart suddenly stopped beating. The only doctor on duty in the emergency room had just left for the day, since it was Memorial Day. The nurses on duty called him back and immediately began using an AED to bring me back to consciousness. The doctor returned and a specialist was called to perform an angioplasty. This was the first of several close calls when an AED would revive me and help restore my heart.

Six Minutes to Live or Die: Automatic External Defibrillators (AEDs)

In the United States each year, sudden cardiac arrest occurring outside of a hospital kills 250,000 people, which is approximately 685 people per day (Appenzeller, 2005). Studies have shown that two out of three deaths occur before the victim even reaches the hospital, usually at home, work or in a public place such as a golf course (Appenzeller, 2005). In fact, according to the American Heart Association, the top five places where people suffer cardiac arrests are airports, jails, stadiums, golf courses and shopping malls. The most determinant factor in whether an individual suffering from cardiac arrest lives or dies is elapsed time until treatment. For years, expert opinion stated that help must arrive within ten minutes, but new findings from the Mayo Clinic show that lives actually are saved or lost within six minutes (Appenzeller, 2005). The installation of automatic external defibrillators (AEDs) in public areas is quickly becoming an invaluable tool to rescuers and victims alike in reducing response times and increasing lifetimes.

Potential users of AEDs must be able to understand when to use the device, how to use it, and where it is located. *Risk Management in Sport* (2005) cites a *USA Today* article that tells the story of a person who collapsed at a gym where the staff was trained in AED use. On the day in question, the person who normally worked the front desk was absent and his replacement did not even know what an AED was when asked to retrieve the device. The victim died as a result of not being treated in time (Appenzeller, 2005).

High School Running Back Suffers Cardiac Arrest

Hayward Demison, a running back at Central Catholic High School in Portland, Oregon, scored a winning touchdown and then collapsed after he told his coach he was having trouble breathing. Lisa Lyver, a cardiac nurse, who was a spectator at the game, rushed to his side and started CPR on him. She said that Demison was in cardiac arrest without a pulse. His heart was stopped for two minutes by the time Lyver reached him. Through her efforts, he recovered. Demison was scheduled for heart surgery and doctors expected him to play the following season. This incident received national attention, and due to the quick action of a cardiac nurse, Demison lived to play another day (*AB Newswire*, 2010).

CPR Saves Coach's Life

Tim Blakeney, a soccer coach at Oakbrook Preparatory School in Spartanburg, South Carolina, was struck by lightning during soccer practice. Alexander Holland Holbein, the school's student body president, and only one day shy of his 18th birthday, was also struck by a bolt of lightning.

Coach Blakeney went into cardiac arrest. He later credited his survival the quick response of school administrators who performed cardio-pulmonary resuscitation and saved his life. After Blakeney was struck by lightning, his players, "most of whom had been knocked to the ground by the bolt, ran inside the school calling for help." Athletics director Marie Tewkesbury found Blakeney and Holbein on the ground, not breathing. Tewkesbury began administering CPR on Blakeney, while another administrator attempted to revive Holbein. An automated external defibrillator (AED) was used to shock Holbein's chest in an attempt to restart his breathing. Then they resumed CPR on both men. Blakeney survived; however, Holbein did not respond to the attempts to revive him and died at the scene (*From the Gym to the Jury*, 2007).

Defibrillator Saves Life

Matthew Keene, a 17-year-old high school student, collapsed during football practice in New Hampshire. Keene suffered sudden cardiac arrest, stopped breathing and had no pulse. Coaches and athletic trainers immediately performed CPR and shocked his heart into beating with a portable defibrillator. The quick response led to Keene's survival and recovery, and he now is leading a campaign to provide AEDs in every school. Keene realizes that he was given a second chance to live. He said, "I don't want to hear [that] this happen[ed] to anyone and [that] they [did] not survive." Keene competed as a football lineman, a baseball catcher and as a hockey goalie. He is an inspiration to everyone (*From the Gym to the Jury*, 1997).

Defibrillator's Location Unknown, Athlete Dies

Mike Ndiribe, a basketball player at Grayson County College in Texas, collapsed during halftime and died less than an hour later. There was an automated external defibrillator on campus at the time Ndiribe collapsed, but no one knew where it was located. The athletics director at the host school said that there was an AED on campus, but he did not know where it was when they needed it. Paramedics arrived five minutes after they received the urgent call, but it was too late. The athletics director said, "We don't have (an AED) in the gym. Steps will be taken to get one in there" (McCloskley, 2007).

Ethical Questions

1. What are the problems relating to the pre-participation physical examinations?
2. What areas of the pre-participation physicals are important but neglected in many instances?
3. Discuss sickle cell trait in athletes.
4. Discuss the death of Jospin Milandu.
5. Why have concussions been a "hot topic" among the NFL and football at all levels?
6. What is the Zackery Lystedt Law?
7. What has the NFL done to curb concussions?

8. Discuss the situation of Armistice Day, 1941, in the high school game of Weequahic vs. South Side. What did the Newark Star Ledger do?
9. Discuss this statement by Fred Mueller: "There are no excuses for heat-stroke deaths."
10. What was the problem associated with "Dr. Death"?
11. Discuss the importance of AEDs and CPR.

Chapter 6

Legal Issues

"The Constitution does not stop at the public school doors like a puppy waiting for his master, but instead it follows the student through the corridors, into the classroom, and onto the athletic field."—Neuhaus v. Torrey *(1970)*

Participation in sports continues to increase every year and today we witness interest in every type of sport. High school, college and professional football have found a place on national television and it is not unusual for television to sponsor football each and every day. Football coverage begins as early as 9:00 a.m. on game day and goes on after midnight. The 2010 World Cup Soccer Championship drew record numbers of spectators in South Africa, the host country, and on television. It seems that the United States, as well as the rest of the world, cannot get enough golf, football, basketball, baseball, soccer, rugby, tennis and just about every sport known to the world.

At the same time as worldwide interest and participation in sport activities, litigation involving sports-related activities is at an all time high. Damage awards have grown accordingly and large awards are not the exception today, but more likely the rule. Lawsuits involving sports will continue to flood the court dockets as people are more knowledgeable of their legal remedies and individual rights. It is apparent that sports and the law have entered a new era in the 21st century.

Administrators, coaches and anyone associated with sports activities question their authority over the litigation that confronts them. Civil rights continue to plague those who are called upon to defend their policies, such as Title IX, Americans with Disabilities Act (ADA) and other legislative and constitutional acts. It is common practice for litigants to claim that their constitutional rights are violated in sport-related lawsuits. Sport litigation will not tolerate rules and regulations that are arbitrary, capricious or unreasonable. The key word in sport litigation seems to be *reasonable*. The court expects and even demands action by sport leaders that exemplifies reasonable conduct, action and judgment.

Courts have made it clear that not every rule that is challenged, nor injury that is sustained will result in a lawsuit or unfavorable decision to a defendant in a sports-related lawsuit. Once again, however, courts have made it clear that they will not tolerate outmoded rules, arbitrary regulations and grossly negligent conduct by those in positions of authority. The courts in the 21st century appear to place emphasis on the welfare of the individual, and this represents a dramatic change regarding the law. All 50 states have abrogated or modified the doctrine of governmental immunity that protected sport organizations and schools alike from suit. This doctrine used as a defense in sport-related cases began to erode in the 1960s.

Since Title IX was passed in 1972, and other legislative fiats, the court will not permit a double standard to exist regarding race, creed, color, sex or disability. Although litigation frustrates people involved with sports-related programs, such litigation and exposure to the public eye have proved to be beneficial to sport as a whole. They lead to the provision of conditions that make sports safer to all concerned and, in reality, what educators, spectators and participants want it to be. Sport and the law in the 21st century truly represent a "whole new ball game" and one that should be the best ever.

Rosenfield Opposes Immunity

Harry Rosenfield, an opponent of sovereign and governmental immunity, opposed an outmoded doctrine that placed injured students in an unfair position, as parents often faced impossible situations when medical bills exceeded their financial resources and, at times, their children, through no fault of their own, were facing a limited life because of their conditions. Rosenfield expressed his objection to the immunity doctrine by protesting that:

> The present rule, in my judgment, is completely inconsistent with all modern concepts of justice and social responsibility. It is unreasonable to require an injured person to bear a disproportionate part of the normal operating cost of activities undertaken by the entire community. (Appenzeller, 1978)

Rosenfield continued his dissent by pointing out the following:

> The whole community pays for the school building, for light, heat, books, school contracts, etc. Why should the injured pupil or coach pay out of his pocket for an item that is an operating cost of the school budget—in fact, if not in law. If a school breaks a contract, it is liable in law. If it breaks someone's neck, it is not. I submit that this does not make sense. (Appenzeller, 1978)

Because of Rosenfield and a growing number of educators who opposed the doctrine, states began to abrogate or modify the doctrine and permitted themselves to be sued when negligence was present.

Four Cases Could Set a Trend

Recently, four court cases in the Supreme Courts of Massachusetts, Wisconsin, Ohio and Arkansas surfaced that could possibly set a trend that could lead to a return to the doctrine of sovereign and governmental immunity as a defense in sport-related injury cases.

For years, the common law principle, which protected school districts with immunity, was successfully used as a defense by school districts without regard to the circumstances of the case in question. In the 1960s, only four states abrogated the immunity doctrine in sport-related cases involving alleged negligence. California, Connecticut, New Jersey and New York were the states that passed legislation that permitted lawsuits against them. In the majority of states that relied on the immunity doctrine, no matter how much negligence led to the injury, the school district could not be found liable.

12-Year-Old Boy Injured by Unanchored Goal

Dustin Welch, a 12-year-old boy, was injured when an unanchored soccer goal fell on him and broke his leg. The Supreme Court of Massachusetts held that not securing the soccer goal was ordinary negligence and fell within the broad immunity conferred upon nonprofit associations by the state. The court held that "nonprofit associations conducting sports programs for youths are to be treated differently from ordinary land owners." Furthermore, the legislature had "made the judgment that the elimination of liability for negligence in nonprofit sports programs is necessary to the encouragement and survival of such programs" (*Welch v. Sudbury Youth Sport Soccer Association*, 2009).

Consider the implications of this court ruling on the safe conduct of sports. An insurance company sent an e-mail to all the YMCAs they insured, asking that they anchor all soccer goals immediately. The Consumer Products Safety Commission (CPSC) reported that from 1979 to 2008, there were 34 deaths and 58 serious injuries caused by unanchored soccer goals. Shortly after the report was issued, two 10-year-old boys in Arizona died from unanchored soccer goals that killed them on a school playground.

High School Cheerleading Is a Contact Sport

Brittany Noffke was a ninth grade cheerleader who fell and injured her head while "practicing a cheerleading stunt on a hard tile floor prior to a high school basketball game" (*Noffke v. Bakke*, 2008). Three students were taking part in the stunt, in which Noffke was the flyer, Hillary Hall was the base and Kevin Bakke was the post and spotter. There were no secondary spotters and no mats on the tile floor. Noffke fell backwards and severely injured her head. Her coach was supervising another group of cheerleaders and not where Noffke fell. Noffke sued the insurance company alleging negligence on the part of her coach and teammate Bakke.

The Supreme Court of Wisconsin held that "high school cheerleading is a contact sport and therefore its participants cannot be sued for accidentally causing injuries." The court also ruled that "a high school cheerleader cannot sue a teammate who failed to catch her while practicing a stunt." In addition, the court held that the injured cheerleader could not sue the school district (Foley, 2009).

The district court of appeals had previously ruled that cheerleading did not qualify as a contact sport "because there's no contact between opposing teams." However, all seven members of the Supreme Court of Wisconsin agreed to overturn that decision. Justice Annette Ziegler said that cheerleading involves "a significant amount of physical contact between the cheerleaders that at times results in a forceful interaction between participants." She cited, as an example, stunts that have cheerleaders being tossed in the air (Foley, 2009).

In essence, the Wisconsin Supreme Court's decision "means cheerleaders can only be sued for acting recklessly or intentionally in causing injuries." Regarding the school district, Ziegler said it "cannot be sued for the coach's behavior under a Wisconsin law that shields government agencies from lawsuits for the actions of employees" (Foley, 2009).

In North Carolina, researchers found that two-thirds of the approximately 100 cases of catastrophic injuries to high school and college females every year since 1982 were caused by cheerleading. Injuries are on the rise in part because of the increasingly difficult stunts (Foley, 2009).

Cheerleader Injured Doing the "Big K"

Angela Crace and her parents appealed the decision of the Ohio Court of Claims that granted judgment to Kent State University (KSU) on the basis of KSU's defense that "primary assumption of the risk barred appellants' negligence and loss-of-consortium claims against KSU" (*Crace v. KSU*, 2009).

Angela Crace, a junior at Kent State, was the captain of KSU's cheerleading team. Her coach, Lenee Buchman, positioned team members to practice a stunt known as the "Big K," which was described as "essentially a human pyramid that consisted of a base, a middle layer/base, and flyers." The pyramid was two and one-half people high with spotters assigned on the ground to catch the flyers when they came down. The "Big K" had the highest degree of difficulty that the NCAA permitted.

On the day of Angela's injury, the KSU cheerleaders had varying experience and expertise. Angela was assigned the position of flyer, and in the two attempts to perform the "Big K," she fell twice from 15 feet in the air. Her spotter caught her both times. Buchman substituted a different spotter as her rear spotter. The spotter she chose "had neither seen nor participated in the 'Big K.'" He told Buchman that he felt uncomfortable spotting this stunt. The new spotter failed to catch Angela when she fell 15 feet. Instead, "he panicked, shielded his eyes, and moved out of the way." As a result, Angela fell to the floor and suffered "catastrophic injuries, including immediate paraplegia" (*Crace v. KSU*, 2009).

The injured cheerleader filed a lawsuit against KSU, alleging negligence on the part of the coach. A bench trial was held and the trial court granted judgment for KSU. An appeal was filed immediately. The appellant and her parents had signed an informed consent before the season started, but KSU did not include on its release "any exculpatory language releasing KSU from liability" (*Crace v. KSU*, 2009).

The appellate court held that "under primary assumption of the risk, a person assumes the inherent risks of the recreational activity and cannot recover for injuries unless another person acted recklessly or intentionally." The Supreme Court of Ohio commented:

> Acts that would give rise to tort liability on a city street or in a backyard are not negligent in the context of a game where such an act is foreseeable and within the rules ... Thus a player who injures another player in the course of a sporting event by conduct that is a foreseeable, customary part of the sport cannot be held liable for negligence because no duty is owed to protect the victim from that conduct. Were we to find such a duty between co-participants in a sport, we might well stifle the rewards of athletic competition. (*Thompson v. McNeill*, 1990)

The court believed that the appellant "was injured by an inherent risk of cheerleading." It also ruled that the coach did not act recklessly or intentionally.

From these recent court cases, it appears that the three Supreme Court decisions have concluded that "where injuries are sustained in a sporting event, there is no liability for injuries caused by negligent conduct" (*Crace v. KSU*, 2009).

An Unfortunate Opinion by a Federal Judge

The parents of Christy Hardaway sued the Newport Special School District. The plaintiffs claimed that their daughter was dismissed from the team because of the parents' dissatisfaction with the coach. The parents had been upset at the racial epithets from opposing fans during road games and the coach's failure to take appropriate action. This is a federal case, according to the plaintiffs, because their daughter has a property interest in continued participation, and is therefore entitled to due process. The district court held that "an injustice may have occurred when Ms. Hardaway was dismissed from the basketball team. However, it is not within the power granted to federal courts to right every wrong that may be inflicted on individuals in our society" (*McFarlin v. Newport Special Sch. Dist.*, 1992).

Judge Stephen M. Reasoner also took issue with the plaintiff's request for reinstatement and meaningful participation. Judge Reasoner questioned whether he was to leave the Federal Bench for a place on the team bench beside the coach to ensure that the young lady would achieve meaningful participation. The judge added:

> If individuals are going to participate in sports, ... they must be willing to submit themselves to the authority of another individual in the role of a coach ... It is a virtual certainty that they will be subjected, on occasion, to arbitrary and unjust treatment. Anyone who has ever operated under someone else's supervision or authority has been frustrated at one time or another by some decision which directly affected them, but over which they had no control whatsoever ... For many of us, the first such experience came as part of our participation in high school athletics. However, the mere fact that a coach may be wrong does not convert the matter into a federal case. (*McFarlin v. Newport Special Sch. Dist.*, 1992)

The Court denied the plaintiff's motion for an immediate hearing, a temporary restraining order and a preliminary injunction.

As a sports participant and coach from the 1940s through the 1960s, I witnessed injuries and even deaths caused by negligence, with little opportunity for the injured participant to win a case due to the defendant's reliance on the immunity doctrine. Like Harry Rosenfield, an anti-immunity advocate, I believe this is wrong. The question remains, will other states return to immunity for sporting events? If so, I believe blanket immunity will deprive injured athletes of the fairness they deserve. Only time will tell if we are going to return to unqualified immunity in a state's attempt to protect carelessness and failure to provide a safe environment for participants in sporting events.

The above four cases could set an alarming trend for other states eager to protect those who fail to provide a safe environment for sport participants. It goes along with recent judicial decisions that say a student who participates in extracurricular activities has no constitutional rights because the activities are a privilege not a right.

Few Lawsuits against Coaches

Back in 1945, there were very few lawsuits brought by players or coaches on every level. One exception was a lawsuit against our Wake Forest football coach, Douglas Clyde "Peahead" Walker. Mac Grandy, a speedy halfback on the 1945 football team, was injured during a game against the University of Chattanooga. Grandy was put on the sidelines during a rain-soaked evening and covered with a blanket throughout the game. He claimed that he was denied medical help for his injured knee during the train ride back to the Wake Forest campus. As a result, he claimed, he was unable to participate in baseball and prevented from a future career as a pitcher in organized baseball.

Mac Grandy was an outstanding athlete with exceptional speed, and was a potential professional player in major league baseball. He was also very popular with his Wake Forest teammates. However, when word got out that he had filed a lawsuit for our coach's alleged failure to provide immediate medical assistance, our players did not support his contention of negligent conduct by our coach. No one on the team felt that a coach should be sued for practically any reason. In 1945, coaches were just not sued. The court agreed with that and favored our coach and not our teammate.

Do Courts Intimidate Critics?

Jennifer Batoon, a San Francisco marketer, "decided to vent on Yelp.com," an internet rating site where she described a difficult session she had with her dentist, Gelareh Rahbar. Rahbar responded on Yelp that Batoon complained on Yelp only after Rahbar turned her into a credit bureau for a delinquent bill. Various people supported Rahbar, who sued Batoon for alleged defamation, claiming her complaint on the internet led to a decline in her revenue. Batoon was aided by a California law designed to protect free speech and a judge dismissed Rahbar's defamation lawsuit. The judge ordered Rahbar to pay Batoon's legal fees of $43,000. While Batoon may have won this case, free speech may have suffered a major blow because, once a prolific reviewer, Batoon "now limits herself to occasional reviews and only positive ones. The internet community lost one voice" (*USA Today*, 2010).

There is considerable speculation that the fear of lawsuits may limit honest criticism on the internet. In 1992, California came up with an anti-SLAPP law (strategic lawsuit against public participation) as a solution. The law makes it easier for defendants to seek early dismissal of such lawsuits at no cost. Twenty-six other states followed California with similar anti-SLAPP laws. "People who are unfairly attacked could still fight back. They'd just have to rely more on the court of public opinion, where they'd prevail only if the facts are on their side" (*USA Today*, 2010).

Critics of the anti-SLAPP law predict the following:

> The prospect of getting sued for the Internet blog post is scary, but is no less scary for small-business owners, such as dry cleaners Jin and Soo Chung, who faced an economically crippling $54 million lawsuit in Washington, D.C., over allegations that they had lost a customer's pants. Applying anti-SLAPP rules to all lawsuits would not eliminate such abusive cases, but it would make them far less frequent. (*USA Today*, 2010)

A Blueprint for Success: 15 Risk Management Strategies for Coaching in the 21st Century

For the safety of student-athletes and spectators, the successful operation of their institutions and programs, and protection of coaching and professional staffs, we suggest the following simple, but critical risk management strategies:

1. Always put the welfare of the individual first. If you err, err on the side of conservatism.
2. Do not issue equipment until the following items are completed:
   a. Participation in a physical examination;
   b. Confirmation of insurance coverage;
   c. Confirmation of eligibility; and
   d. An agreement to participate.

3. Inform athletes of the inherent risks of the sport and the ways they can protect themselves.
4. Develop a medical response plan according to the resources available. Conduct practice drills occasionally to determine everyone's responsibilities and response times.
5. Following serious injury, rely on qualified medical personnel to decide on the athlete's reentry into a game or practice session.
6. Develop a policy for athletes with disabilities (one eye, one kidney, one testicle, etc.) that still might allow them to participate in sports.
7. Inspect equipment and facilities when appropriate.
8. Post signs regarding safety and behavioral expectations in locker rooms and gymnasiums.
9. Check your insurance coverage, including travel and liability. If you are not qualified to evaluate the coverage in force, seek the assistance of qualified advisors.
10. Always supervise high-risk activities.
11. Avoid terminology such as "suicide drills, death run, death pads and hamburger drill." These terms could come back to haunt you in court should an injury occur.
12. In the event of an injury, always follow up with a telephone call or personal visit to check on the athlete's condition. However, during these visits, never, never admit fault.
13. In the event of a serious accident or injury that could lead to potential litigation, alert the athletics director or principal immediately. Follow up with a call to the insurance company and then to the attorney.
14. Isolate and keep under lock and key any equipment involved in serious injury (helmets, protective pads, etc.), as these may become evidence in any litigation that may follow.
15. Be aware that you may be sued in the course of performing your duties. Do not panic, be prepared and coach with confidence (Appenzeller, 2005).

The Controversial Hair Cases

One of the most controversial sport issues in the 1970s centered around student-athletes' hair. In 1971 alone, there were 104 cases related to hair. I was scheduled to speak on liability to coaches and athletics directors at a conference in Minnesota. All the speakers before me talked passionately about a case at Redwood High School in California where a group of track athletes refused to comply with the athletics department's regulation that every athlete be neat and well-groomed, clean-shaven, with the hair off the collar and at a reasonable length. The penalty for refusing to comply was automatic suspension from the sport. The athletics director promised that a verdict by the court upholding the students would bring athletics department regulations down and change sports as we knew them. The next speaker was just as adamant about athletes who wore sandals and flip flops.

By the time I was to speak, I was disappointed at the unusual emphasis on appearance and I told the group that if they had no interest in safety for our athletes, they could leave right then. It appeared hair was the big issue at this conference, and I was not their man. Dr. Art Gallon, a noted athletics director in California, later told me that my talk got the conference back on track from the previous speakers who put emphasis on the wrong topics.

The California court in *Neuhaus v. Torrey* (1970) upheld the athletics department's regulations, but emphasized that each case needs individual consideration based on its own merit, according to the background and setting of the situation. It is interesting to note that the athletes at Redwood High School were the only students with short hair. The school's student body was described as "Bohemian" and the athletes in question were cross-country runners.

A Vermont court viewed the issue in a different way when three tennis players at Brattleboro High School challenged a rule they believed violated their constitutional rights (*Dunham v. Pulsifer*, 1970). The high school had a code that regulated extracurricular activities such as athletics. The athletics department formulated regulations that were intended to promote good morale and team spirit. They specified, among other things, that for males, hair must be tapered in the back and on the sides of the head, with no hair over the collar. Sideburns should be no lower than the earlobe and trimmed.

The Vermont court, however, warned against conformity and uniformity, which, it noted, students experience soon enough when they graduate and go into the world. It ordered the school to reinstate the three boys to the tennis team without penalty and raised a question that many athletes also asked: why every sport could not have its own rules on hair length, which could be reasonably related to performance in that particular sport.

The court concluded with a familiar quote: "The Constitution does not stop at the public school doors like a puppy waiting for his master, but instead it follows the student through the corridors, into the classroom, and onto the athletic field." Of the 104 cases reported related to hair, school officials won 58, while the students won 48. It is clear that the courts were not unanimous in their rulings on the hair issue (Appenzeller, 1980).

Due Process

Due process, or lack of it, has raised questions for years in court cases in which the issue has been litigated. In a 1978 case in Nebraska, *Braesch v. DePasquale*, due process was the issue and the case attracted national attention. Five senior athletes were expelled from the boys' and girls' basketball teams for violating good conduct rules. The athletes sought and received a permanent injunction prohibiting the school from denying them participation on the teams. The school officials appealed the decision and people everywhere waited for the decision to learn what guidelines the court would set regarding good conduct rules and extracurricular activities.

By the time the case came to court, the athletes had graduated from high school and tried to get the case dismissed because it was moot. The school officials refused to drop the case because the issue involved was of such great public interest. The court agreed and decided to hear the case. The Supreme Court of Nebraska made the exception to hear it, contending:

> In the context of disciplinary action in the field of interscholastic athletic competition, almost no case could reach this court for decision before it became moot if we refused to decide all cases where no actual controversy still exists between the parties at the time of appellate hearing and decision. The motion to dismiss is not well taken (*Braesch v. DePasquale*, 1978)

The court noted that recent decisions varied regarding the question of whether athletic participation was a privilege or constitutional right. It recognized the fact that while the state of Nebraska provided students with the opportunity to engage in athletics, there were far less constitutional decisions concerning sports than academic programs. It raised the question of whether the school, in light of constitutional implications, could legitimately deny the students the opportunity to participate in sports. The court then considered whether the defendants had observed due process and referred to the *Goss v. Lopez* (1975) case, in which the U.S. Supreme Court set guidelines for suspending students for disciplinary reasons. In *Goss*, the U.S. Supreme Court held that a student subject to suspension be given due process that included "oral or written notice of the charges against him, and, if he denies them, an explanation of the evidence the authorities have and an opportunity to explain his side of the story" (*Braesch v. DePasqule*, 1978).

The court concluded that the students were given due process with the right to appear at a formal hearing, but declined and chose to seek an injunction instead. Therefore, the court reversed the action of the district court in granting the students injunctive relief and favored the administration. It was clear that due process was extended to the students, but they decided to bypass the hearing.

Congress passed the Civil Rights Act of 1871 to protect emancipated blacks with the guarantees of the Federal Constitution. The flood of litigation under this Act compels our courts to interpret the rights guaranteed by the Fourteenth Amendment. Today's athletes have become aware of their rights, not only under the Fourteenth Amendment, but also under the First, Fourth, Fifth and Ninth. Student-athletes are sensitive to issues that affect due process, personal rights and equal protection, and exhibit a willingness to seek judicial remedy when they feel their rights are violated (Appenzeller, 1980).

Coach Unaware of Due Process

I once received an emotional telephone call at 1:30 a.m. from our women's basketball coach following a loss to a rival team. She explained that several members of the team reported that the loss was due to the misconduct of three starters who were violating established good conduct rules. She told me she had scheduled an early morning meeting with the three students, during which she planned to suspend them indefinitely from the team. I could not go back to sleep because something seemed wrong. Suddenly, it became clear. The coach was taking the word of other student-athletes to suspend the three starters without affording them due process. I called her to discuss due process procedures prior to her meeting with the students. When she met with the students who had allegedly violated good conduct rules, she extended procedural due process by observing the following:

- An individual must have proper notice that he or she is about to be deprived of life, liberty or property.
- An individual must be given the opportunity to be heard.
- An individual must be afforded a fair trial or hearing with the right to appeal an adverse decision.

In this situation, the students admitted fault and accepted the temporary suspension. If they had not admitted guilt and were not satisfied with the punishment, they would have followed this appeals procedure:

- Appeal to the athletics director.
- Appeal to the athletics committee.
- Appeal to the school president, whose decision is final.

Jason Rabon, in *Managing Sport and Risk Management Strategies* (2nd ed., 2003), writes, "From detailed research into the due process claims made nationwide by high school and college coaches who have been dismissed, a violation of procedural process is the most common form of litigation." The majority of the coaches claim that "their due process rights were violated and a breach of fair and reasonable procedures occurred." Rabon advises those who have the responsibility of administering due process:

> Follow appropriate due process procedures, and treat all individuals with fairness and impartiality to avoid litigation on behalf of the organization. Simply put, it isn't always what you say, but how you say it. (Appenzeller, 2003)

The United States Supreme Court decided that students have a constitutional right to know why they are being suspended and, in turn, have the right to a hearing (*Greensboro Daily News*, 1975). The hearing may be simply a meeting between the student and the disciplinarian.

It is obvious that the issue of civil rights in all areas, including athletics, is being recognized by the courts. For one reason or another, many people associated with athletics become irritated when student rights are mentioned. It may be due to past memories of student rights, barricaded doors and the takeover of facilities. Whatever the memories are, the fact remains that athletics in the seventies were subjected to much litigation involving questions of due process (Appenzeller, 1975).

The courts, however, confused the issue of whether sport is part of the curriculum and covered by constitutional rights when it commented that sport participation "remains a privilege founded upon a right to participate in what admittedly are activities forming an integral part of the school curriculum" (*Brown v. Wells*, 1970).

In another instance, the court held:

> The privilege of interscholastic competition is outside the protection of due process and a student is not given a federally 'constitutional right' to participate in a sport unless his rights under the equal protection clause are violated. (*Wellsand v. Valpariso* 1971)

Many of these cases were litigated in the 1970s, but the debate over due process is still being treated differently in the courts today. As in the 1970s, more and more questions are being raised that require consideration of due process, such as:

1. Should athletics be classified as a right or a privilege?

2. Should an institution be penalized for the illegal action of a coach or athlete?

3. Should all sports in a college program be penalized for the illegal action of staff or participants in one sport, such as basketball?

4. Should coaches and athletes be subjected to signed statements and polygraph tests to prove their allegiance to institutional and association rules?

These questions asked in the 1970s are still being asked in the 21st century and will continue to raise ethical questions until definitive action is taken by the courts.

A Lack of Due Process

We once recruited a young man for our basketball team who had narrowed his choice of schools down to two, and we were the one he finally chose for enrollment. The neighboring school did not take the student-athlete's choice very well and reported us to the Conference Commissioner, saying that our student had gone to class at their school and was therefore ineligible for sports participation at our school. It appeared that we could lose all the games the student in question had played and go from first place to last in the conference race.

All of this was done behind our back, as no one told us the details of the investigation. I finally learned the name of the professor who had stated that the student came to his class. I went to see the professor, who said he had wondered why the coaching staff came to his class and pressured him to say that the student had attended his class. "No way did he ever come to my class and I have my grade book to prove it. I will testify in your behalf," he said.

After two weeks of secret meetings behind our back, we were cleared of any wrongdoing. We learned the hard way about a lack of due process. Incidentally, this student-athlete made All-America and was inducted into our Sports Hall of Fame years later.

Fair Play Policy Implemented

During the 2009 football season, I had the opportunity to observe charges against a school regarding alleged illegal recruiting. Text messages accusing the athletics department of recruiting violations were rampant and brought statewide attention to a very good program.

After a year of investigations and interrogations of coaches, athletics directors and administrators, a "Fair Play Policy" was initiated. According to the policy, anyone can call, email or text a message alerting the county school office of illegal recruiting or other illegalities the person wants to report and can do so anonymously.

In my opinion, this is not Fair Play because the person complaining does not have to sign his or her name. Can you imagine the unfortunate things that can be said when they can remain anonymous? My high school principal had a simple, but fair policy: if the call or letter was unsigned or anonymous, he refused to listen or read the letter. In my opinion, this is preferable to accusing someone without signing or giving a name. Talk about unethical behavior!

However, the reason many school districts endorse a Fair Play Policy that does not require a person to sign his or her name is because they believe many people will not complain if they must sign their names, for fear that the person involved may retaliate against their children. They insist that the letters and calls should be kept confidential, which means the allegations of misconduct will be investigated without affording the person accused of wrongdoing due process.

Fair Play Questioned

Regarding situations that are unethical when anonymity is the rule, I remember a situation that could have led to the firing of an excellent, dedicated professor. Our president called me in and I realized something was definitely wrong. He said a student had given him an audio tape in which he accused the professor of sexually abusing him. He wanted the professor fired immediately. The president said he knew that as I was the football and track coach, the players confided in me, and he asked if I had heard any negative comments about this particular professor. I told him, "Not at all," and that the students really respected this man and always talked about how much they admired him.

Later that month, the president called me to tell me that the same student came into his office to tell him that he had made up the charges on the tape because he hated the professor and hoped his lies would get him fired. The professor stayed on until he retired with honor for his long and valuable service to the college. He probably never knew of the complaint by a disgruntled student and the confidence our president had in the positive things said by the faculty and staff he interviewed about the professor.

New Jersey Interscholastic Athletic Association's Due Process Policy

The New Jersey State Interscholastic Athletic Association (NJSAA) recently passed legislation to address the many eligibility issues that often lead to litigation over illegal recruitment. In their handbook (Section 8, p.70), the rule reads as follows:

Any member school which institutes an unsuccessful appeal before the Commissioner of Education and/or the courts challenging a rule or a decision of the Association, not involving the eligibility of Student-Athletes, either prior to or after having first exhausted the internal appeal procedures of the Association, will assume the full cost of such litigation, including costs and counsel fees incurred by the Association and members school(s).

The exception comes when the case involves eligibility. In cases involving public schools, the appeal goes to the Commissioner of Education, while an appeal from a non-public school goes to the Superior Court. Mike Hebert, the NJSAA attorney, said that the number of appeals declined when the legislation was passed, but today there are still a number of lawsuits filed (*New Jersey State Interscholastic Athletic Association Handbook*, 2010).

Penny Postcard Ends Scholarship

I was a junior who had played two years of varsity football and two and one-half spring practices. My first two spring practices consisted of 33 days of offense and defense without injury, but in my third spring practice I suffered a severe injury to my knee that ended my career. I was one who unexpectedly received one of the infamous penny postcards in the spring of 1946. As soon as I received the card on a Saturday morning, I heard a knock on my dormitory room. It was our defensive line coach, Tom Rogers, an All-America lineman at Duke University, who came to talk with me about the postcard. He said apologetically, "Herb, I am truly sorry for the card, but I have good news for you—my friend at Glenville State College in West Virginia has a full football scholarship for you. I know you can play for them and you can start at tailback for them." This really helped me at a time when I was at an all-time low. However, after thanking Coach Rogers, I told him I planned to stay at Wake Forest University and graduate. I also told him I would get a job to pay my way through. After all, I was majoring in Latin under the top Latin professor in America, Dr. Hubert Poteat, and wanted to complete my degree with him as my major advisor.

The decision to stay was one of the best I ever made. Wake Forest did more for me than I ever could repay, during my time as a student and as a coach. They gave me uniforms for the first high school football team I coached and their outstanding athletic trainer volunteered to come to all our Friday night games when Wake Forest had a Saturday home game. It was unheard of to have the services of a college athletic trainer at a small high school. When I coached at

Chowan Junior College in Eastern North Carolina, Wake Forest once again furnished jerseys for us to wear, plus other equipment. The athletic trainer enabled our injured players to come for rehab whenever needed. When I desperately needed a game, Wake Forest's coach sent a JV team to play us at our home field.

In 2008, I received a call from the provost, probably the most celebrated Wake Forest graduate, Ed Wilson, who told me I had been unanimously voted into the Wake Forest Sports Hall of Fame to join Tim Duncan, Brian Piccolo, Arnold Palmer and many other legendary figures whom I had admired for years. I knew of course that the selection was not for my prowess in football or track, but other accomplishments through the years. I wish my old coach who cut my scholarship my junior year was alive when this honor came.

Twenty-one years after my scholarship was cut, ten other Wake Forest football players had their scholarships abruptly terminated, and no one had any recourse for their loss and no one challenged the unethical action by their coach. Almost all transferred to other schools. Ironically, one was named Little All-America at Appalachian State University, another Little All-America at Atlantic Christian College and a third was named captain of Muhlenberg College's football team. From all reports, the men who left Wake Forest all achieved success in football at other schools.

Athletic Scholarships and Due Process

In 1967, Gregg Taylor signed an agreement to receive a full football scholarship at Wake Forest under rules set by the Atlantic Coast Conference (ACC) and the National Collegiate Athletic Conference (NCAA). At the end of his first semester, during which he participated in football, Taylor earned a 1.60 grade average. Wake Forest required a 1.35 average. To get his grades up, Taylor did not report for spring football practice and improved his grade average to 1.90. When he completed his third semester, he achieved a 2.4 average and did not return to the football program at the university. The Faculty Athletic Committee met with Taylor to determine the school's validity in canceling his athletic scholarship. The university held a hearing and decided that his scholarship should be withdrawn. In *Taylor v. Wake Forest University* (1972), Taylor sued the university for expenses incurred after the termination of his grant-in-aid. He argued that the university violated the contract between himself and Wake Forest University (Appenzeller, 1985).

Judge Robert Campbell stated that the court did not agree with Taylor because the scholarship was awarded for academic and athletic achievement. Participation and attendance, the court reasoned, were required to maintain his physical ability. When he refused to do so in the absence of an injury, and only to devote more time to his studies, Taylor was not complying with his contractual obligations. The court concluded, therefore, that the university met its obligation to the athlete and that Taylor did not meet his obligation to the university (Appenzeller, 1985).

As late as 1976, the NCAA had a rule that students who signed athletic grant-in-aids could not lose them once they started their first semester. To me, this raised an ethical question: why should an athlete be able to just decide he or she does not want to practice or play, but instead choose to devote all his or her time to his or her studies, and still retain his or her athletic grant? Later, this rule was changed by the NCAA, and the institution was required to extend considerable safeguards for athletes in hearings and other requirements before coaches could decide to arbitrarily cut a student's athletic grant without procedural due process. Due process is now in force.

Very little has been done to eliminate the ills that are often found in sport. It took 58 years for the court to reverse *Plessy v. Ferguson*'s separate but equal doctrine with the *Brown v. Topeka* decision that ended racial segregation. Racial discrimination did not end because of the church, school or other social agencies. It ended by judicial action. In like manner, the court may be the dominant force to end discrimination, negligence and violence in sports. The courts are making sport participation its best ever.

The sport administrator faces legal issues in the 21st Century that did not exist in the past. Today, the courts hold the sport administrator responsible for situations involving tort, criminal, employment, contract and constitutional law. A risk management program is necessary to meet the demands of a litigious society. It is essential that both administrators and coaches understand how to manage risks and make it a top priority. The courts require school personnel to operate a reasonable, safe program, although they recognize that the safest program can never avoid accidents. The sport administrator should rely on the school's attorney for guidance regarding school law and the applicability of individual state law.

Ethical Questions

1. What were Harry Rosenfield's reasons for opposing the immunity doctrine?
2. When did most states modify the immunity doctrine?
3. Do you favor immunity for cases involving sports?
4. Discuss the *Welch*, *Noffke*, *McFarlin* and *Crace* cases, and the reasons given by the courts for their decisions.
5. In the *McFarlin* case, do you agree with the opinion of the federal judge?
6. What is the anti-SLAPP law?
7. List the 15 "Blueprint for Success" risk management guidelines.
8. Discuss due process in the *Braesch* case in Nebraska and the case's outcome.
9. Discuss the "hair cases."
10. Discuss anonymity in reporting alleged violations.
11. Discuss the "penny postcard" incident as opposed to the 1972 Gregg Taylor case.

Chapter 7

Hazing

"In the sixth century BC, Emperor Justinian of Byzantine outlawed the hazing of first year law students. There is no mention of hazing in written records again until the Middle Ages. Scholars propose that the practice was successfully eradicated until university members found old documents of codified Roman law detailing Justinian's decree. It was then that students of the Middle Ages document hazing practices of first year students. From then until the present there has been a continuing issue with hazing."—Hank Nuwer, Wrongs of Passage: Fraternities, Sororities, Hazing, and Binge Drinking *(1999)*

Introduction

Hazing presents an ethical behavior problem for many athletic administrators and coaches in today's sports programs. Chuck Huckabee, writing in *The Chronicle of Higher Education* (2008), reported that a large study sponsored by the National Center for Hazing Research and Prevention found that "nationwide, more than half of students who belong to campus organizations, including performing-arts groups, experience hazing."

This chapter will highlight the prevalence of hazing as early as middle schools, up to professional sports. Although 40 states prohibit hazing in its schools, many graduates defend hazing as a traditional rite of passage in various organizations that have membership requirements. Those who favor hazing say that hazing should be fun, not a violation of somebody. A report in the *Las Vegas Review-Journal* (2006) cites some former athletes defending hazing in sport, saying that "it's humorous, and a little cruel, but you think, hey, you know what, they [the seniors] did the same thing to me a couple years ago" (Kalil & Dewey, 2006).

A former college athlete in Colorado stated that the younger athletes were targeted for hazing. He said, "There was no hitting in the face or the groin … We just basically beat them in the arms and legs, so they'd be sore but not seriously hurt." He went on to describe how he too was hazed as a junior varsity player: "They all just kind of took a turn. It was like a senior's privilege ... Maybe 10 or 15 guys would come and give you three or four licks each, then they'd help you up, and one of them would give you a ride home. It was just a tradition" (Kalil & Dewey, 2006).

A former high school athlete said "he witnessed players getting 'swirlies,' where a person's head is dunked into a toilet that is then flushed." One former female athlete said she observed hazing going on but described it as practical jokes against "male athletes their own age rather than their younger, female counterparts on junior varsity teams." She said, "We feathered this one athlete's car and rubbed peanut butter all over this one guy's truck" (Kalil & Dewey, 2006). Is this a healthy viewpoint of hazing? Or just a way to justify the act in today's society?

Many experts continue to be alarmed over the rise and justification of hazing practices in sport organizations. It is commonplace these days to turn on the news and see the latest story on a hazing or initiation activity that occurred in the region. The public frequently learns of hazing incidents via the local media or by watching ESPN, which frequently reports on the hazing or initiation exploits of professional teams. A recent example of this was the coverage of Denver Broncos rookie quarterback Tim Tebow's new hairstyle in the preseason. Many other examples exist as well, such as stories of NFL rookies having to carry the luggage of the veterans during training camp or singing their favorite songs at team dinners. These activities may seem mild and cause little to no harm, but each time these stories occur they send mixed messages about the role of hazing in sport. When you take a close look at the coverage of recent hazing incidents at all levels, it seems that as long as no one got injured, hazing is an acceptable practice, even in the professional ranks. Only when hazing gets "out of control" do people become outraged enough to speak out against the practice. It is no wonder that hazing continues at all levels of sport when there is no clear, consistent message regarding hazing and/or initiation in sport. This leaves the doors open to debate if hazing is an ethical practice in sport. It is therefore essential that those individuals that guide the sport experience at all levels understand the various aspects of hazing in order to protect the virtues of sportsmanship. This chapter will discuss several areas associated with hazing, including how it is defined, the prevalence of hazing practices at different levels of sport, legal concerns, myths regarding hazing and examples of how hazing is being handled in sport.

Defining Hazing

Hazing is a broad term that encompasses many activities, situations and actions that an individual must tolerate in order to become part of the group or team. When trying to construct a definition of hazing, one must consider many different viewpoints. The definition and meaning of hazing often varies from one person to another. For example, an individual who is performing an act of hazing may define the term very differently than the person being hazed. Similarly, an administrator may perceive hazing and the various acts involved differently than a coach or parent. Furthermore, some individuals may only consider physical bodily acts as hazing, while others may include mental and sexual acts as hazing activities. The definitions of hazing become the central focus when administrators are put in a position to decide if hazing occurred or if the activity was a case of horseplay gone wrong. While hazing has been acknowledged for centuries, there is no universally accepted definition. This may be due to the many forms and the variety of ways in which initiations and rituals take place within different organizations.

In 1999, the following definition of hazing was postulated by Dr. Nadine Hoover: "Any activity expected of someone joining a group that humiliates, degrades, abuses, or endangers, regardless of the person's willingness to participate" (Hoover & Pollard, 1999). Hoover's definition brings to light one of the common myths associated with hazing. There is an underlying myth that if a person participates in an initiation ceremony voluntarily, then the initiation process cannot be considered "hazing." Hoover's definition proposes that an activity that humiliates, degrades, abuses or endangers another is an act of hazing, regardless of the individual's willingness to participate.

In addition, several state laws dispute this myth, including Texas law, which states, "It is not a defense to prosecution for the offense under this subchapter that the person against whom the hazing was directed consented to or acquiesced in the hazing activity (Sec. 4.54)." Moreover, these definitions provide a more detailed explanation of what hazing entails, making it easier for policy makers and athletics directors to effectively illustrate the activities that may be considered as hazing (McGlone, 2008).

Types of Hazing

In their groundbreaking study on hazing in 1999, Hoover and Pollard suggested there are two distinct categories of hazing: physical and mental. The physical form of hazing may include activities such as beatings, branding, paddling, excessive exercises, excessive drinking and/or drug use, and forced sexual activities. In addition, activities involving sexual activities and/or sexual assaults are considered forms of physical hazing. Sexual hazing often includes simulated sex acts, sodomy and forced kissing. Mental hazing often goes overlooked or undetected, but is just as dangerous as physical hazing. Mental haz-ing occurs when initiates feels that they are in a dangerous situation or that there is a high degree of embarrassment involved with the activity. Types of mental hazing may include verbal abuse, being blindfolded, and being cap-tured and locked in small places (Nuwer, 2000).

Other common forms of mental hazing include being denied team privi-leges, being excluded from team activities, being denied food or beverages dur-ing team activities and simulating sexual activities. Mental and physical hazing can occur separately or in conjunction with one another based upon the ac-tivities and the perspective of the person being hazed (McGlone, 2008).

Hazing as a Tradition

Hazing has been in existence since the time of ancient Greece. As time has passed, these traditions have continued and evolved. In modern times, if high school students are asked why they participated in hazing, they report that it "was fun and exciting." Other reasons include, "it brought us closer together as a team" or "I got to prove myself." Still other high school students report, "I had to go through it last year, so now I get to do it to someone else," or that it is a "tradition" (Hoover & Pollard, 2000).

In fact, many groups try to keep traditions alive by adding on to the tradi-tions of the past in order to leave their personal mark on the group. It is this add-on effect that makes hazing more dangerous today than in years past. By adding a new element to hazing, older experienced members get to add a new twist and expand on the tradition. For example, when first-year athletes joined the team, they were each required to drink a beer in order to become part of the team. The following year, the new athletes were required to drink a six-pack of beer in order to become part of the team. As time passes, the six-pack becomes a gallon, until the tradition becomes a "drink until you pass out" rite of passage. The add-on effect has made hazing more dangerous and some ac-tivities may be life threatening.

Furthermore, hazing is typically planned and carried out behind closed doors or in secret. The silence is characteristically only broken after someone has been injured so severely that medical attention is required. At this point, the secret is revealed and the activities become public. The school or organi-zation, as well as the athletes themselves, may be put under the media micro-scope and the effects of the hazing activity may be intensified by the amount of attention being given to the incident. This attention may cause great diffi-culty for the image of the school, its athletics programs, the coaches and the athletes, and thus becomes a public relations issue for the entire institution (McGlone, 2008). Sport administrators need to discuss the moral and ethical decision-making process that takes place during these activities. If hazing has to be planned in secret in order for people stay out of trouble, is it something that would resemble an ethical practice in sport?

The State of Hazing Today

Hazing has been troublesome for centuries. However, only in the last decade has hazing been researched in the area of sport. As previously mentioned, Hoover and Pollard conducted and led the first large-scale study regarding hazing practices on college campuses in 1999. This study became known as the Alfred study, and was initiated after Alfred University had the unfortunate responsibility of dealing with a hazing-related death on its campus.

This landmark study provided the first empirical data showing how prevalent hazing was on college campuses across the country. The Alfred study established baseline figures for the prevalence and severity of hazing. As a result, many colleges and universities have established policies and procedures in an effort to reduce the number of hazing incidents within intercollegiate athletics. While society has recognized the issue of hazing in athletics, the prevalence and severity of the problem may not be fully known, nor understood (McGlone, 2008).

Prevalence of Hazing

The research on hazing in the last decade suggests that anywhere from 50% to 100% of athletes have been exposed at some point to some sort of initiation. Breaking down the numbers further, 66% of those surveyed were subjected to humiliating rituals, including but not limited to being dressed up in costumes, having food and other miscellaneous substances thrown on them, being yelled at in public and having to perform embarrassing acts in public. Furthermore, 25% of those who reported being hazed participated in unacceptable illegal behaviors, which include trespassing, theft, vandalism or destruction of property, underage drinking (and driving), drug use and sexual assault. These hazing activities are gender blind as well, as women and men both reported being hazed at an equal rate. However, women were more likely to be involved in alcohol-related hazing than their male counterparts. In addition, 16% of the female athletes reported being involved in activities that carried a high probability of risk or that could result in criminal charges (Hoover & Pollard, 1999).

Hazing Is Not Just an Athletics Issue!

A recent study by University of Maine researchers reveals that hazing is commonplace in all kinds of college student organizations, and that most students don't recognize that some forms of dangerous, even illegal, behavior constitute hazing. The survey, known as the "National Study of Student Hazing," is by far the largest and most comprehensive study of its kind. Part of a three-year research project, it includes responses from 11,482 college students at 53 institutions around the U.S. A research advisory group helped define a list of forced behaviors that constitute hazing. A partial list includes: attendance at a skit night or roast where team members are humiliated; wearing clothing that is embarrassing and not part of the uniform; being yelled, screamed or cursed at by other team/organization members; acting as a personal servant to other organization member; enduring harsh weather without proper clothing; drinking large amounts of a non-alcoholic beverage such as water; drinking large amounts of alcohol to the point of passing out or getting sick; watching live sex acts; performing sex acts with the same gender (Allan & Madden, 2008).

Stereotypes often shape perceptions of hazing as only a problem for Greek-letter organizations and athletes, and hazing behaviors are often dismissed as simply harmless antics and pranks. The study also reveals that one-quarter of those who experienced hazing believed that coaches and/or advisers were aware of the activities. A similar percentage of respondents reported that alumni were present when hazing occurred. In more than half the incidents reported by students, photos of the activities were posted on public Web sites and roughly 25% of students reported that hazing occurred in public spaces on campus (Allan & Madden, 2008).

High School Hazing

Hazing is often thought of as harmless fun, where "boys will be boys and girls will be girls." This misconception can lead to troubling results. Hazing at any age can be troublesome, but hazing in high school and earlier can have devastating hidden harm that often goes unnoticed. Middle school and high school students are at various stages of development within their adolescence, and are vulnerable to peer pressure due to their intense need to "belong" (Nuwer, 2000).

We would all like to think that hazing is a thing of the past, and that all the recent media attention regarding hazing has somewhat reduced the prevalence of hazing on our teams and at our schools. In an idealistic world, this would be the case; however, reality sets in when you take a look at the recent headlines.

Hank Nuwer, one of the nation's foremost experts on hazing, states:

> Hazing at any age can be exceedingly harmful. Hazing at the high school level is particularly troubling because the developmental stages of adolescence create a situation in which many students are more vulnerable to peer pressure due to the tremendous need for belonging, making friends and finding approval in one's peer group. Further, the danger of hazing at the high school level is heightened by the lack of awareness and policy development/enforcement around this issue. While many colleges and universities in the U.S. have instituted anti-hazing policies and educational awareness programs related to hazing, very few secondary schools have done the same. (Nuwer, 2008)

The National Federation of High Schools has publicly addressed hazing and views it as cause for concern. The organization has developed many resources for their member schools, and has developed numerous educational components to help schools, coaches, administrators and students deal with hazing. Included in these components are recommendations for creating an anti-hazing policy, which includes seven separate sections: 1) purpose, 2) a general statement of policy, 3) the definition of hazing, 4) reporting procedures, 5) school district action, 6) reprisal, and 7) dissemination of the policy (NFHS, 2009).

National Federation of High Schools' Policy: High School Hazing Statistics

Hazing is prevalent among American high school students. Research suggests that 48% of students who belong to groups reported being subjected to hazing activities. In addition, 43% reported being subjected to humiliating activities and 30% reported performing potentially illegal acts as part of their initiation. Both female and male students reported high levels of hazing, although male students are at highest risk, especially for dangerous hazing. Moreover, the lower a student's grade point average, the greater his or her risk of being hazed. Athletes are not the only group at risk in high schools; almost every type of high school groups had significantly high levels of hazing. For example, 24% of students involved in church groups were subjected to hazing activities.

Intercollegiate Hazing and College Hazing Statistics

Research indicates that more than 250,000 students experienced some sort of hazing to join a college athletic team between 2001 and 2005. In addition, 2.5% of all college students admitted to being hazed, while 40% admitted to knowing about hazing activities. Again, it was reported by 40% of the athletes surveyed that a coach or club advisor was aware of the hazing and did not attempt to stop it. Furthermore, 22% reported that the coach or advisor was involved in the hazing, which brings up another discussion on whether this should be labeled as hazing or harassment. Hazing in college affects both men and women, with research indicating that 50% of the female NCAA Division I athletes reported being hazed, and 20% of females that reported being hazed were subjected to alcohol-related hazing. However, an even higher percentage admitted to "mental hazing," which ranged from singing to being kidnapped. Ten percent of the female NCAA athletes were physically hazed, including being branded, tattooed, beaten, thrown in water or having their heads forcibly shaved. Furthermore, another 6–9% of the female NCAA athletes were subjected to sexually-related hazing, including harassment, actual assault or being expected to simulate sex activities (McGlone, 2005).

Women's Athletics

In 2005, another landmark study was conducted, becoming the first (and to date only) study to examine the prevalence of hazing in National Collegiate Athletic Association (NCAA) Division I (DI) women's athletics, based on the perceptions of current female student athletes (SAs), athletics directors (ADs) and senior women administrators (SWAs). The findings revealed that overall, 48.5% of the athletes reported they had been hazed. Furthermore, nearly 39% percent of the athletes reported they had known about hazing occurring on women's teams at their institutions. In addition, 31% reported they had witnessed acts of hazing on their current teams, and 34% percent reported that they had hazed other athletes on their current teams. This study brought to light that hazing is occurring in women's NCAA DI athletics. The fact that nearly one out of every two athletes in this survey indicated that they have been hazed suggests that hazing has become part of the culture of women's NCAA DI athletics. There appears to be an overall awareness that hazing is occurring; however, there is also a widespread perception that hazing is not a problem on one's own campus. The prevalence of hazing combined with the perceptions revealed in the study indicate that athletes, coaches, administrators, athletic departments, institutions and the NCAA are in a vulnerable position in regard to hazing (McGlone, 2005).

Hazing in Recreational Sport

Recreational sport seems to get overlooked, as it is not typically in the forefront of campuses or news headlines, and many times the administrative oversight of college recreational sports is not as structured as those in high school and college. However, recreational sports are very popular and the number of people participating in recreational leagues continues to grow. It would seem odd, then, that these leagues would not have the problems associated with hazing that their athletics counterparts do on the same campuses.

In their study regarding the prevalence of hazing in NIRSA sport clubs in 2006, Martin & McGlone found that hazing is indeed common in recreational sport at the college level. In fact, nearly 38% of club sport participants indicated they had been hazed, while 31% of participants indicated they knew of hazing occurring in other club sports on their campuses. Furthermore, 27% of those surveyed stated that they had personally witnessed acts of hazing on their own sport club teams. It is an interesting finding that team club sports had higher rates of hazing than individual sports.

A follow-up study was conducted by Allen & Madden in 2008, which revealed the most common hazing behaviors: 41% participated in drinking games; 20% drank large amounts of alcohol to the point of getting sick or passing out; 20% sang or chanted by themselves or with others in public situations not related to an event, game or practice; and 19% drank large amounts of non-alcoholic beverages. Furthermore, 17% indicated they had been screamed, yelled or cursed at by other members of the team as an initiation practice, while 12% endured harsh weather conditions without appropriate clothing as part of a hazing activity. Other common forms of hazing within the club sport structure included sleep deprivation and sexual acts (McGlone & Martin, 2006).

Hidden Harm

As previously mentioned, there are different viewpoints on what constitutes an act of hazing, which makes hazing difficult to control. It is important, no matter what one's personal viewpoints are on any type of hazing or initiation activity, that sport managers understand and recognize that hazing, even in its mildest forms, can and often does lead to harm. It can be related to basic physics that every action has some type of reaction. Simply stated, hazing hurts children, emotionally and physically.

Studies show that 71% of the students subjected to hazing reported negative consequences, such as getting into fights, being injured, fighting with parents, doing poorly in school, hurting other people, having difficulty eating, sleeping or concentrating, or feeling angry, confused, embarrassed or guilty. In one study, 1% of those who had been hazed reported that they wanted to harm themselves, and 25% indicated they considered quitting the team as a direct result of hazing.

None of the outcomes listed above are what sport participation is supposed to lead to, and in any other context, these harms would be addressed. However, when it comes to hazing, the response is often to ignore the situation and sweep things under the rug. The question is why we would continue to allow this to occur in our schools and programs.

Another scary fact is that hazing starts young, and continues through high school and college. In fact, 25% of those who reported being hazed were first hazed before the age of 13. Dangerous hazing activities are as prevalent among high school students (22%) as among college athletes (21%). Substance abuse in hazing is prevalent in high school (23%) and increases in college (51%). Recently, it has been reported that sexual hazing incidents are on the rise as well.

Legal Aspects

As the number of reported hazing incidents has increased, so has the number of states that have passed legislation to deter hazing from occurring. Currently, there are 44 states with anti-hazing statutes, while six states have not developed or introduced anti-hazing laws. Only the states of Alaska, Hawaii, Montana, New Mexico, South Dakota and Wyoming lack any type of specific hazing law (Nuwer 2008). While many in those states have called for hazing laws, it is important to note that a specific hazing law may not be necessary, as most activities associated with hazing fall under laws that are already in place. For example, many hazing activities could fall under the auspices of assault and battery legislation. In 1969, 35 states had laws regarding hazing, and this was the last year that no fraternity-, sorority- or athletics-related death occurred in the U.S. (hazing.hanknuwer.com).

Hazing is punishable under criminal law in 40 states. Since hazing is considered a criminal act, the judicial system has established many other legal definitions that address and define hazing. Current hazing legislation varies from state to state, and the punishments for hazing may include a fine, imprisonment or both, depending on the state and the severity of the hazing incident. With the various definitions of hazing, the average individual may have great difficulty determining what types of behaviors constitute hazing. Similarly, when one looks at the legal definitions of hazing and anti-hazing statutes, it becomes increasingly difficult to develop legislation that encompasses all aspects of hazing without compromising constitutional rights.

The ambiguity in hazing laws, combined with the continuance of hazing activities, has created the call from many anti-hazing activists for the establishment of national anti-hazing legislation. This legislation may create consistency in determining the legal threshold for hazing, as well as the penalty for hazing. In 2005, a National Hazing bill was proposed. This bill has failed to make it though the system. However, the proposed bill has not been forgotten and many advocate groups whose purpose is to help reduce hazing continue to try and lobby for national hazing legislation (McGlone, 2008).

NCAA Policy

The National Collegiate Athletic Association (NCAA) does not have any written hazing bylaws or policies addressing hazing. In fact, they leave hazing policy up to the conferences and schools that make up their membership. According to Pollard, "Colleges ... have a greater liability with athletic hazing than with [fraternities and sororities]. After all, we recruit them. They wear our uniforms, and we went to their families to encourage them to be part of our campus community." This is surprising since research indicates that if the NCAA penalized teams, schools and students for hazing, it would get their attention and go a long way to reduce hazing within NCAA athletic teams (McGlone, 2005).

I find it surprising that with the knowledge and the admission by student-athletes that if the NCAA stepped in and created some sort of penalty for teams who haze, the NCAA has not created a policy. I applaud the NCAA for taking a stand and addressing the issue in a hazing symposium during the 2008 NCAA National Conference. In addition, the NCAA has developed hazing prevention materials (McGlone, 2008).

Recommendations for Athletics Programs

The fact remains that hazing continues on our campuses. The question is, how do administrators handle and deal with hazing and initiation practices?

While there is no one perfect answer, the recommended approach is to develop a multi-faceted program. The foundation of this approach centers around education. Administrators need to address the issue in a clear and open fashion. In addition, hazing needs to be discussed with students, administrators, parents, coaches, health care teams and anyone involved with school organizations in order to ensure everyone is on the same page. Too often schools establish a policy, put it in the handbook and rely totally on the fact that those that need to understand the issue will read about it in the manual. Education programs need to squarely address the topic, address the myths associated with hazing, offer alternatives to achieve the cohesion it is often associated with, and establish reporting procedures and ramifications for being associated with hazing practices.

Education programs can include a variety of components, from having open discussions, issuing pamphlets and watching anti-hazing videos, to coming up with an anti-hazing contract and having each person sign it. At minimum, every high school or college should have a written anti-hazing policy. This policy should be explained and discussed with each team by the athletics director or individual coach. In most instances, freshmen are the victims of hazing of every type. Many coaches turn their heads when athletes haze members of their teams. Coaches need to be alert to hazing and enforce anti-hazing polices that are known to team members. Zero tolerance should be observed (McGlone 2008). These education components should include explanations that when hazing occurs, it creates a losing situation. For example, it may cause losing a player due to injury, losing the right to be on a team, losing the season due to cancellation, and losing the respect of the community, school, parents and friends.

In addition, education should "Kill The Myth." The most vital concept is that hazing does *not* build team unity. The myth that hazing can be good must be killed. There is nothing helpful about hazing. Rituals and traditions that cause any person to feel less worthy (i.e., at the bottom of the totem pole) merely maintain the status quo, solidifying those in power. Even the brightest, most ethical student leaders can and do misuse their power in a hazing situation. If you truly believe that hazing can destroy your team, then you are ready to prevent hazing.

It is also suggested that each organization have in place a reporting procedure. This procedure needs to be simple, safe and offer anonymous reporting. It should also include wording that informs those who know about an upcoming hazing activity that it can be reported prior to an incident occurring. It is important that you completely investigate any incident that is reported, even if it is just a rumor. In any case, administrators, coaches and parents need to discuss what hazing is, any consequences of hazing, the hazing policy, and how to prevent hazing.

In terms of legal aspects, administrators need to keep good records of all anti-hazing efforts in case of a lawsuit. Litigation has increased in the area of hazing under various laws, and it is always good policy to ensure all safety and education actions are documented. It is also important to protect those who report hazing, as they often fear a backlash for their actions. Remember that even when a student comes to you and asks you not to say anything, confidentiality cannot be assured when harm or risk of harm is involved. Finally, if an incident has taken place, be fair and appropriate in your response. It is never okay to ignore policy for your favorite player or starter; be consistent in upholding all policies. When necessary, you may need to report the incident to the local authorities or health care providers. Often, this leads to some sort of media story. Remember, if the media become involved, you have certain legal responsibilities, including not releasing certain information. Ensure you know these policies for your organization prior to discussing any incident with the media. It is a good idea to write a statement if necessary and have only one person deal with media. Do not get wrapped up in questions, and let the media know that as more details are available, you will let them know. Try to avoid saying nothing; while this might be good legal advice, it may appear that you are trying to hide something.

Lastly, when preventing hazing, offer alternatives. It is a myth that hazing brings teams closer together or builds trust. However, if this is the desired outcome and why hazing occurs, then offer alternatives that achieve or build the same ideals. For example, if a team wants to learn to trust each other, take them to a ropes course or do team building exercises. If a team desires to become closer to each other, try working together on a community project, like cleaning up a local playground or working with a charity. Chances are that if a group has the opportunity to spend time with each other outside of normal practice and school schedule, they will find a new level of bonding and this may decrease the likelihood of hazing.

Court Cases Involving Hazing

Ousted Athletics Director Gets $567,500 Settlement

A New York school district agreed to pay $567,500 to a former high school athletics director who claimed that he was demoted because he criticized the district's failure to address locker room misbehavior. In October 2001, the

Averill Park Central School District, made headlines when a high school student reported that he was the target of a lewd hazing ritual. The school's athletics director, Lou Cioffi, appeared at a news conference and claimed that he had repeatedly warned the district of the behavior, to no avail. Cioffi's position was soon eliminated, and he was forced to return to teaching before ultimately moving to another district. Cioffi claimed that his demotion was retaliatory, and though the district disagreed, the parties negotiated a settlement. *(From the Gym to the Jury,* 2008).

The High Cost of Hazing: Family of High School Victim Wants $1 Million from Town

In the summer of 2006, a football player at Fairhaven High School in Massachusetts was reportedly physically and sexually assaulted by older members of the football team while at Camp Wishbone. The crime was also videotaped. Eventually, four members of the team were charged with hazing and assault, but not before the entire town turned against the victim and his family for reporting the incident. Now the family has informed the town of Fairhaven that it wants $1 million in compensation, and if it does not respond to the demand within six months, they will file a civil complaint against the town. So, they hadn't filed a lawsuit yet, they were just asking nicely for the money. Seems very civil, doesn't it? A letter sent by the family's attorney to the town claimed the hazing incident at Camp Wishbone was not an isolated occurrence, but rather it was part of a "culture of ongoing criminal hazing by Fairhaven football players" and, specifically, "it was common knowledge that, in prior years, football player students were required to stand naked in wash tubs while other team members urinated on them" (Anderson, 2008).

RIT Hazing Case

Five Rochester Institute of Technology students were accused of pressuring others to drink dangerous amounts of alcohol in 2007. Charged with first-degree hazing and unlawfully dealing with a child were: Jennifer P. Salavarrieta, 21, of Piscataway, N.J.; Marie E. Krysak, 21, of Endicott, Broome County; Kerry E. Gallagher, 20, of Stratham, N.H.; Katelyn M. Temple, 20, of Henrietta, N.Y.; and Lindsay L. Thompson, 22, of Mamaroneck, Westchester County. The charges stemmed from a party in May 2007 where six RIT students were hospitalized after binge drinking. The victims were allegedly pressured into consuming dangerous levels of alcohol to join the school's rugby clubs. The victims were taken to Strong Memorial Hospital. They all recovered, but some spent time in the hospital's intensive care unit. Both the men's and women's rugby clubs were suspended and were eligible to reapply for recognition in the fall of 2010. Eight players on the men's and women's rugby teams were charged in the case. The men and women chose to have separate trials (Loudon, 2008).

Hazing Leads to $3 Million in Medical Bills

The mother of a 15-year-old student filed a lawsuit against a school district alleging that her son was abused by his teammates at a summer football camp. In the suit, the mother sought unspecified damages. Court documents state that the boy accrued $3 million in medical bills and other costs. The plaintiffs contended that the boy was sexually attacked, held down, punched, kicked and sodomized with an object, all in the presence of several other students. The boy is undergoing counseling and psychological treatment, along with on-going medical care (*From the Gym to the Jury*, 2008).

Catholic University Forfeits Lacrosse Games

Catholic University forfeited three women's lacrosse games in the 2006 season, and placed the team on probation for the following season. The forfeits were the result of an investigation of an off-campus freshman initiation party where hazing took place. School officials learned of the hazing after photos were posted on the Internet under the title "Catholic University Women's Lacrosse Initiation Party 2006" (*The Associated Press*, 2006).

Prank Leads to Tragedy

A player on the Bradley University soccer team died of smoke inhalation after a fire started in a room shared with four roommates. The boys lit a roman candle under the door after a night of drinking. The fire was so intense that the boys could not save their friend (*From the Gym to the Jury*, 2008).

Bands Gone Wild

The University of Wisconsin at Madison suspended its marching band in 2008 for "serious hazing allegations," "alcohol use" and sexualized behavior." This came at a time when the *San Francisco Chronicle* reported that Tom Slabaugh, marching band director at the University of California at Davis, filed a sexual harassment complaint against his own band. The marching band at Prairie View A&M University was suspended after an anonymous person claimed "band members had been hit and had their heads shaven during hazing rituals" (Stripling, 2008). Edwards, director of the Prairie View band, said, "It is part of the culture [of marching bands], and it's got to stop." He added that "it's not just small schools ... it's large schools as well." Susan Lipkins, a psychologist who studies hazing and author of *Preventing Hazing*, called the suspension of Wisconsin's band for hazing allegations "a huge statement." However, she questions "whether colleges have created systems to truly deal with hazing and abuse" (Stripling, 2008).

Wisconsin's band had been placed on probation in 2006 for hazing and harassment. School officials did not comment on whether the university had instituted any educational programs for band members in response to the 2006 probation.

Six Arrested in Possible Hazing by Band Members

Six members of the marching band at Southern University at Baton Rouge were arrested and faced criminal charges for alleged "battery over ritualistic acts" in connection with injuries to two band members. Officials at the university said they are cooperating fully with the investigation and cited their "zero tolerance policy." The injuries occurred prior to the Southern Bayou Classic football game against Grambling State University. The Baton Rouge television station WAFB, a CBS affiliate, reported that the two victims were beaten with a two-by-four as part of an initiation into the band's french horn section. A third person elected to stop participating after he was hit over 50 times with the two-by-four. The other two band members were hospitalized (*From the Gym to the Jury*, 2008).

Additional Hazing Incidents Reported in From the Gym to the Jury *(2008)*

- Summer 4-H camp children nine to thirteen years of age were ordered to fight or be confined to their cabins. Admission of $1 was charged and the limit on betting was $4. The counselors were 14 to 18 years of age. A parent said the boys were pitted against each other like a cockfight.
- Parents of a boy who was taped to the ceiling of a bus during a football road trip in Alberton, Montana, debated whether or not to sue the school. The remainder of the football season was cancelled.
- Glenbrook High School North in Chicago engaged in hazing activity, in which senior girls assaulted junior girls during a powder puff football

game. As a result of the hazing, 33 senior girls were expelled, two juniors were expelled and two parents were charged for providing alcohol to minors.

- Eleven lacrosse players, also at Glenbrook High School South, paddled thirteen new players off campus, and underage drinking was encouraged. School officials cancelled the rest of the season.
- At a summer camp in Pennsylvania, 15-, 16- and 17-year-old boys were sodomized by three varsity athletes with broomsticks, pine cones and golf balls in front of teammates. As a result, the junior varsity and varsity football schedules were cancelled for one year.
- In Chico, California, the girls softball schedule was cancelled for the 2006 season after an underage girl recruit was made to drink at a team party. She was later hospitalized and almost died.
- A backup quarterback in Smithfield, Utah, was taped to a towel rack by his teammates and his girlfriend was brought the locker room to watch. When he objected to the hazing, his football coach refused to take him on the road trip for the next game. His parents sued the school claiming that it created a hostile environment for their son and that his rights had been violated.
- Seven wrestlers in Thousand Oaks, California, were suspended for one year for pinning a girl on a mat and probing her buttocks with a mop handle. The wrestling season was also cancelled.
- Seven rugby players were indicted for a prank in the dorm that backfired, leading to the death of a student.
- In South Dakota, a coach approved of a letterman's invitation in which a student-athlete was made to lie on a metal mat (grid) that was wet. The mat was connected to an electrical cord and the student was electrocuted when he was lying on the mat (*From the Gym to the Jury*, 2008).

Massachusetts Coach Hit by Hazing Claim

Law offices representing a former Marblehead High School soccer player announced their intent to file a legal complaint against the town, school department, superintendent, athletics director and high school principal for negligence in hiring soccer coach Steve Ingemi. Attorneys Robert K. Rainer and Chris O'Connor claimed that their client, Jacob Rainer, and other varsity soccer players were subjected to hazing rituals under the direction of Ingemi during the 2004–2006 seasons. In a letter, they alleged that Ingemi ordered each player accepted to the team to participate in the right of passage ritual known as "branding." The player was asked to stand inside the goal and face midfield.

Ingemi then kicked a soccer ball at "great velocity" toward the player with intent to leave a mark or imprint of the ball across his chest. If the player moved or attempted to protect himself from the ball, the process was repeated until the player could withstand the blow.

"This so-called drill willfully and recklessly endangered Jacob's and other players' physical and mental health," the legal presentment read. "Having allowed Ingemi to employ this dangerous form of hazing for so many years is unconscionable ... Apparently those in authority in Marblehead never supervised Ingemi or trained him to understand his obligation as a coach and representative in the town of Marblehead not to organize this hazing ritual."

Rainer and O'Connor planned to also file a civil action against Ingemi for assault, battery, false imprisonment and intentional infliction of emotional distress. Marblehead Superintendent Paul Dulac questioned why the complaint came two years after Rainer graduated. O'Connor said that the issue was something Rainer had been thinking about for some time and only recently became comfortable coming forward with it. "It's an interesting case from my perspective," O'Connor said. "You only hear about incidents of hazing when something awful happens ... It's an opportunity for us to get the issue out prior to something bad happening." O'Connor said that if found responsible, damages would be paid to the former student, as is the case for all civil complaints. "But the bigger picture is [beyond] the scope of what the courts can award," he said. "Awareness is the real goal here" (*The Daily Item*, 2008).

Tallmadge, Ohio Teen Gets Probation in Hazing Case

A 17-year-old former Tallmadge High School football player was placed on probation for one year and ordered to undergo psychological counseling for an attack on a younger teammate at school the previous summer. Robert Underwood, who was found guilty last month of juvenile delinquency charges of rape and hazing in connection with the incident, turned to face the 16-year-old victim and his family in court and tearfully read a written letter of apology: "It was never my intention to cause you harm in any way. I thought that what I was doing was nothing more than a silly prank to get people to laugh. I realize now the severity of what I did, and it was nothing to laugh about" (Meyer, 2008).

The victim, who was 15 at the time of the attack, testified in Summit County Juvenile Court that he was accosted by several teammates after football practice. He said he was forced to the ground, his pants were pulled down and he was jabbed repeatedly in the buttocks with a plastic drinking straw. Special prosecutor Dan Riedl of the Ohio Attorney General's Office, who was appointed to handle the case, told Juvenile Judge Linda Tucci Teodosio before sentencing that Underwood "picked up that straw and pushed it multiple times into the victim's rectum ... That was an intentional act. It wasn't merely something that got out of hand. It was an intent to cause a real violation ... of another person" (Meyer, 2008).

As part of Underwood's sentence, Teodosio ordered the teen to be classified—under mandated state guidelines for the offense of rape—as a Tier 3 sexual offender, the most serious sex offender classification under Ohio law. It will require Underwood to register his address with the sheriff's office every 90 days for life.

Underwood also was ordered to undergo an alcohol assessment and treatment program, to write a letter of apology and make amends to the victim and his family and to perform 40 hours of community service. If he violates any of those terms of probation, then he could be sentenced to incarceration in a Department of Youth Services facility for a period of at least one year up to his 21st birthday, Teodosio said. Riedl asked the judge to prohibit Underwood from returning to Tallmadge High as another part of his sentence, but Teodosio declined the request, saying she would leave that decision to school officials. Underwood has not attended classes at the school since the incident, the judge noted.

Underwood's mother and father accompanied him to court, and Teodosio praised them in her concluding remarks, saying "it took a lot of courage to take this case to this level ... If more people would step forward and be brave enough to come into court to speak about these kinds of things, then hopefully ... they will not occur to other young men and women" (Meyer, 2008).

High School Students Allege Sexual Hazing

Local high school baseball players in Indian River County, Florida claim they were touched sexually as a part of their team's initiation. A report detailing the investigation revealed the disturbing details. The investigation began after claims that a player on the Sebastian River High School baseball team was sexually hazed by teammates.

The report revealed, "They pinned him on his back and pulled his shorts up exposing his butt and someone said get the bottle [a two-liter bottle]." The report went on to say that students then touched the player sexually with that bottle. Five students were suspended and at least two expelled from Sebastian River High School. The head coach, George Young, was released from his coaching position, and suspended from teaching for three days. Young is accused of hiding some details of the assault from the school's athletics director (Gonzalez, 2008).

The report showed that when asked why this was the first he had heard of the bottle, Young looked at the parents and said, "I thought we agreed not to mention this last night in order to protect [an unidentified person's] privacy." Students claimed this type of hazing had been ongoing with the Sebastian River High School baseball team for years. The report revealed, "One player indicated that he had witnessed 'up to twenty incidents.'" Some players said they were embarrassed to come forward. Others explained that they were urged by other players to keep quiet. According to the report, one victim told investigators, "A sophomore told me to keep my mouth shut about this, 'if you say something, they will get kicked off the team.'" Victims urged the school to take action. The report showed one teen saying, "Yes stop it of course. They shouldn't do it to anybody. It is a horrible thing to do to someone." According to investigation records, plans were underway to re-train all Sebastian River High School coaches about hazing prevention. The school also hoped to require players to attend training each season about how to prevent and report hazing (Gonzalez, 2008).

New Mexico High School Hazing Case

New Mexico state police conducted a criminal investigation into the incident in which six juniors at Robertson High School allegedly hazed and assaulted six freshmen at a summer football training camp. New Mexico is one of six states that does not have an anti-hazing law, according to a report by New Hampshire attorney Linda S. Johnson at the National Association of Independent Schools. But in 2006, the state's Public Education Department issued a mandate for all schools to have written "bullying prevention" rules, to include hazing and harassment.

The Robertson incident is not the first time hazing at a New Mexico high school has been in the news. In 2005, a teen reporter with *The New Mexican*'s Generation Next section reported on "freshmanizing" at Santa Fe High School; in one case, it led to a freshman with a broken arm, according to the principal. In 2002, a Robertson baseball coach was fired, allegedly after a hazing incident on a school bus. In 1997, 11 Santa Fe High School students were suspended after a 14-year-old student drank himself unconscious and ended up in the hospital with alcohol poisoning; school officials called it hazing (Robertson, 2008).

Teen Gets Nine-Month Sentence for Hazing

A tearful 17-year-old Jerek Padilla was sentenced to nine months in juvenile jail, followed by three months of parole for his part in a football team hazing and rape. Several members of the Robertson High School, New Mexico, football team, including Padilla, used broomsticks to sodomize their teammates at the team's training camp in Gallinas Canyon, New Mexico. Padilla pleaded

guilty to one count each of second degree criminal sexual penetration and conspiracy to commit sexual penetration. The teen was led away in handcuffs from
the state district court in Santa Fe. Padilla apologized to the victims, saying, "I
know what I did was wrong, and I am ashamed of what I have done" (*Journal
Northern Bureau*, 2009).

Judge James Hall rejected a plea by a juvenile probation and parole official for a suspended sentence in the Padilla case. He said that "what happened to the victims at the camp was 'horrific' and that Padilla took part in
an assault that was done in the most demeaning way possible." Padilla, an
honor student at Robertson High School, began serving his sentence at the
John Paul Taylor Center in Las Cruces, New Mexico (*Journal Northern Bureau*, 2009).

The verdict is a signal to coaches and administrators that the courts will not
give a slap on the wrist anymore for hazing incidents. "Zero tolerance" should
be an accepted policy for all athletics programs.

"Kids Will Be Kids"

DP was in the sixth grade in Michigan and had been the victim of both
physical and verbal bullying for several years. DP's parents reported the harassment and a school administrator said, "Kids will be kids, it's middle school."
The parents responded by filing a Title IX suit, naming the school district and
superintendent as defendants for "failing to take reasonable action to halt or
prevent such bullying."

During the seventh grade, DP's locker was broken into and students "uri-
nated on his clothing, and threw his shoes into a toilet. His locker was also
covered with sexually-oriented graffiti." DP's parents reported the incident and
the students responsible for the harassment were punished by school officials.
This helped stop those responsible for a time; however, other students continued to harass DP. During junior varsity baseball practice several months
later, DP was "sexually assaulted in the locker room by a teammate." DP reported the incident to his coach, who "in a team meeting," instructed "the student-athletes, in the presence of DP, not to joke."

DP transferred to a Catholic elementary school and took courses at a local
college. The U.S. District Court granted summary judgment to the defendants
and the plaintiffs appealed. The appellate court held that school officials knew
that the school's action in the harassment was ineffective, but they continued
to do the same thing over and over. The district court had ruled in favor of
the parents but kept summary judgment on the plaintiff's claim of "deliberate
indifference" against the school district. As a result, the appellate court re-

versed the district court's ruling on "deliberate indifference." A federal jury then awarded $800,000 to the parents against the school district (*Patterson v. Hudson Area Schools and Mainar*, 2009).

In the *Journal of Physical Education, Recreation and Dance* (2010), Michael Carroll and Daniel P. Connaughton write about the *Patterson* case and give ten risk management tips that are valuable for anyone who is responsible for creating a zero-tolerance bullying policy designed to eliminate situations that DP and his parents endured during his years in middle school. The tips are as follows:

1. A strict, zero-tolerance anti-bullying and harassment policy should be developed and communicated to all stakeholders. Students and sport participants should know that bullying of any kind will not be tolerated and will result in strong disciplinary action.
2. The *Patterson* case illustrates that even some teachers at the school downplayed the bullying and harassment as normal joking behavior among students. Teachers, administrators and coaches need to be aware of the adverse effects of bullying, including depression, social isolation and suicidal thoughts.
3. Athletes and participants should be required to sign a contract.
4. Strong disciplinary and corrective measure should be taken for known cases of bullying. The consequences for such behavior should be used to dissuade other students from engaging in similar behaviors.
5. Ensure proper supervision of physical education classes, recess and after-school or weekend sport activities. Research has shown that bullying often occurs in these settings due to a lack of proper supervision.
6. Establish an easy-to-implement reporting system, as well as a protocol for conducting a fair investigation of reported bullying behavior.
7. Be aware of anti-bullying statutes that may exist in your state and make sure to comply with the legislation.
8. Keep a thorough record of reported instances of bullying and of the action taken. Maintain these records for at least the statute of limitations in your state.
9. Evaluate the school's or organization's bullying practices and their effectiveness. The *Patterson* case demonstrates that an institution whose response to bullying has been ineffective but keeps doing the same things may be found to be "deliberately indifferent" and could be held under Title IX.
10. Additional anti-bullying information may be obtained from the following websites: www.stopbullyingnow.hrsa.gov/adults/, www.schoolssafety.us, and www.naspoline.org.

For years as an athletics director, I tried to implement a zero-tolerance hazing program. One of the problems I witnessed in visiting many high school and college campuses was the "deliberate indifference" of coaches. "Kids will be kids" has been a prevailing attitude for years, which makes the victim the bad guy for reporting harassment. Another important factor is for the administrator to take immediate action when abuse is reported, and not try to delay it or sweep it under the rug to avoid adverse publicity. A great part of hazing and bullying can and will be stopped if coaches and athletics directors take a positive step to stop abuse.

Parent Takes on Bullying

Tom Harrison is a parent who wants to prevent tragedies that are caused by bullying. His 16-year-old son, Alex, endured harassment at school, and as a result took his own life with a shotgun he planned to use on a skeet shooting trip with his father. A note was left by Alex telling his parents he loved them and that he was very sorry. He said, "I can't take it any more." Alex was described as "extremely brilliant." At 13 years of age he was already studying college-level anatomy and built his own computer. Alex had just gotten his driver's license, had a girlfriend, a core group of friends, was a long-time boy scout and a member of the ski team, and he played tennis. Harrison speaks at gymnasiums about his son's tragic suicide using a photo slideshow about his son. He tells his audiences about his son's reluctance to tell others about the harassment he endured and urges them to help stop bullying, which has become a serious problem nationwide (Irvine, 2010).

Fraternity Ordered to Pay $16.2 Million to Parents of Dead Pledge

The *Austin American Statesman* reported that a state judge in Texas "ordered a University of Texas at Austin fraternity chapter and its national parent organization to pay $16.2 million to the parents of a freshman pledge who died." The pledge was made to drink one half-gallon of hard liquor. He became intoxicated and fell from the fifth-floor balcony of his off-campus apartment. The incident took place after a night of hazing by the Sigma Alpha Epsilon fraternity.

The parents of the deceased filed a lawsuit against the local fraternity and its national organization. John Dietz, a district judge, ordered the two organizations to pay the $16.2 million after they refused to respond to the initial claim made by the parents. Judge Dietz issued a "default judgment" with the understanding that state law permitted "the fraternity to seek a new trial if it could explain its failure to respond initially" (Mangan, 2008).

Hazing Prompts School to Fire Wrestling Coach

Nine wrestlers at Asheboro High School in North Carolina allegedly bound seven teammates' hands and feet with duct tape and photographed them with their cell phones. Asheboro police charged the wrestling coach, Dennis Johnston, with "aiding and abetting assault, a misdemeanor." Johnston told the police that he had knowledge of the incident that took place in the school's wrestling room. The police did not know if Johnston was present during the hazing or in the vicinity. Asheboro High School fired the wrestling coach and the police charged the nine upperclassmen with misdemeanor assault (Bell, 2008).

Larry Riggan, the Asheboro High School principal, said that "Asheboro City Schools does not have a written policy against hazing," which is generally viewed as "any activity expected of someone joining a group that humiliates, abuses or endangers someone, regardless of the person's willingness to participate" (Bell, 2008).

St. Ignatius College Prep Sued for Alleged Hazing Incident

Christopher Connolly, a water polo player at St. Ignatius College Prep in Chicago, was hazed by his teammates, leading him to become a quadriplegic. An assistant coach called Connolly "Flounder," and instructed the teammates to throw "snowballs, kickboards, buoys and other pool equipment" at Connolly. Another coach ordered him to get into the pool to avoid the harassment by his teammates; when he dove into the pool, Connolly's head collided with the bottom of the pool, fracturing his vertebrae (Mack, 2009). Connolly's parents sued the school for negligence and sought undisclosed monetary damages from St. Ignatius. The coaches were not named as defendants (Mack, 2009).

Hazing in the NFL

Hazing can be a harmless NFL ritual, a rite of passage punctuated by laughter and bonding. Veterans tape rookies to goal posts, douse them with ice water and Gatorade, and spray them with shaving cream. Dumping rookies in a tub of ice-cold water is another popular staple. That was the rich tradition of the Baltimore Ravens for several years under former coach Brian Billick, at least until new coach John Harbaugh basically halted the practice altogether. With the exception of center Jason Brown and offensive guard Chris Chester mildly taping up rookie linemen Oniel Cousins and David Hale in the middle of the field, there was no public special treatment directed toward the rookies other than the normal initiation into professional football through hard hits in blocking and tackling drills "We haven't had any hazing," Harbaugh said days before breaking camp. "We talked about that. We're not a hazing team" (Wilson, 2008).

Harbaugh's stance on hazing mirrors the approach of many younger, progressive coaches. Perhaps they're mindful of the uglier side of hazing, or they're simply following the precept of treating every member of the team equally regardless of tenure and status. Although I believe it's more a case of the latter, there's a disturbing history in NFL circles involving hazing that has no place in the sport.

Jeff Danish, a former New Orleans Saints defensive lineman, was forced to endure running through a gauntlet of 20 fist-swinging teammates while wearing a pillowcase on his head. He was hit with a bag of coins, kicked and elbowed, suffering facial bruises as well as a cut on his arm that required 13 stitches. Danish never named names to former coach Mike Ditka, but his stitches busted open in a game. He wound up being cut from the team despite his wounds. Saints tight end Cam Cleeland also suffered eye damage during this hazing incident. That wasn't just a case of "boys being boys." It's called assault and battery. It's serious criminal behavior that should never be tolerated in the sports realm or anywhere else. According to the NFL, there is no formal policy on hazing and the league leaves it up to the individual teams to oversee as they see fit. Last year, San Francisco 49ers coach Mike Nolan issued this comment as a proponent of hazing: "It builds team unity if it's done correctly," he said. "It can be done in a way that's kind of fun. They may not enjoy it necessarily, but it builds some camaraderie among the team if done properly" (Wilson, 2008).

Haircuts for Sports Teams: Do They Promote Unity or Are They Hazing?

What started as a simple complaint about an unauthorized haircut at football camp has turned into a raging debate that has put one mom against dozens of area residents and coaches. But one national expert says the mom is right: football camp haircuts are a kind of hazing.

The mom, whose son attends Goodrich High School in Michigan, was upset and complained to the Board of Education when her son came home from football camp with his head shaved—a haircut she didn't authorize. Coaches and other teammates said all the players agreed to the cuts. So, where do you draw the line? How do you differentiate bonding from hazing? The expert says even with the boys' consent, the act is out of line. "With the issue of hazing, consent doesn't matter because in most states, hazing is against the law," said Norm Pollard, dean of students at Alfred University in New York. "Someone can say they wanted to do it, but that really doesn't matter" (Mullen, 2008).

One area coach said many high school sports steams have some type of tradition—but for solidarity, not as hazing. "It's something the team does. It's kids being kids," said Joe Delaney, varsity football coach at Grand Blanc High School. "My kids come back on a regular day with haircuts that look strange and I know they did it to each other," he said. "It's not hazing. It's something they enjoy, and they ask each other to do it" (Mullen, 2008).

Pollard noted that hazing may start with minor acts such as haircuts, but it can evolve into something more serious. "Shaving of the head may seem simple, but it escalates from there. Sometimes it results in death," Pollard said (Mullen, 2008).

Title IX Comes to a Hazing Victim's Rescue

The plaintiff, known as John Roe, signed a waiver to participate in a preseason football camp for Gustine High School (GHS). The camp was supervised by the coaches at GHS. Roe was "assaulted in the locker room and then held down while teammates inserted an air pump into his rectum; while in the shower, he was grabbed and pushed while being called sexual names; he was subjected to a pillow fight in which pillow cases were filled with heavy objects and used to attack teammates" (Hopf & Wolohan, 2010). Upperclassmen also exposed their genitals to him and verbally harassed him on and off the field.

During the camp, 15 other students were assaulted by upperclassmen, and one of the incidents was even observed by the team's head coach. The head coach reprimanded the boys and took the air pump from them. An assistant coach later heard the boys talking about what they had done to Roe and reported it to the school's principal, who reported the incidents to the Gustine Police Department.

Roe transferred from Gustine High School because of the hazing he endured at the football camp. He filed a complaint against the school district for "negligent supervision, sexual battery and sex discrimination." He also filed a federal complaint under Title IX for sexual discrimination. The school district and coaches, who were also named in the complaint, claimed immunity from all state and federal claims under the California Education Code. The code provides that "all persons making the field trip or excursion shall be deemed to have waived all claims against the district, a charter school, or the State of California for injury, accidents, illness or death occurring during or by reason of the field trip or excursion" (Hopf & Wolohan, 2010). The court ruled that "the statute and case law clearly intended to extend this immunity to school-sponsored activities such as camps" and granted the district and coaches "summary judgment for all of Roe's state-law actions." The court, however, held that "if the district and coaches violated federal law, they could not hide behind the state field trip immunity statute" (Hopf & Wolohan, 2010).

Joelle Hopf and John Wolohan, writing about the case in *Athletic Business* (2010), noted that the head coach "did not take the appropriate steps after he observed the gym incident involving another student." They concluded:

> Even though the school district and coaches were able to shield themselves from liability under state law via California's field-trip immunity, it is important to note that school administrators may still be potentially liable under federal law … Therefore, as preseason camps become more common, it is essential that coaches actively prevent all types of hazing and, if incidents are noticed, that they take immediate remedial action to prevent future incidents. (Hopf & Wolohan 2010)

Education

Dr. Susan Lipkins, a psychologist and a leading expert in the field of hazing, discusses the importance of education when it comes to hazing in *NFHS Coaches' Quarterly* (2007). According to Lipkins, a system-wide educational campaign needs to be created in order to repeatedly and thoroughly define hazing and its consequences. You cannot simply say "no hazing" once or twice and expect that to be sufficient. In order to change a culture, continuous anti-hazing programs need to occur. Such education must extend beyond the locker room, beyond the athletic field, and must occur in classrooms and at home. Prod the administration to share the responsibility of hazing education. They need to develop appropriate prevention and intervention strategies (Lipkins, 2007).

Ethical Questions

1. How many students in campus organizations are hazed? How do students justify hazing in college?
2. Explain "as long as no one gets injured, hazing is acceptable."

3. How would you define hazing?
4. What are the types of hazing?
5. Discuss hazing and tradition.
6. Besides athletics, what are other kinds of hazing?
7. Discuss the expression "boys will be boys and girls will be girls."
8. Compare high school and college hazing.
9. Discuss female athletes and hazing.
10. Discuss hazing in recreational sports.
11. Discuss hazing on the state level.
12. What is the NCAA's policy on hazing?
13. How can high schools and colleges curb hazing?
14. Discuss "hazing brings teams closer."
15. Discuss some of the court cases involving hazing.
16. What is your opinion on whether hazing bonds professional teams?

Chapter 8

Violence in Sport and Child Abuse

"Youth athletes spend an average of 326 hours of practice time per season under the supervision of their coach, dwarfing time spent with teachers, health educators and physicians."—CAPPAA (Child and Adult Physical and Psychological Athlete Abuse) Report (2010)

The game started out all right, but before long it got rather bloody. This is when my English visitors started asking questions. "Is the object of the game to injure as many players on the other team as possible?" the husband asked. "No, that is not the object of the game," I said. The wife said, "Do you get more points for breaking a man's leg or his neck?" "You don't get points for breaking either his leg or neck. You get penalized for it." "Oh," said the husband. "What is the penalty?" "Your team is penalized 15 yards." "Do you mean to say if you break an opponent's leg, you only get 15 yards against you?" "What do you think he should get?" I said, trying to hold my temper. "In England, I believe it's three years in prison," the wife replied. "It's a game!" I said. "The men who play expect to have their legs broken. That's what makes it so exciting." "How civilized," the wife said. I couldn't keep my temper any longer. "What do you think we are—barbarians?" "Quite," the husband said. (Buchwald, 1977)

The above passage, in my opinion, describes the rising violence in American sports in the 21st century. Teri Engler, a professor of law at the University of Chicago, wrote on violence in sports in *Sports and Law: Contemporary Issues* (1985):

Americans turning to the newspaper's sports section or turning in to television news are likely to run across enthusiastic accounts of violence on playing fields and rinks around the world. The images are enough to make a tender-hearted non-athlete (and even some seasoned jocks) squirm with discomfort: football players ramming their helmets into their opponents' bodies or batting them with their taped-up forearms ... hockey players maiming each other with their sticks ... baseball players sliding into base with their spikes intentionally aimed at the infielders ... fans streaming out of the stands for mass assaults on officials, players and other fans. Most of these have become increasingly violent, too. Violence, some contend, is becoming part of the game, just as it is becoming a part of our everyday life. (Appenzeller, 1985)

Many social and psychological studies, according to Teri Engler, "have agreed on the course of increased violence today: 1) a greater emphasis on winning than on sportsmanship; 2) a surge in spectators demands for brute force" (Appenzeller, 1985).

Violence Is Learned

Sports psychologist and Utah professor of health Keith Henschen says that "violence is learned." "Kids don't come into this world violent. They learn it from you and me. And we reward that violence in so many subtle ways." Henschen believes, for instance, that "coaches and parents often show youngsters that they care more about the product (winning) than the process of learning about a sport and developing the skills necessary to play and enjoy it to the fullest" (Appenzeller, 1985). Henschen blames part of the problem on the reverence coaches and parents give to competitiveness and the rationale that it leads to other positive characteristics. Thomas Tutko and William Bruns, authors of *Winning Is Everything and Other American Myths* (1976), agree with Henschen:

One of the strange beliefs that underlie competition is the assumption that if a person is competitive, he also possesses more positive characteristics. The athlete can throw a racquet, start fights, use "gamesmanship" to disrupt his opponent, throw tantrums, deliberately roughhouse a competitor or curse the officials, and its dismissed because "He's a hell of a competitor. He wants to win." The athlete can be immature or childish or destructive, but because he "wants to win" this excuses his behavior. We surely wouldn't give the same consideration to a bank robber who beat up a teller and three customers if his legal defense was, "He's a hell of a competitor. He really wanted to rob that bank. He's the number three ranked bank robber in Colorado." (Tutko & Bruns, 1976)

Henschen wants a new set of heroes (like Tim Tebow, the All-America and Heisman Trophy winner at University of Florida) to replace what he calls the anti-heroes. He feels that the media gives too much attention to violence in sports. This elevates the status of those who use violence in their particular sports and get the attention of young sport fans who want to emulate their heroes (Appenzeller, 1985).

On a Personal Note

After seven decades of active involvement in sports, I definitely agree with the sentiments of Henschen, Tutko and Bruns. I get tired of hearing individuals who say, "I'm a competitor. I don't care if it's a sport or playing cards or Ping Pong, I've got to win because I'm a competitor." The finest competitors I coached or observed on the court or playing field were men and women who were dedicated and determined to excel, and yet quiet in their manner and presence and very good sports—a man such as Ralph Nelson, who, as captain of our football team, refused to further injure a player who should not have been in the game.

Violence can often lead to developing a rivalry between two schools. Our big rival at Wake Forest was traditionally NC State University. When I enrolled in school, all I heard was, "We must beat NC State in every sport." Tradition had it that the annual Easter Monday baseball game always began with a fight. If the game was at Wake Forest, NC State students would come on a train from Raleigh and get off at the depot at Wake Forest, where a group of Wake students would be waiting and a fight would break out. The next year, Wake Forest men would get on the train and the same situation would occur.

Violence on the court and field led to a change in rivalry. Wake Forest's legendary basketball coach, Horace "Bones" McKinney, spoke to the students prior to the game against nationally-ranked University of North Carolina. He implored the student body to observe good sportsmanship at the game that night. However, the hotly contested game ended in an on-the-court brawl in which both players and fans participated.

During the same year, the Wake Forest football team got into a wild brawl after a UNC end hit the Wake Forest quarterback, who was playing the safety position. From that moment on, the game was little on football and more on fighting, which extended to after the game. After that day, UNC rather than NC State was the heated rival of Wake Forest.

Violence in Pompeii

Sport violence is not new today. Spectators of games in Pompeii "broke into wild sword fights which resulted in many deaths." The Roman Senate banned all gladiator contests for a decade. In 1985, a riot between Italy and England broke out during a World Cup game in Brussels, Belgium. British fans stormed the Italian section, described as "one of the worst acts of violence in the history of sports. Forty people were killed and 267 were injured" (Appenzeller, 1985). The mere act of putting on a uniform and entering the sports arena should not serve as a license to engage in behavior which would constitute a crime if committed elsewhere.

Violence in the National Hockey League

David Forbes of the Boston Bruins and Henry Boucha of the Minnesota North Stars got into a fight when they left the penalty box. Forbes reportedly attacked Boucha from the rear with his hockey stick and inflicted severe injuries.

Boucha filed a lawsuit against Forbes and the Minnesota North Stars in a highly publicized suit. Forbes stated, "I'm disillusioned with the whole system, I just don't see, no matter how wrong the act is, how anything that happens in an athletic contest can be criminal" (Appenzeller, 1980). On the other hand, the attorney for Boucha took issue with Forbes and replied:

> If a participant in a sporting event were allowed to feel immune from football and reasoned that even if his opponent had violated a duty he owed the plaintiff, there could be no verdict in favor of the injured player because the level of violence and frequency of emotional outbursts in NFL football games are such that [the injured player] must have recognized and accepted the risk that he would be injured by such an act as that committed by the opposing player. (Appenzeller, 1980)

The court then expressed its opinion regarding violence in professional football when it said, "The character of NFL competition negates any notion that playing conduct can be circumscribed ... by any standard of reasonableness" (Appenzeller, 1980).

Sport Litigation Is Varied

Sports litigation can involve participants in any sport. Cases on record arise from football, soccer, basketball, softball, baseball, ice hockey, bowling, skiing, tennis, golf, track, fishing and an unbelievable number of hazing-related incidents (Appenzeller, 1980).

A New Era of Tort Law

Tort law received impetus in 1975 when Julian Nabozny, a goalkeeper in Winnetka, Illinois, was kicked in the head by an opponent in a soccer game. Witnesses testified that Nabozny was kneeling in a non-contact area when he was kicked in the head by the opponent who could have avoided the accident (Appenzeller, 1980).

The trial court routinely followed the precedent in earlier cases and held that the defendant was not negligent, since Nabozny had assumed the risks inherent in soccer. The Illinois court took an unusual and bold step when it reversed the trial court's ruling and sent it back to them for reconsideration, emphatically declaring that, "The law should not place unreasonable burdens on the free and vigorous participation in sport by our youth. However, we also believe that organized athletic competition does not exist in a vacuum. Rather, some of the restraints of civilization must accompany every athlete on to the playing field."

The court then added, "A reckless disregard for the safety of other players cannot be excused … it is our opinion that a player is liable for injury in tort action if his conduct is such that it is deliberate, willful, or with a reckless disregard for the safety of the other players as to cause injury to that player" (Appenzeller, 1980).

This landmark case was settled out of court for a reported $65,000 by the insurance company of the parents of the boy who inflicted the injury on the plaintiff (*Sports and the Courts* 1980). This case opened the door for participants who were injured and faced the well-worn defense that they assumed the risk inherent in the sport. It was a breakthrough for redress in injuries. There will be those like Boston Bruin Forbes, who still believes that no matter how wrong the act is, "how can anything that happens in an athletic contest be criminal?" (Appenzeller, 1980).

However, today, ethical behavior in sports exists and decisions like the one in *Nabozny* set a precedent for liability when a participant deliberately injures another participant and liability is possible. The ethical question remains: should sports at any level be immune from reasonableness and immune from lawsuits?

An Example of Sport Violence

In *Sports and the Courts* (1980), we reported the case of *Hackbart v. Cincinnati Bengals* (1977), in which Denver Broncos defensive back Dale Hackbart was watching another player intercept a pass, when he was hit from behind by Booby Clark of the Cincinnati Bengals with a forearm. Hackbart sued the Bengals, claiming that the blow that injured him constituted reckless conduct. The Colorado court made several comments that are worthy of consideration by any sport participant, particularly those who participate in collision sports such as football. It declared that Hackbart had assumed the risk of injury by playing football and reasoned that even if his opponent had violated a duty he owed to the plaintiff, there could be no verdict in favor of the injured plaintiff because "the level of violence and frequency of emotional outbursts in NFL football games are such that the injured player must have recognized and accepted the risk that he could be injured by such an act as that committed by the opposing player" (Appenzeller, 1980).

The court then made an interesting observation of coaches in the NFL when it mentioned "the action of the coaches in the NFL to arouse their players to a state of 'controlled rage.' It felt that players obeyed rules to avoid penalties rather than to prevent injuries to their opponents." The court then made a comment that, if true, could cause countless injuries on all levels of sports: "The character of NFL competition negates any notion that playing conduct can be circumscribed by any standard of reasonableness" (Appenzeller, 1980). Such was the attitude of the courts in 1980. However, NFL Commissioner Roger Goodell is attempting to change all that. Emphasizing safety, he is addressing the problem of concussions by preventing illegal helmet-to-helmet contact. Goodell wants referees to enforce the rules pertaining to head injuries with the hope that serious head injuries can be reduced in future seasons.

NFL Fines Players for Illegal Hits

Gary Mihoces, writing in *USA Today* (2010), discusses the NFL's dramatic approach to violent blows. James Harrison, Pittsburgh Steelers linebacker, was fined $75,000 for his high-profile hit against a Miami Dolphin. Atlanta Falcon cornerback Dunta Robinson and Brando Meriweather of the New England Patriots were fined $50,000 each for violent tackles. Roger Goodell served notice that illegal hits to the head and neck would result in more significant punishment, including suspension (Mihoces, 2010).

The potential fines and suspensions brought about heated discussions from players, coaches, fans and just about everyone who follows the game. ESPN's Tom Jackson said, "Tackle properly and quit trying to get on SportsCenter's Top 10 plays." Terry Bradshaw, Fox NFL analyst, said the league was "very smart" to protect itself against lawsuits from injured players that could be "devastating." Bob Costas, speaking on Monday Night Football, disagreed with Chris Collingsworth prior to a game between the Minnesota Vikings and the Green Bay Packers. Costas believed, unlike Collingsworth, that some players do try to injure opponents. Costas felt that the NFL's tough stand on vicious hits to the head proved that the NFL was doing everything it could to avoid catastrophic injuries if an injured player attempted to sue for huge damages. The main reason for toughened penalties was strictly to prevent liability, in Costas' opinion (*Monday Night Football*, 2010).

The increased emphasis on the prevention of concussions made the NFL's action timely as well as a preventable measure. In 2010, the NFL gave a $1 million dollar grant to Dr. Robert Cantu's Boston Center for Brain Injuries to conduct research in this important area.

Rule 12, Section 2, Article 8 of the NFL rule book describe illegal hits as the following:

1. "Forcibly hitting the defenseless player's head, neck or face with the helmet or face mask, regardless of whether the defensive player also uses his arms to tackle the defenseless player by encircling or grasping him."
2. "Lowering the head and violently or unnecessarily making forcible contact with the 'hairline' or forehead part of the helmet against any part of the defenseless player's body."
3. "Launching (springing forward and upward) into a defenseless player, or otherwise striking him in a way that causes the defensive player's helmet or facemask to forcibly strike the defenseless player's head, neck or face— even if the initial contact of the defender's helmet or facemask is lower than the defenseless player's neck." (Mihoces, 2010)

On a Personal Note

Years ago, our junior college football team traveled to an away game to play a very strong military prep school that was a feeder school for major Division I colleges. I remember well running our double reverse kickoff return that had a high success rate. In over six games, one version or another of the return had scored a touchdown. We elected to receive the kickoff to start the game and our third option broke into the clear, heading for a spectacular touchdown. Suddenly, a player came from the sidelines and tackled our ball carrier. In those days, it was only a five-yard penalty.

From that moment on, the game degenerated into a slug fest. Three of our players were taken to the hospital with serious injuries, and our 6'6" All-America star basketball player who played wide receiver came to the sidelines holding his mouth. His front teeth had been knocked out and the opposing player who had launched into his neck laughed and said, "I didn't have to do that—I just wanted to!"

The opposing coach said our men could have fought back and the violence would have stopped, as it did earlier in the year when both sides retaliated. Both teams had said, "That's enough rough stuff—now let's play football."

About the opening kickoff, the opposing coach laughed and said, "I counted and had only 10 men on the field so I pushed one of my players on the field to make 11 as your runner ran by." In all my years of coaching football, this was the only time an opponent ever played our team at this low level. It was the last time, as this school dropped its football program at the end of the year. This incident was not at all an example of ethical behavior.

Can the NFL Save Football?

President Teddy Roosevelt campaigned against violence in football because of the number of injuries and, at times, deaths. Robert Lipsyte, in *USA Today* (2010), wrote that Roosevelt answered the "rising call for banning the game and helped institute new rules that improved the game." Lipsyte notes that the emphasis today is on "helmet-to-helmet" hits that can cause concussions and spinal injuries, which can lead to dementia and other health issues. Many critics call for eliminating football or federal intervention to curb violence.

Football is our national pastime and the violence of the game, especially at the college and pro levels, has always been one of its main attractions. Highlight reels have routinely been a collection of breathtaking collisions. "But it wasn't until recently, as the roster of damaged brains was revealed, that watching football began to feel more like a guilty pleasure" (Lipsyte, 2010). Last season, three particularly vicious hits in three games led NFL officials to fine players a total of $175,000 and threaten suspension for illegal hits.

Football is the most brutal of our popular team sports, featuring "ferocious gladiator behavior." Former linebacker and union official Dave Meggyesy said, "Typically, the greater physical domination and degree of violence a team does to its opponent, the more likely that team will win the game" (Lipsyte, 2010).

One thing is clear: our nation realizes there is a serious problem with the injuries that have long-term effects on the men who play the game. Certainly, the NFL has recognized the health problems football can present and is attempting to meet the challenges with rule changes and enforcement. In lieu of Congressional involvement, and "unless or until it seems clear that the professional leagues cannot regulate themselves," Lipsyte notes that the responsibility is our own, and concludes with the following questions:

> Should we allow our kids to play football and start that risky pounding early, when their heads are particularly vulnerable? And should we continue to watch it as it is, accomplices to a violent cartoon of warfare that sacrifices young men for entertainment? (Lipsyte, 2010)

"Can Sports Kill You?" by Gil Fried

I have practiced sport law for almost 20 years. I think I have seen it all, when out from my peripheral vision comes a new issue or concern that I previously was not as focused upon. That was until I was asked by the Center for Disease Control (CDC) to help chair a task force designed to reduce workplace injuries in the sport industry. To be honest, the task force does more than look at the sport industry. My purview is NAICS Sector 71, which includes arts, entertainment, and recreation. Nestled within this large sector are all professional sport, sport facilities, and a slew of other employees. In total, there are almost 2 million employees in the sector. I thought I knew how people were injured. I thought I worked in a relatively safe industry. Boy was I wrong.

To provide an example, the Bureau of Labor Statistics highlights the following number of employees in the sports industry during 2008:

- 12,450 athletes
- 36,710 coaches and scouts
- 29,900 life guards and ski patrollers
- 42,290 usher/ticket takers
- 158,560 fitness and aerobics instructors
- 25,640 recreation workers

Some numbers are harder to calculate. For example, there is an estimated equivalent of 146,625 full-time employees in 2004 in the horse racing industry. The numbers are hard to pinpoint since there are so many independent contractors working in the industry. In the industry alone, there were 79 workplace related deaths from 1992–2006 including 28 trainers, 26 jockeys, 8 exercise riders, 7 grooms, and 10 employees classified as other. From 1998–2006, there were 14,200 workplace injuries in the horse racing industry as well. Some professionals might think that horse racing is completely different than the sport they manage. But the numbers highlight that our field is just as or even more dangerous.

Deaths

In 2008, there were just over 5 thousand workplace related deaths. In Sector 71 alone, there were 229 deaths. Forty of those deaths were in the category of performing arts/spectator sports. There is not a most common age for people to die on the job. It would be assumed that younger, inexperienced workers would make more mistakes and would be more likely to pass away. However, the 45–54 age range followed by 55–64 age range was the most frequent range of deaths. The statistics are pretty consistent across numerous areas that 75% of the deaths would occur to Caucasian workers, 12–14% would be African-American, and 10–12% would be Hispanic.

People die various ways, but the most common reason for death is transportation related accidents. Transportation related examples include: a boss sending a worker on an errand and they get into an accident, a broadcast truck gets into an accident on the way to broadcast a game, and sporting goods on a truck that gets into an accident. A total of 81 deaths in our sector are attributable to transportation related incidents. Surprisingly, while being struck by or against an object would seem to be a frequent cause of death, it is not the second most common cause of death in our sector. That title would go to workplace violence and assaults. In the performing arts/spectator sports area, there were 14 assaults leading to deaths in 2008. Drowning was also the cause of six deaths in the amusement and gambling area.

Some managers might think that these deaths only happen to the grunt workers. In the art, entertainment, and recreation category, there were eight managers who passed away. In 2008, the most common occupation in which a person passed away in our area was on the media side, where 25 people died. These media individuals could include reporters traveling to cover a story. There were also 20 ground maintenance staffers who died.

I do not want to frighten everyone, but I think it is important to highlight the risks that exist, and the bigger risk is not deaths, but serious injuries.

Injuries

Injury rates are compared by industries based on a relative incident rate. The incident rate for all private industries in 2008 was 113.3%. Injuries in the sport industry occurred at a much more frequent rate as highlighted in the chart below:

Category	Incident rate	Perct. Higher than Norm
Spectator Sports	163.4	44.2
Golf Courses	138.2	21.9
Skiing Facilities	320.7	183.0
Marinas	178.3	57.3
Fitness & Recreation	81.5	(28.1)
Bowling Centers	103.7	(8.4)

Thus, the injury rate in most sectors of the sport industry significantly exceeds the national average. The most common nature of injuries is often strains or sprains. However, some locations have much higher injury rates based on the type of job. Golf courses, for example, had 95% more cuts injuries and 195.5% more machine related injuries, possibly from working on golf carts, retooling clubs, and working with vegetation cutting machines. Other major concerns at golf courses included a 58.3% increase in injuries associated with chemical and hazardous material exposure and 84.3% increase in transportation related injuries. Chemical and hazardous exposures can also range from electrocutions to oxygen deficiencies (such as drowning) and are not unique just to golf courses where pesticides are frequently used. The number of chemical related injuries at marinas was 537.5% higher than the private industry rate.

One of the shocking numbers was the number of injuries associated with violence. The sport industry had a rate 216.6% higher in 2008 than in private industry. That number was not a fluke and the numbers for the past several years have shown a steady growth in violence related injuries. Thus, violence did not just produce a number of deaths, but also numerous injuries that possibly could have been prevented through an anti-violence campaign.

The numbers clearly highlighted skiing as the most dangerous industry for workers. Sprains and strains were 257.3% higher and fractures were 341.5% higher than the private rate. The most common body part injured for those working in the ski industry were shoulders (+370.5%) and knees (+797.9%). the most frequent activity that caused skiing related injuries were falls on the same level (possibly slipping on wet or icy surfaces or falling on the slopes) which were 731.3% higher than the private industry rate.

What to Do

These numbers are shocking and they show that, as an industry, we need to do more to protect ourselves and our employees. What can a sport industry professional do? It is easy:

- Be vigilant and look for hazards in your workplace.
- Take workplace violence seriously and take steps to minimize the potential and train employees how to respond.
- Provide employees with appropriate training so they know how to use their equipment.
- Track workplace injuries and return to work programs.
- Bring in a workplace hygienist to help evaluate the workplace for safety issues.
- Subscribe to the NIOSH/NORA free newsletter which tracks industry injuries and provides some useful hints to reduce injuries (email the author to get your name on the list).

Our Goal with the CDC/NIOSH/NORA is to reduce art, sport, and recreation injuries by 30%. Please join us in trying to reach and exceed this goal.

Gil Fried is a Professor of Sport Management at the University of New Haven. He has written numerous books and articles on facility management, sport finance, and his passion—sport risk management. He can be reached at gfried@newhaven.edu.

Violence in Sport

The sports world was horrified after San Francisco Giants baseball team fan Bryan Stow was beaten nearly to death in a parking lot near the Los Angeles Dodger Stadium. Two men took violent exception to Stow wearing Giants gear to a Dodgers game and attacked him. One attacker has been apprehended, while one is still at large. A large reward has been offered for their arrest. As a result of the attack, the Los Angeles Dodgers have cancelled half-price beer night. Security in and around Dodger Stadium has been increased, and the Los Angeles Police Department has also greatly increased the number of uniformed officers assigned to Dodger home games (Brady et al., 2011).

Several years ago, I was a guest at a suite in the opening game of the Washington Redskins season. Those of us in the suite were assured that the Redskins had very good security and we were comfortable with safety procedures. However, one of the men who was to join us at the game never showed up.

We learned after the game that he had been assaulted on the way to the stadium by a group of men and was in the hospital suffering from a brutal beating. We later learned that another spectator had been seriously injured when he was hit by a bus in the stadium parking lot. Before the game began, seven people were burned by fireworks that were used as part of the pre-game festivities. All seven were taken to the hospital for treatment of their injuries. From our observations, poor lighting in the stadium parking lot created an unsafe environment that led to several injuries. The latest rumor is that the seven were considering litigation against the Washington Redskins.

Sadly, our experience was not unique. In recent years, there have been a number of similar incidents and injuries that have occurred at several sporting events:

- Seventy-five people were involved in a parking lot brawl before a UCLA-USC football game. Two people were stabbed and three were arrested.
- A 49-year-old woman slapped a 57-year-old man during an altercation at the US Tennis Open in 2010. Her 75-year-old father stepped into the altercation, causing the two men to fall over several rows of seats. Both men were taken into custody by police.
- A 24-year-old man put two fingers down his throat and intentionally vomited on a 11-year-old girl at a Philadelphia Phillies baseball game.
- A "ten-cent beer" promotion at a Cleveland Indians baseball game in 1974 led to a forfeited game due to the violence it caused. (Brady et al., 2011)

Joel Fish, Director of the Center for Sport Psychology, observed that recent violence is not just an American issue, but also a worldwide problem with numerous cases of fan violence in Europe, Asia and South America. He notes, "There is just something about sports that pushes buttons in people and activates a lot of emotion" (Brady et al., 2011).

Various Examples of Sport Violence

Oregon Cheerleader Suffers Concussion

Katelynn Johnson, an Oregon University cheerleader, suffered a concussion when she was hit in the head by a water bottle thrown from the stands after Oregon's double-overtime victory against the University of Arizona. Arizona football coach Mike Stoops called Oregon's athletics director Mike Bellotti to express concern for the injured cheerleader. Johnson was carted off the field and taken to a hospital, where she was treated and released. An apologetic coach Stoops commented that the university would continue to look at security at its home games. We often hear reports of Mascots being assaulted at games, but not many incidents are reported about cheerleaders (*The Associated Press*, 2009).

Red Sox-NY Yankees Argument Leads to 20 to 40 Years in Prison

Ivonne Hernandez, 45, was convicted of second-degree murder in the death of 29-year-old Matthew Beaudoin. Hernandez killed Beaudoin because he taunted her for being a NY Yankee fan. Police reported that an argument took place outside a bar over the NY Yankees & Boston Red Sox rivalry. Hernandez testified she was terrified after Beaudoin and others beat on her car windows when she compared the number of NY Yankees World Series wins to those of the Red Sox. She was sentenced to 20 to 40 years in prison (*The Associated Press*, 2010).

Mother Charged with Assault

East Millbrook Middle School basketball coach Chris Kwolak took a player out of a game and the boy's mother was charged with assault after she struck the coach. The woman yelled at her son's coach, and came out of the stands and hit the coach on the back of his head. The assistant principal and an off-duty deputy witnessed the assault and the deputy pressed charges (*News & Record*, 2009).

Player Gets 10 Years for Assault on Referee

Leon Woods, 23, pleaded guilty to a felony of first-degree assault. After a semi-pro football game in the North American Football League (NAFL), Woods ran up to official Peter McCabe, Jr., 54, and swung his football helmet repeatedly with a brutal and unprovoked blindsight hit. McCabe "suffered a fractured skull and underwent facial reconstruction surgery. He still hasn't recovered his sense of smell or taste." Woods was sentenced to a prison term of ten years with five years of post-release supervision. Woods' teammates refused to let McCabe's fellow officials use their cell phones to call 911 for medical assistance (*Referee*, 2010).

Consequences of Running on the Field

One of my respected colleagues told me that he and two other high school boys went to a Brooklyn Dodgers game in the 1940s after cutting school. During the game, not between innings, they jumped off their outfield bleacher seats and proceeded to run around the bases. A policeman and behind-the-plate umpire caught them when they reached home plate. Their punishment was to be escorted out of Ebbets Field with a stern warning not to ever do it again. That incident remains fresh in the mind of my friend fifty years later.

Quite a different situation occurred in the present day. A 17-year-old boy ran onto Citizens-Bank Park in Philadelphia, where the Phillies were playing the St. Louis Cardinals. A police officer used a Taser gun to stop the boy. The American Civil Liberties Union of Pennsylvania (ACLU) said the action of the policeman was "completely out of proportion to the situation." The boy's mother "apologized on her son's behalf and said he regretted his actions" (Livingstone & Nightengale, 2010).

In a *USA Today* survey of fans asking whether it was appropriate for the police to Taser the fan who ran onto the field, the results of 15,630 votes were:

Yes	63%
No	26%
Unsure	11%

(Livingstone & Nightengale, 2010)

In 1971, Baltimore Colt linebacker Mike Curtis got a tremendous ovation from the fans after "he showed a fan 'some frontier Justice' when he hit a fan running on the field during a game." No other fan disrupted a game after Curtis stopped the fan with a vicious tackle; his hit was as devastating as a Taser could have ever been.

Adult Player Attacks 17-Year-Old Referee

Andres Diaz, 34, became upset when the referee was going to penalize a fellow soccer player. He ran across the field and tackled the 17-year-old referee. Diaz was held on $5,000 bond and charged with aggravated assault, which could be a felony depending on the extent of the young referee's injury. The referee was taken to the hospital, where he did not respond to the tests he was given. Douglas Weh, president of the Edison United Soccer Association, said the league was formed as a way "for adults to stay in shape and have fun while training young referees how to officiate games" (*Referee*, 2011).

Peewee Teams Suspended after Brawl

Two peewee baseball teams in Houston, Texas, the Hurricanes and the Patriots, were banned from the playoffs because their coaches got into a fight. A parent filmed the incident, in which two players were scuffling after a play and the coaches from both youth teams were "chasing and struggling with each other on the sidelines." The League officials suspended both teams from the playoffs. Daniel Petty, an 11-year-old player, told the *Houston Chronicle* that "it's basically the coaches' fault" (*The Associated Press*, 2010). The parents asked the League officials to let the teams play, since the coaches and not the players were the problem. The situation raises the question: should the young players be penalized because of their coaches' misconduct?

Coach Suspended for Alleged Misconduct

Paul Furlong, baseball and football coach at Allegany-Limestone High School, was accused of "instructing two pitchers to throw at a Wellsville batter during a game." Superintendent Diane Munro said, "Athletes have a lot of emotion and Paul reported a bad decision." A former player said, "We were never told to hit someone in the head, but if someone showed us up, we were told to hit them, but never in the head." During a game, Furlong allegedly told his starting pitcher to hit an opposing player with a pitch. The pitcher did not hit the player and left the field one pitch later. A relief pitcher replaced him and Furlong also told him to hit the opposing player. Both pitchers refused to throw at the player and later reported the incident to school officials. Furlong has been suspended from coaching, but is still employed as a physical education instructor at the school (Schiano, 2010).

Child Athlete Abuse

In a report dealing with issues involving youth sports, a Washington court made the following statement:

> Teachers and coaches assigned to protect and supervise children during school sponsored curricular or extra-curricular activities have a duty to exercise that degree of care that ordinarily prudent teachers or coaches engaged in the supervision of students or athletes of like age would exercise under similar circumstances. It is the same for non-school coaches. Parents and guardians do not sign up their children or relinquish their children's rights or waiver consents for non-inherent risks of athletic practices, competitions, games and contests that include maltreatment, endangerment, serious injuries and for death caused or allowed to be caused by coaches. (*McLeod v. Grant County School District*, 1953)

"Sport in America: A New Crisis" by Dr. Tom Appenzeller

When most Americans think of the excesses of sports, the ancient Romans come to mind. We see images of Russell Crowe or Kurt Douglas fighting in the Coliseum or Charlton Heston driving a chariot in the epic movie Ben Hur. There is a vision of 50,000 men and women screaming for blood as the gladiators fall or 100,000 fans cheering passionately for their favorite race team and driver in the *Circus Maximus*. Americans have been fascinated and also critical of the Roman lust for blood and violence in their sporting spectacles and for their use of sport for political control. However, the Romans never exploited their children for the purpose of entertainment. We have no evidence of children ever performing in the arena or the Circus Maximus. There were no mini gladiators fighting to the delight of the crowd, no junior chariot-racing league competing for prizes and glory. The Romans put the spectacle in spectator sports, using the games for political and social control Panis et circus—bread and circus. The contests in the arenas and circuses were serious business and the risks to the participants was life threatening and very real. Fame and glory to the victor, pain, agony and even death went to the loser. The participants were adults who understood the consequences of their actions, not children.

Historically, organized sport has been a test of physical skill, speed, agility, endurance and the ability to withstand pain. To the victor went glory and adoration and to the loser, humiliation, agony, and even death. Sport began as combat challenges to select the best leaders and insure survival. There have always been risks in sports, but the benefits to the winners outweighed the chance of serious injuries for the participants. In ancient Rome, sport was an adult activity that came with great reward and danger. Today in America, we encourage and are entertained by children playing adult games. From 2000 to 2006, Little League Baseball had a seven million dollar contract with ESPN to broadcast games. In January 2007, Little League Baseball signed an eight-year contract extension with ESPN to expand national coverage of its baseball and softball tournaments to at least 49 games in all eight divisions. Little League games will be on ABC, ESPN HD2, ESPN Classic, ESPN Deportes, ESPN News, ESPNU, ESPN International, ESPN Radio, ESPN.com, ESPN 360 and Mobile ESPN. ESPN's Publishing Division will offer licensed products including hats, t-shirts, pins, banners, bobble heads, collectable dolls, instructional and inspirational videos. Little League Baseball is a nonprofit business with a budget in 2006 of over 16 million dollars. Little League is just one example of an organization that has turned children and the games they play into a big business. Pop Warner, American Athletic Union (AAU) and a host of other national organizations have served to put children on center stage and into the world of adult sport. We have always had child actors entertaining adults on the silver screen or television.

Think back to the Our Gang Series, the Hardy Boys, the Mouseketeers, Opie Taylor, Leave It to Beaver and all the movies and television series that have showcased children. However, Hollywood and television created rules very early to protect children from being misused and abused by companies seeking to turn a profit. The Coogan Laws, named after child star Jackie Coogan, date back to 1939 and the Screen Actors Guild revised the law in 2000. Coogan's Law limits how many hours children can work per day in the film and television industry. The laws are very specific about limits placed on child actors and they regulate work schedules and create academic expectations. However, the same level of concern is not exhibited by national youth sport organizations as much as it is the for profit based organizations that are making money from children in sport. Travel teams, select teams, all-stars, camps, academies and training facilities see children as revenue sources. Now there has evolved a new youth sport professional who makes his income on children playing sports and training for athletic futures. Like ESPN, these for profit businesses rely on children playing and practicing a particular sport.

Child labor is not new. The United States had serious issues with child workers in mills, factories and mines at the beginning of the 20th century. Eventually the Federal Government stepped in and limited the hours that children could work and minimum ages of employment in hazardous and non-hazardous jobs. There were different hours of employment for school days, weekends and summer vacations. The emphasis was to protect the children and to stop their exploitation as cheap labor by their employers. Parents were often forced to seek work for their ... children to supplement their meager family incomes. One of the most famous child laborers of that era was "Shoeless" Joe Jackson who worked in a textile mill in Greenville, South Carolina, while never learning to read or write. Maybe if Jackson had learned to read, he would not have signed the confession admitting to taking money to throw the 1919 World Series.

In the old days, employers paid children for their labor. However, today parents gladly, almost without hesitation, pay the salaries of youth sport entrepreneurs. Tom Sawyer would be proud of the current youth sport coaches who get thousands of dollars to give young boys and girls the opportunity to play sport. Remember that Tom convinced his friends to pay him for the opportunity to whitewash his Aunt Polly's fence. Recreational sports are often not good enough for today's parents, many of whom feel pressured to enroll their children for travel teams or all-star competitions. Today, parents are paying to ensure their son's or daughter's athletic success will lead to a treasured college scholarship or Olympic gold. Many parents believe that with extra tutoring, better coaching and more exposure, fame and glory will follow.

The Youth Sport Entrepreneur Law has created quite a business model on the backs of young children and it is the parents that are the revenue engines. In his 1976 book, *Sports in America*, James Michener stated, "Laws exist to protect children at work and in school, but then play governed by adults goes unchecked." Maybe it is time we start protecting our children in sport.

Ethical Questions

1. To what do experts in sport law and risk management attribute violence in sport?
2. What role do parents play in violence in sports?
3. Discuss some examples of sports-related violence in the chapter.
4. Discuss any acts of violence you have witnessed in sport.
5. Discuss the article by Gil Fried on sport violence.
6. Discuss Tom Appenzeller's article on child abuse in sport.

Chapter 9

Parents and Booster Clubs

"I recruit good, ethical parents as much as good, talented kids because, in the end, there's a connection between the two."—Joanie Milhous, *field hockey coach at Villanova University, quoted in* The New York Times *(2008)*

A day after a school's basketball season ended, the coach resigned. His team had just lost in the second round of the state playoffs. His decision was made three weeks before the season ended and he attributed his action to the following:

1. Constant stress that was put on his kids and staff.
2. The concept of team play was negated by parents' emphasis on playing time, points and statistics.
3. All sports at schools have added input and participation by parents. It was extreme at his school.
4. The situation became stressful in his house and in his day-to-day workings; it was not enjoyable. (*News & Record*, 2010).

Playing Time a Problem

A father argued with his six-year-old son's coach during a youth football game. The father was upset over the lack of playing time his son was getting. The father pulled a gun on the coach and was charged with aggravated assault, simple assault and reckless endangerment (*MSNBC.com*, 2006).

Parents Are Often the Problem

Kay West, in *How to Raise a Gentleman* (2001), writes about sportsmanship and comments, "Some of the most blatant exhibitions of bad sportsmanship ever witnessed have taken place, not in professional sports, stadiums and arenas, but at children's soccer, basketball, hockey, softball and baseball games.

Even worse," she said, "the ugly outbursts have come, not from children, but from their parents" (West, 2001).

Rock Brinkley, a youth sports coach, described a scene at a championship Little League football game in Winston-Salem, North Carolina. The teams were in the middle of the field after the game, shaking hands and exchanging congratulations on the well-played game. On the sidelines, parents of the players on both teams were involved in a violent brawl.

In Utah, a high school state basketball championship game could not be completed because spectators were involved in a fight. The game was moved to a gymnasium whose location was unknown to parents and fans, and played before only referees, score-keepers, clock operators and the players.

Parental Influence: Good or Bad?

Former high school basketball coach Mac Morris, of Page High School in Greensboro, North Carolina, made an interesting observation when asked about parents and the issue today of playing time for their sons and daughters on sport teams. Morris coached Danny Manning, who not only won a championship under Morris, but also a national championship under legendary basketball coach Larry Brown at Kansas University. Morris had little, if any, tolerance for parents who expected more playing time for their sons and daughters. Morris emphatically said that "as far as he was concerned, the best high school coaching job was at an orphanage where he would not have to hear complaints from unhappy parents." Coach John Roscoe, a football coach for forty years, agreed with Morris and added that coaching at prisons would be ideal.

Three Complaints in 40 Years

I coached for four years at two high schools in the same county. The only time I was confronted by parents was a real surprise to me and totally unexpected. I found out that several students in one of my classes reportedly cut school and instead got off the school bus to drink alcohol on trips to Raleigh, North Carolina.

The principal was afraid of parents and made many decisions he knew would not bring about parental criticism. Even when he was expected to take action, he wavered on justified punishment. I told the principal that I did not want the absent class-cutting students back in class without punishment. He agreed. I was summoned to the principal's office the day after he carried out my suggestion. As I entered his office, he rushed past me and told me to go on in. I was confronted by four of the angriest parents I had ever experienced. They ranted and raved about my lack of teaching experience, and used whatever derogatory remarks they could think of at the time.

One of the parents transferred his son to another school in the county, while the others accepted several days of suspension for their wayward sons, but let me know of their anger toward me. This incident was unpleasant, but was also a part of my education as a classroom teacher and coach.

At Chowan Junior College, I never had to deal with unhappy parents, possibly because our men won championships and four post-season football games during my tenure. Winning does prevent and solve many problems. At Guilford College, I was a coach for six years and athletics director 31 years, the longest tenure for a college athletics director in the state of North Carolina at that time. I had just a few incidents with parents during my long tenure as a professor, coach and athletics director.

"We Want You to Fire the Coach or We Will!"

To my surprise, I had a conference call from the mothers of the tri-captains of our soccer team. They told me I had to fire the soccer coach and to do it immediately. I explained that I was aware of their unhappiness with our coach, and assured them that I would handle the situation. I had warned our president of the situation prior to the call from the three mothers. I then called the tri-captains in and warned them that I would suspend them from the team if their mothers called again. The three men were excellent leaders and expressed disappointment with the telephone call. All three assured me that I would not receive any more calls from their parents.

Several weeks later, one of the three mothers called to tell me that she was going to get the parents of the entire team to get the coach fired. My immediate reply was that she needed to get two men fired. She asked, "Why do I need to get two fired?" I responded, "Because you will also have to get me fired, and I know you will never get it done because the college will not fire me!" That was the last time I heard from the mother.

A parent of one of our student-athletes called to tell me that her son's medical bill for a football injury had not been paid. She said she was going to call the state's commissioner of insurance and report me for not paying the bill. I told her that the problem was with her son, who ignored three letters to ask him to stop by our office and sign the claim form. He never paid attention to our letters and we could not send the claim to the insurance company. That ended the mother's complaint.

Parent's Concern Leads to Major Upset In Football

When I was a student at Wake Forest, we lost an important homecoming football game against N.C. State's Wolfpack. My roommate, Rock Brinkley, was a fullback who led the Southern Conference in scoring in 1944. He fumbled twice near N.C. State's goal line and the fumbles led to our disappointing loss.

During a team meeting in preparation to leave for Tennessee to play the No. 1 ranked team in the nation, an incident occurred that shocked everyone in the town. As the film of the game came to the part where Rock fumbled, an assistant coach shouted, "There goes Rock fumbling again!" Rock, a young man with a temper, answered in a loud voice with some uncomplimentary remarks, and our head coach told him to leave the meeting and not come back.

When the team got on the bus for the airport the next day, Rock was nowhere to be found and the team left without him for the upcoming game.

The following Saturday morning, Rock received a telephone call from Leroy Martin, the father of Sid Martin, a tackle on the team. Martin was a highly successful businessman with close ties to Wake Forest. He came to the town of Wake Forest, put Rock in his car and took him to an airstrip nearby where he had a private airplane. They flew down to Knoxville, arrived at the stadium and, as the team came out of the locker room to warm up for the game, Rock entered the locker room with Martin. The team was excited and Rock found his equipment waiting for him in a locker. The rest is history and it is a memory that Wake Forest alumni remember with pride. Rock scored two touchdowns as Wake Forest upset heavily favored Tennessee. This was the only loss for Tennessee that year and Tennessee dropped all future games with Wake Forest from 1946 to the present time. A parent's unusual act of kindness created a legendary moment in Wake Forest football history.

"Philosophical Differences," Claims Principal

Ron Barba, head coach of St. Joseph High School's girls' basketball team, was told his contract would not be renewed. Barba's teams had five successful seasons and won a sectional championship. Barba told reporters that he was fired because parents bypassed the coach and athletics director, and instead complained about his coaching to the principal. They threatened to keep their daughters from playing for Barba the following year. The principal said the school had a policy that hired coaches on a year-to-year basis. Barba was informed that he wouldn't be retained for the reason of "philosophical differences." Barba felt that some members of the undefeated junior varsity team would beat out the upperclassmen. This opinion, he said, was what had the parents up in arms (*Santa Maria Times*, 2009).

Parental Involvement in Sport

Some years ago, the Sport Studies Foundation conducted four workshops in the state of North Carolina dealing with sport from ages 5 to 20. Youth from these ages playing sport during non-school hours was the major concern, but attention was also accorded the many important relationships between inter-scholastic athletics and non-school programs. The four workshops held in Greensboro, Charlotte, Raleigh and Fayetteville culminated in a report called *Youth Sport: A Search for Direction* (1981).

A proposition that created lively discussion suggested that parents operate the youth sports programs. A dissenter, who was a director of a sports program, said "it had taken him 15 years to wrest control from parents and well-meaning citizens in order to institute programs of equality." Other directors were resistant to suggestions that parents and other citizens be included in decision-making; they felt that parents created problems. Those who favored the proposition said that parents have the most intimate involvement with the prime participants. They know more about the youngster's concerns than any other group. Parents could ensure that the youngsters remained the prime objective of a program, and would not allow outside influences to divert a program from its central purpose or philosophy.

The conference participants voted on the controversial proposition to give control of the program to parents. The results of the vote were: 25 for the proposition, and 76 against it. It was interesting to note that the comments gave the impression that the major problem was not to protect children from harassment by their own parents. Much attention was given to controlling overzealous parents (*Youth Sport: A Search for Direction*, 1980).

A Sad Situation

I recently heard of a situation that involved a mother and father of a college junior in a major Division I school. The student had been a cheerleader on the 2009–2010 squad, but when tryouts for the 2011 team were held, a committee did not vote for this cheerleader to continue in 2011.

The parents of the disappointed cheerleader became upset over the decision of the committee and put the blame on the head cheer coach. A request was made and granted for the parents to meet with the athletics director. At the meeting, the parents demanded that the cheer coach be fired and demeaned the coach in unbelievable terms. The cheer coach was present and had to listen to the charges against her.

The athletics director asked the cheer coach to take her back as an alternate, a request the coach turned down. Her response to the athletics director was, "If I am as bad as the parents claim, why would they want her back to cheer with me?"

As an athletics director, at times a particular team wanted to meet with me and a coach they wanted to have fired. I never let a team of men or women come in and try to lambast a coach. Instead, I would meet with the captain without the coach present and discuss the situation.

The Parents Aren't All Right

Thirty-five years ago, Lyle Mitchell, along with several other doctors at Children's Hospital Boston, founded the first clinic in the United States for children who participate in sports. Instead of the usual ankle sprains or hyper-extended shoulders, Mitchell and his fellow doctors found a different profile of injuries. Many children tend to suffer injuries from "chronic overuse." Their bodies are overtrained to a degree that they can't take it anymore. Mitchell estimates that "three quarters of the youth players seeking care at the clinic have been damaged by doing too much too fast, often when they were too young." In contrast to the problem of obesity in youth, "there's definitely a group of kids that are too active" (Hyman, 2009).

Mitchell and his colleagues say that the problem can be prevented. By "introducing variety, moderation and rest into an everyday sports routine, a child's risk can be cut to nearly zero." Mitchell's group emphasizes that the kids are not the problem; rather, it's the parents—the great enablers. One of the doctors, an orthopaedic surgeon, reported that a mother of a tennis player went into a rage when told that her 10-year-old daughter had a stress fracture in her shoulder that could interfere with her growth. The indignant mother refused to accept the doctor's recommendation to let her daughter rest until healing took place. The mother said her daughter just needed physical therapy so she could play in an important competition in two weeks. Therefore, a six-month rest period was out of the question. The doctor made an interesting comment: "Do parents think I get a thrill out of shutting a kid down? You can go to a chiropractor. Wish on a star. Try a magnet. Wear garlic. The fact of the matter is your child needs rest" (Hyman, 2009).

"I Learned a Lesson"

Andrew Kniceley, Chairman of the Fairmont State University (FSU) Board of Governors, resigned and apologized for his verbal attack against football coach Gary Lanham. Kniceley is the publisher of *The Times West Virginian*.

Lanham started all his seniors on Senior Day at FSU, except Kniceley's son, Josh. After the game, Kniceley was angry because his son had been a starter for two years and did not get much playing time his senior year. Lanham tried to get away from the angry parent, and a police officer intervened to separate the two men.

Later, Kniceley wrote an apology to Lanham and school officials that he published in *The Times-West Virginian* (2009): "I have learned a lesson that I should have known beforehand. I regret any embarrassment or discomfort that I have caused FSU, my newspaper and my family–especially my son Josh."

FSU officials regretted Kniceley's resignation from the Board. They praised Kniceley for his valuable contribution to FSU. Kniceley's apology says it all and parents should take heed of his uncalled for action after his son's final game.

One of the complaints of coaches today is that they are pressured by parents over a lack of playing time for their sons or daughters. A very successful coach in Nebraska resigned after she watched parents of her players use a stopwatch to check the amount of time their daughters got in practice and games.

Parents' Negligence

I once attended a middle school football game during which a 13-year-old quarterback blacked out. After the game, several parents encouraged the boy's parents to take him to an emergency room for a medical checkup. The boy's father did not believe that it was necessary to check his son out. This is typical among many parents. The next day, the parents took their son to a local hospital, where they learned that their son could not practice or play until the school received approval by a licensed physician for the boy to practice or play. The boy in question may be the benefactor of a new procedure in North Carolina in which medical approval is necessary for practice or games after a concussion is suffered.

Risks High in Youth Sports

The Columbus Dispatch (Ohio) reported that "a year-round five billion youth sports industry is pushing some children too hard and pressuring families to spend big money traveling the country for games, specialized training and the pursuit of elusive college scholarships" (*USA Today*, 2010). The *Dispatch* spent a year studying youth sports and found the following:

1. Non-school leagues are largely unregulated and can leave children more susceptible to injury. At a minimum, many kids are robbed of their childhood.
2. Youth sport is marked with physical, emotional and financial minefields for children and families.
3. Some parents are driven by fear that their children won't be good enough for a varsity or college team.
4. Families easily can spend up to $50,000 a year in youth sport programs.

The Dispatch surveyed about 1,000 Ohio high school students and 213 coaches, along with 70 athletes and 33 coaches from Ohio State University. Half of the athletes reported that they started playing sports as early as six years of age and "quickly felt the need to press on if they wanted to someday earn a spot on a high school varsity team or win a scholarship" (*USA Today*, 2010). The study revealed that "more than 40% [of the athletes] said their parents pressured them to play, and 10% said their parents' behavior during games embarrassed them." David Klontz, baseball coach at Heath High School, said, "Too many parents today want to be agents instead of parents" (*USA Today*, 2010).

Sandy Baum, an economics professor at Skidmore College in Saratoga, New York, said, "Your kid is much better off studying and doing well academically than spending all the time on the soccer field." An expert on financial aid, Baum feels that "parents were making the wrong investment" today with their emphasis on youth sports (*USA Today*, 2010).

Parents Sue Principal and Coach, Alleging Civil Rights Violation

The parents of a student at Wyoming Valley West High School (WVW) filed suit against the school principal and swim team coach on behalf of their son alleging a violation of his civil rights. The parents claimed that the defendants violated his Fourth Amendment rights and due process-protected property interest.

During the 2002–2003 school year, Dominic M was a sophomore at WVW and a member of the swim and water polo teams. During this period of time, Irvin DeRemer was WVW's principal and Frank Tribendis, the swim coach. The parents produced evidence that the coach requested that they take their son for a drug screening. The coach conditioned a negative finding on the drug screening in order to allow their son to continue participation on the swim and water polo teams. The drug test screening was negative. At a summer practice session, the coach told Dominic M that he did not approve of his work ethic and that he was "uncoachable and no longer wanted at swim practice" (*Dominic v. Wyoming Valley West High School, et al.*, 2005). He then scheduled a meeting with the principal and parents, where he informed the parents that he believed their son engaged in the use of illegal narcotics. He gave the parents the name of a counselor for Dominic M to see. The coach told the parents that their son could not participate on the water polo team and informed the water polo team that Dominic M was "in need of drug rehabilitation and not to associate with him" (*Dominic v. Wyoming Valley West High School, et al.*, 2005). The mother attempted to speak with the coach and she was told that he would call the police if she did not leave the facility.

Dominic M underwent an evaluation at a drug treatment facility and the result was that Dominic M was not suffering from a substance abuse problem. The principal denied the parents' request for a meeting in an attempt to reinstate their son to the swim team. Someone cut the lock off Dominic M's locker and searched its contents. The parents claimed that the coach was the only one who could have done this.

The defendants responded to the lawsuit by the parents of Dominic M and filed a motion for summary judgment. The United States District Court for the Middle District of Pennsylvania noted that "in order for a municipality or other governmental entity to be liable under the doctrine of *respondeat superior*," a plaintiff "must establish a deprivation of a constitutionally protected right resulting from a policy, practice, or custom" (*Dominic v. Wyoming Valley West High School, et al.*, 2005).

The court concluded that the plaintiffs did not provide any evidence of constitutional violations. The court considered the plaintiff's contention that their son's civil rights had been violated and concluded:

1. Parents lacked standing to assert federal claims against school defendants since parents, whose son remained on swim team after passing the drug test, did not allege any injury relating to federal claims.
2. Coach's interference with affiliations involving team member and his peers at school did not violate team member's First Amendment right to free association.

3. Compulsory drug screening of student did not violate student's Fourth Amendment rights.
4. Student did not have a due process-protected property interest in participating in extra-curricular activities such as interscholastic athletics.

The court granted defendants Wyoming Valley West High School, Irvin T. DeRemer and Frank T. Tribendis' motion for summary judgment (*Dominic v. Wyoming Valley West High School, et al.*, 2005).

This 14-page case covers many constitutional issues that are important to coaches and administrators alike. Due to its length, we are not able to discuss all of them. However, we recommend that everyone who is interested in the opinion of the court on such a timely issue read the case in its entirety.

Parent Urges Emphasis on Good Character and Behavior in Youth Sport

Debra-Lynn B. Hook writes in the *Milwaukee Journal* (2006) that parents and coaches alike "need to save room in athletics for kids who play by the rules." Hook describes the girls who play with her daughter on the community soccer team: "These girls make good grades, sing in the school choir, act in school players. These are also the kind of girls who make cookies for their teachers when they are having a bad week. They include a non-soccer girl who sits at their lunch table because they did not want her to feel left out" (Hook, 2006).

Hook goes on to describe the feeling she experienced when an opposing team was guilty of misconduct. The coach of her daughter's team pulled her aside and told her that this is the way it is and will only get worse. The frustrated parent notes that sport on every level seems to tolerate bad conduct and violence, and TV records such bad and unethical behavior. She writes: "Never mind the rise of poor behavior on the sidelines—parents second guessing and physically attacking coaches, fans throwing water bottles at pro-baseball players" (Hook, 2006).

Hook adds: "Turn the TV channel to most any pro football basketball and football games and you will see players fighting, taunting and intimidating other players, players engaged in roughness, players pandering to the crowd and the TV." Hook refers to sports analysts who cite "diminishing societal standards as well as the glare of media attention and the athlete's sense of being larger than life" as part of the problem. She contends that parents should not be afraid of being labeled meddlers or puritanical if they call for ethical and proper behavior in sports. Hook believes that character and ethics may take on the greatest importance on the fields of play. She reasons that "the sports arena provides a safe and controlled environment for displays of physical prowess and attempt at victory … Without rules of behavior, without character and integrity, the field becomes nothing more than the Roman Coliseum, a free for all, where the heat of competition gets carried to the worse possible outcomes" (Hook, 2006).

In conclusion, Hook calls on coaches and athletes alike to put "greater emphasis on the ethical and character building aspects of athletic competition." She insists that "sports are a major social force that shapes the quality and character of the American culture" (Hook, 2006).

Parents: Have Faith, Don't Hover

Stephen G. Emerson, President of Haverford College, has a daughter in college. He is also responsible for 1,182 students at Haverford. He attended Parents Weekend where his daughter was and Parents Weekend at Haverford. He writes in an article about how "he gives advice to parents from his experience of two decades and three-plus years as a college president." His advice covers a lot of ground for parents of college students. He suggests the following:

1. Do not hover over my now-adult daughter.
2. Avoid taking control out of concern for my daughter, who is smart, independent and capable of handling things on her own.
3. Hovering may be our generation's greatest sin.
4. Young people have what it takes to make it on their own.
5. We will be behind our children and they will be leading us.
6. Our changing world is going to need all the skills and passion and sensibilities they may have to offer.
7. Do all you can to enable them to become independent adults.
8. Have faith and they will use their independence well.

President Emerson noted that our students will meet the challenges of a changing world and succeed (*News & Record*, 2010).

Booster Clubs

Parents support booster clubs to provide funds for athletics programs. I have seen both good and bad regarding booster clubs on the high school and collegiate levels. I remember the firing of a successful coach when he refused to buy his groceries from a store owned by a powerful member of the high school's booster club. I have witnessed the firing of coaches who were excellent teachers and role models, but failed to post winning records. Members of booster clubs can exert heavy pressure on administrators and school board members. The potential for good is present. I have witnessed many acts by booster clubs that provided positive support for student-athletes, coaches and administrators.

When I began my tenure at Guilford College in 1956, I started the Quaker Club. The college had existed for 132 years without an athletics booster club and many on campus preferred it that way. From a modest beginning, the Quaker Club has become a vital factor in the successful operation of the athletics program. It is a club that supports, but does not interfere, with the operation of athletics, never attempting to influence the hiring or firing of a coach. Through the years, the attitude has been that it exists for the sole purpose of helping young people prepare for careers and life. Some of its activities include:

- Hosting tailgate parties at home football games for parents, faculty and friends
- Selecting members for the Sports Hall of Fame committee and sponsoring the induction banquet
- Hosting receptions at selected home basketball games for men's and women's teams
- Sponsoring the leadership awards banquet
- Distributing a quarterly newsletter
- Sponsoring the end-of-year awards banquet, and providing awards for individual athletes, coaches and teams
- Assisting the college in financing special projects, such as purchasing video equipment, renovating the field house and purchasing a soccer/lacrosse scoreboard
- Renovating the weight training rooms
- Raising endowment funds for future program enhancement
- Helping with and hosting various athletics events
- Underwriting the travel costs by charter buses for the sport teams (Appenzeller, 2003).

With such altruistic projects, one wonders why booster clubs get such criticism. The answer seems to be the illegal conduct of overzealous alumni and fans who will do almost anything to have a winning program. A coach (who was eventually fired for getting his institution on probation) was so popular with members of the booster club that he received a new automobile each year and a stipend that corresponded to his former salary.

In another situation, a booster club was paying the salaries of four coaches at one time. Three of them had been fired, but they had years left on their contracts. Many coaches are fired each year and accept their fate as the institution pays the remaining years on their contracts. The problem lies with perquisites promised by the booster clubs. Several lawsuits have revealed that some coaches are promised membership in three or four country clubs, a new car each year and other attractive perks. The coaches often sue for the perks promised by the booster club. The end result is usually a financial settlement.

Booster Clubs Require Expensive Perks

Booster clubs require expensive donations for its members. For example, the Arkansas Razorback Foundation will put your picture in its football game-day program for $5,000. A $10,000 donation to the booster club at Syracuse University will give you the opportunity to attend a VIP reception with the athletics director and the head coaches. Stanford University will allow you to go on a road trip for an away football game for $50,000 (Clotfelter, 2010).

Overseeing the Booster Club

In the early days of the Quaker Club, the funds raised were placed in an account in a local bank. The goal was to have control of the funds, and we tried to safeguard the programs by requiring three signatures before a check could be written. This process was cumbersome, but, more than that, it caused people to become suspicious of fund usage.

When I was asked to oversee the total operation of the Quaker Club, including finances, I agreed on one condition: all booster club funds had to go through college channels. When we had needs, the request would go from the athletics director to the business manager for approval. An important addition was that all funds would be audited by the college auditors. This system works and eliminates adverse perceptions about the use of funds. I was flattered when three athletics directors called to inquire about our booster club. Each reported that the club had been singled out as a model and they wanted to copy the guidelines. All went well until I explained the financial arrangement we followed. They replied that they, not the school, wanted to have control over their funds and would use local banks for that reason.

That was twenty years ago, and isn't it interesting that the Knight Foundation published a report in March 1991 with one of its concerns being the financial structure of booster clubs? The 2000 report reinforced their concerns and recommended the following: all funds raised and spent in connection with the intercollegiate programs should be channeled through the institution's general treasury, not through independent groups, whether internal or external. The athletics budget should be developed and monitored in accordance with general budgeting procedures on campus (Knight Foundation Commission on Intercollegiate Athletics, 1991 and 2001). While the Knight Foundation's recommended approach is one of the best, it may be the most difficult to implement.

Ethical Questions

1. At the Sport Studies Foundation workshops, it was proposed that complete control should be vested in the parents, as opposed to the association or league. Should parents have involvement in youth programs since "parents know their children best?"
2. Should coaches recruit "good, ethical parents as well as talented athletes?"
3. What can be done to prevent parents from emphasizing playing time for their children on practically any level of sport?
4. Do you agree that the best environment for coaching is in orphanages or prisons?
5. In the situation of the cheerleading coach being asked by parents to reinstate their daughter, what suggestions do you have to handle the request?
6. How would you handle a parent's attempt to fire a coach?
7. Discuss "chronic overuse" in children's sport-related injuries.
8. Discuss the statement by Sandy Baum that "parents are making the wrong investment today with their emphasis on youth sport."
9. Discuss the case of Dominic against Wyoming Valley West High School involving allegations by the parents of Dominic that his civil rights had been violated. Do you agree with the decision of the court?
10. Discuss the role of parents in the operation of booster clubs.
11. What are the functions of booster clubs?
12. How would you handle the control of booster club funds?

Chapter 10

Equipment and Facilities

"I promise you, John, if you come to Wake Forest, there will be a Catholic church in town." — Douglas Clyde "Peahead" Walker, former Wake Forest football coach

There are many instances of unethical behavior when dealing with the need for top safety equipment and the purchaser elects to save money by ordering cheaper equipment. In one instance, a sport administrator decided to save money by electing not to purchase mats for the concrete walls of the new gymnasium. Unfortunately, in a pick-up game of basketball a participant was inadvertently pushed into the unpadded concrete wall. He sustained a serious head injury, sued and received $250,000 in an out-of-court settlement. In other cases, failure to anchor soccer goals has caused many deaths and catastrophic injuries that have led to million-dollar settlements. Failure to obey the new Virginia Graeme Baker federal law regarding swimming pool safety has also led to catastrophic injuries and deaths, which have led to subsequent lawsuits.

In this chapter, other issues such as multimillion-dollar expenditures for lavish facilities to attract "blue chip" athletes will be discussed. Some institutions rename facilities that were named for others so they can gain more money with a new donor; this also presents an ethical problem.

An important responsibility of the sport administrator is to provide and maintain safe equipment and facilities. The safety committee can be a powerful force in developing inspection lists for both equipment and facilities and can also eliminate confusion over who will be the designated inspector. There should be a well-conceived plan for periodic inspections of equipment and facilities for hazards and other dangerous conditions prior to their use. Failure to inspect led to a huge damage award in New York. A school district failed to implement a program of preventive maintenance and inspection of its facilities, and a loose nut and bolt on a ladder led to the death of an employee and a $1,400,000 award to his family (*Woodring v. Board of Education of Manhasset*, 1981). This chapter discusses ways that equipment and facilities, in my experience, most frequently present problems for the sport program.

Indoor Facilities

A student in Alabama was cut around the eye by shattered glass from an unprotected light bulb in the ceiling of the gymnasium. The student filed a lawsuit claiming that injuries to his eye and face were permanent (*Beasley v. Morton*, 1990). The sport administrator should alert staff that all clocks, lights and windows should be properly shielded. In addition, keep unused equipment stored in a safe area and make certain that basketball goals are at a safe distance from walls, unprotected glass doors or windows located behind the goals.

Location of Glass Panels a Hazard

The old gymnasium at Guilford College had panes of regular glass several feet behind the basketball backboard. I used to stand in the lobby and watch basketball games through the glass panes until Bob Kauffman, a 6'8", 240-pound All-America with tremendous speed, started running toward the glass panels with his hands outstretched. He used the window to stop himself. We subsequently replaced the window with a solid brick wall with proper padding. What a case Kauffman, a first-round NBA draft choice with the Seattle Supersonics and three-time NBA All-Star, would have had against the institution if his professional career had been ended by our negligence. I breathed easier when the hazardous condition was corrected.

Ronald Baron, a sport law specialist, cautions the sport administrator to "provide and maintain safe equipment and facilities. Periodically inspect for hazards or other dangerous conditions prior to use. Upon the discovery of hazards, immediately remedy the hazard, remove the defective equipment, or avoid the use of the unsafe facility until the problem is corrected" (*From the Gym to the Jury*, 1990).

Ground Fault Interrupters

A coach decided to enlarge an existing whirlpool so that more than one athlete could use it at a time. The coach sought the opinion of the industrial arts teacher and was assured that it would work and was safe. Three boys got into the whirlpool after baseball practice. Upon hearing their calls for help, a coach disconnected it. Two of the boys recovered, but one died from electrocution. A Kentucky court held that the absence of a ground fault interrupter (GFI) was the cause of the accident (*Massey v. Persson*, 1987).

The death of an amusement park guard and another man could have been prevented, a federal safety official said, if a safety device (readily available in hardware stores for about $10) had been installed (*News & Record* 1991). A representative of the Occupational Safety and Health Administration (OSHA) commented that the device was not required when the park was built. This is a common argument heard when the Center for Sport Law and Risk Management conducts risk reviews in facilities that were built prior to the 1973 Rehabilitation Act. Of course, this is no excuse. Many facilities were built well before the Act, but they must comply with federal law. Compliance with federal law is a must, no mater when a facility was built, unless exceptions to the law are built into compliance regulations.

Sport administrators need to understand the function and need for a GFI. During a risk review at a large midwestern university, we found a lack of GFIs in a training room. The athletics trainer had six whirlpool machines, which student-athletes were using for rehabilitation purposes. None were connected with a GFI. The trainer explained that his athletics director did not want to spend the money (approximately $35 for each GFI) it would cost to provide safety for the users. We find that many areas where water and electricity mix, such as athletics training rooms and locker rooms, do not have GFIs. Electricians can install these safety devices quickly and inexpensively. An awareness of this problem is essential.

When we toured the Dallas Cowboys locker room during a sport law conference in 1997, we saw a large mirror next to the showers. Players standing in water on the concrete floor under the mirrors would plug in their hairdryers. There were no GFI's. One could imagine the enormous damage award that the courts would grant if a high-salaried professional athlete was electrocuted because the area lacked a GFI. Situations like this one are not the exception but often the rule.

Laundries and Dryers

Most schools on the high school and collegiate level have laundries complete with dryers. Most administrators assign a staff member and several student assistants to operate the machines and then pay little attention to their operation. This often overlooked area can create hazardous conditions.

A ninth grader in Louisiana was a student manager assigned to the freshman basketball team. He was in a hurry to get the uniforms washed. In the process, he tried to stop the extractor when it failed to stop spinning. None of the coaches had explained the use of the extractor, although the varsity manager had tried to explain the process to him. He climbed on the machine in an effort to get his foot on the lever. The next thing he remembered he was standing beside the machine, his left leg in excruciating pain. As a result of the injury, the freshman manager was hospitalized for thirty-seven days, and his leg was amputated.

The manufacturer of the extractor testified that when the machine was built, it allowed the user to open the lid while the basket was still spinning, contrary to applicable safety standards. The manufacturer settled with the boy, and the school district was found liable for one-half of the damages because the manufacturer settled before the trial. The 15-year-old boy received damages of $1 million (*From the Gym to the Jury*, 1990).

The late Bill Beale, an attorney and president of Belco Laundry in Charlotte, North Carolina, recommended the following safety tips and hints for the use of athletics laundries:

- Never use any product that does not have the Underwriters Laboratory (UL) Seal on the rear of the machine. The entire product should be UL approved, not just a valve or motor. (Recently, seventeen people were electrocuted by non-UL approved hair dryers).
- Never use or store any flammable products in the dryer room. Never dry any mops or rags that have touched solvents. Mops dipped in flammable solvents for floor cleaning cause most fires. Make sure the salesperson gives you written assurance that the solvent purchased will not burn.
- Never alter or change any parts or "hot wire" a machine to make it run temporarily. Units are made to government specifications for safe use, and reliable sales companies have national service for immediate help. They will also ship any part needed by air freight.
- Keep spare parts in a kit just as you do with your automobile.
- For fast and safe drying, keep the lint screens clean. If cleaned before use, it will save ten minutes in drying time because lint buildup on temperature sensors causes temperature controls to be useless.
- Keep all panels and protective guards in place at all times.
- Keep inspection and maintenance sheets up to date. Notify maintenance when service is needed.
- Never leave machines running unattended for more than thirty minutes.
- Stay until all the items are finished and out of the dryer. Dirty uniforms can be left to soak in water overnight, but turn off dryers at night when no one is present to supervise.
- Avoid heat, rough action, and hurry-up methods, such as high-speed extraction for fast washing and drying.

- Avoid separate extractors—courts hold that they are dangerous and uniform manufacturers claim they tear and damage equipment.
- Avoid commercial laundries if they are not UL approved.
- Many states have laws that require schools to purchase only those electrical products that are UL approved. However, states do not tell salesmen and manufacturers that they cannot sell non-UL approved products to schools. In some ways, it is like drinking laws that permit a store to sell whiskey but penalize drunkenness.
- Follow the rules and your athletics laundry will give you good service. (*From the Gym to the Jury*, 1990)

Locker Rooms

A Minnesota court held a school district negligent for failing "to inspect and maintain the equipment, building, and grounds for the protection of the students" (*Kingsley v. Ind. Sch .Dist., Hill City, No. 12.*, 1977). A piece of metal protruding from a locker tore the skin and tissue from a girl's finger. All that remained of her finger was muscle and bone. Ronald Baron notes that "the locker room should be free of sharp projections and dangerous objects. Surfaces should be kept clean and dry to reduce the danger of slipping and the spread of foot infection. Proper ventilation is important. Lockers should be secured to prevent falling" (Appenzeller, 2003).

Gymnastic Equipment

For years, students attending a summer music camp on our campus became upset with me for not leaving a trampoline open on the gymnasium floor. They insisted they came from a state in which the sport of trampolining was important, and they knew the art of spotting. However, I would not allow the trampoline on the court for anyone to use. If a crippling injury occurred, I explained to them, the institution could not successfully defend a lawsuit in court. I insisted that a member of the music staff, with expertise in the sport, be present to supervise the activity. The conflict was resolved and the activity was carefully monitored by trained personnel. Today, the majority of schools on both the secondary and collegiate level have eliminated the trampoline from their gymnastics programs. Insurance became impossible to obtain, and while the number of trampoline-related injuries was small, the injuries were catastrophic. Too often, equipment such as balance beams, parallel bars, mats and vaulting equipment are left out when class is not in session. The sport administrator should make certain that all gymnastic equipment is kept in a locked area until qualified personnel are available to supervise.

Weight Rooms

Lifting weights has become popular among the general population. Students on all levels use weights in both supervised and unsupervised programs, presenting a need for safe equipment and conditions. The sport administrator should be aware of each team's policies regarding weight training. In Michigan, a high school principal and athletics director were sued for allegedly breaching their duty of care to a student who was seriously injured when heavy weights fell on him. The boy claimed that the sport administrator failed to observe that weightlifting in the summer violated rules when he failed to supervise the program. The Michigan court made an interesting comment when it said that "sport administrators, because of their specialized training, were responsible for enforcing rules and supervising activities and eliminating unsafe practices engaged in by coaches under their direction" (*Vargo v. Svitchan*, 1980).

Spectator Seating

There are many cases in which spectator seating is found to be the cause of injury because the seating is not inspected for defective boards or worn out nuts and bolts. When spectator seating is defective, plaintiffs often succeed in litigation.

I remember an embarrassing incident that happened in our gymnasium when I invited a benefactor of the athletics program to a basketball game. I emphasized the need for a new facility because the 40-year-old, 900-seat gymnasium could not meet present needs. During the game, I looked from the balcony to see if the benefactor was in his seat, when suddenly the foot board and seat board holding him collapsed. As I reached him, he looked at me and said, "I know you need a new gymnasium but this is going too far." We were lucky he was not injured. Instead of a lawsuit, he sent a check for $200,000 to build a new facility. I had requested a thorough inspection of the bleachers before the season and thought they had been approved for use.

A tragic ending to a basketball game occurred when a parent left her infant son on the bleachers so she could go the basketball court to talk with her other son. The "clean-up" crew closed the bleachers electronically without looking for objects or people, crushing the infant to death. It is imperative, therefore, to place a sign on the bleachers warning members of the "clean-up" crew to always check for objects before closing bleachers. Another safety feature of seating involves guard rails on bleacher sections. Most state and federal regulations require guard rails for bleachers over five rows high, and officials recommend that sport administrators comply with seating requirements or face penalties.

Outdoor Playing Surfaces

A Tennessee newspaper reported that a softball umpire sued a city worker and the Metro Nashville government for $25,000. The umpire claimed she suffered physical pain, incurred medical expenses and lost wages when a softball struck a deep furrow near a base and caromed to hit her in the nose. She claimed the field was not in proper shape and the grounds attendant did little to protect participants. The supervisor of the grounds crew apologized for the condition of the field, attributing it to a new man who did not know how to properly drag a field. The sport administrator should delegate a person to check playing fields for holes, glass, rocks, uncovered drains, sockets that protrude above ground and other hazards. Check wire backstops on baseball and softball fields to make certain that holes do not exist that threaten the safety of spectators.

Lack of Warning Track Causes Injuries

Four baseball players ran into an outfield fence because our field lacked a warning track. I put a warning track on the list of priorities, but unfortunately, the price tag delayed its construction. To protect the participants, I used an idea from an athletics director who advised me to cut the grass very low and ten feet from the outfield fence, and paint a white or yellow line around the ten-foot area. We tried it as a good temporary solution. Since then, a warning track has been installed to help alert participants that the fence is near.

Overlapping Fields

Participants in recreation, sport and physical education activities often collide with each other when contiguous fields overlap. It doesn't matter what the sport, overlapping fields can cause problems, injuries and subsequent lawsuits.

A women's softball team reportedly attempted to play a game at a college in Boston when there was a track and field meet the same day. The hammer throw area overlapped with the softball field and hammers fell frequently during the women's game. When the team ended an inning and the players ran toward the dugout, a hammer landed where the shortstop had been standing. The coach, using sound judgment, immediately called off the game and took her team home.

Once during a risk review, I saw a men's and women's track team dodging baseballs. The baseball team used the Astroturf field in the football stadium whenever the baseball field was wet, thus posing hazardous conditions to the members of the track teams. During fall track practice, the members of both the men's and women's track teams dodged footballs rather than baseballs. It seems that the members of the track teams should have been warned, "Track and field can be dangerous to your health." Overlapping fields are a definite hazard and practice of teams from two sports utilizing the same field should be eliminated.

Use of Facilities and Equipment by Outside Groups

For years, our institution leased facilities to various groups, including a summer music festival, and tennis, soccer, lacrosse, basketball and leadership camps. The leasing of facilities has public relations value as well as financial returns, but it also extends the institution's responsibility to provide reasonably safe facilities and equipment. Ron Baron recommends that all equipment distributed to outside groups or facilities be inspected and maintained in a safe condition. All activities by outside groups should be properly supervised by adults representing the group. The number of supervising adults depends on the type of activity, and the age and number of participants. However, the specific number should be spelled out in an agreement prior to the use of the facility. A facility should not be made available until the requisite number of adults is present (*From the Gym to the Jury*, 1990).

Facility Use Agreements

Many schools do not use facility agreements when outside groups use their facilities. The facility and its managers can be named in a lawsuit and possibly held liable for injuries that result from the use of unsafe facilities and defective equipment. To protect a school and staff from liability as a result of negligence or carelessness by an outside group using its facilities and equipment, a facility use indemnification agreement can be used to transfer the risk of loss. The agreement should contain the following items:

- A list of general rules a group should follow when using a school's facilities and equipment.
- A clause requiring the outside group to name the school or organization as an additional named insured on their general liability policy for the dates of the outside group's use of the school's or organization's facility. A certificate of insurance naming the school or organization as an additional insured should be delivered to the school at least one week prior to use. In addition, the outside group or their insurance company should be required to notify the school or organization of any cancellation of the outside group's insurance at least 72 hours prior to the leasing or use of the school's or organization's facilities or equipment.
- A clause requiring the outside group to hold blameless and indemnify the school or organization for any and all claims or lawsuits that may result from their use of the school premises.
- A statement that the school district or organization has absolute right of cancellation without penalty or liability if the facility is unavailable. (Appenzeller, 2003)

The Center for Sport Law and Risk Management

In 1980, I joined Ron Baron, the Director of the Center for Sport Law and Risk Management, to assess from a safety standpoint colleges, universities, high schools and venues nationwide. At a major Division I institution, an ice hockey coach asked us about a situation and questioned who would be liable if a serious injury occurred to one of his players. He had turned in his equipment list to the business manager for approval. He wanted to provide the safest helmets for his players, but the business manger refused to order the helmet the coach requested. He chose, instead, the least expensive helmet that was clearly inferior to the one his coach preferred. The coach believed, as we did, that you do not purchase equipment such as helmets that is inferior and dangerous for the student-athletes. Our opinion was, should a catastrophic head injury occur in which the cause was unsafe head gear, the person who changed the coach's order would be vulnerable to a lawsuit.

For over 20 years, as representatives of the Center for Sport Law and Risk Management, we inspected equipment and facilities at over 100 institutions.

We found that problems existed across the nation, and still do in all too many facilities. In many instances, the problems lead to litigation that not only results in million-dollar awards and but also damages the reputation of the college or venue.

Unanchored Soccer Goalposts Lead to Death and Serious Injury

Two 10-year-old boys in the fourth grade at Rio Colorado Elementary School in San Luis, Arizona, were struck by an unanchored soccer goalpost that fell on them. One of the boys died and the other was treated at a local hospital for a non-life threatening injury. Both boys were playing during an early morning recess in the area of the goalpost when the goalpost struck them. The San Luis Fire Department responded to the accident. Fire Chief Hank Green said that members of the Fire Department treated a teacher who witnessed the accident for shock (*From the Gym to the Jury*, 2009).

On April 10, 1998, 12-year-old Dustin Welch was injured when a soccer goalpost flipped over and struck him on the right leg, causing a fracture. Welch was a participant in a soccer program in the town of Sudbury, Massachusetts. Welch's family commenced a negligence action against the Sudbury Youth Soccer Association, alleging that it owed him a duty to maintain the goalposts in a safe and secure condition, and to warn him of the danger that existed if the goalposts were not properly anchored to the ground. Dustin Welch asserted that the association breached its duties and it was this careless and negligent conduct that led to his injury. The Middlesex Superior Court granted the defendant's motion for judgment on the pleadings and the plaintiff appealed.

The Supreme Court of Massachusetts determined that non-profit associations conducting sports programs for youth are to be treated differently from ordinary landowners. The legislature made the judgment that the elimination of liability for negligence in non-profit sports programs was necessary to the encouragement and survival of such programs. Liability can be imposed on the association for acts or failures to act relating to the care and maintenance of real estate that the non-profit association owns, sponsors or controls and that is used in connection with a sports program and/or any non-profit association activity. Welch argued that the proper use of the soccer goals was to require securing them to the ground. In a modern "catch 22" situation, the Supreme Court of Massachusetts found that because the goalposts were moveable and not permanently affixed to Haskell Field, they therefore could not be considered real estate. The court held that not securing the goalpost was ordinary negligence and fell in the broad immunity conferred on non-profit associations by the State of Massachusetts (*Welch v. Sudbury Youth Soccer Association, Inc.*, 2009).

If decisions like this become routine in the courts of various states, an injustice will be continued that has led to 34 deaths and 58 serious injuries from 1979 to 2008 (Consumer Products Safety Commission). If immunity is automatically given to non-profit organizations, we predict more deaths and severe injuries will occur. We think this judgment of the Massachusetts court is tragic in the extreme and may lead to otherwise preventable injuries and deaths.

Virginia Graeme Baker Entrapment Lawsuit Filed

Bill Stock, a paraplegic, "was swimming in a man-made lagoon at the Hilton Hawaiian Village Beach Resort in Honolulu, Hawaii." He used the lagoon for therapy. His left foot and leg became entrapped in the sole outlet that carried water back to the ocean. Parts of the drain were encased by rocks, which made it difficult to free Stock when he was pinned. It took three adults to free him and he died the following day, a drowning victim.

Stock's family filed suit against the Hilton Resort claiming that it failed to comply with the Virginia Graeme Baker Pool and Spa Safety Act (VGB). An investigation revealed that the drain was blocked by debris. The lawsuit had many charges, including "negligence, wrongful death, failure to protect and violation of the VGB Act." After the victim's death, the Consumer Product Safety Commission began inspecting pools and spas for VGB compliance. Lee Boren, president of the Honolulu-based AquaBlue Pools, Inc., wondered if CPSC would target Hawaii since no inspections to his knowledge had taken place on the islands (*From the Gym to the Jury*, 2010).

It is imperative that pools and spas in every state comply with the VGB Act or remain closed until they are in compliance. Drownings such as the one in the Stock case draw attention to the importance of compliance to prevent tragic incidents like the one in the Stock case.

Pool Accidents Lead to Lawsuits

A young boy was swimming in a motel pool when his head was sucked into the drain of the swimming pool. A subsequent lawsuit was filed against the Seacrest Oceanfront Golf Resort. The plaintiff contended that the grate over the pool drain was not secured properly, leading to injuries to his head, nose and eyes. He also argued that the company that constructed the pool was negligent in their construction of the pool. A jury awarded the plaintiff a settlement of $43,434 (*Burke v. Seacrest, Inc.*, 2003).

In Alabama, Derrick Marshall, a 19-year-old athlete, was swimming in a hotel pool and was involved in an accident with a pool drain. The Montgomery County Health Department had shut the pool down, but the hotel employees told a group that they could use the pool. Marshall died several months after the accident and a jury awarded his family $3.76 million.

Awards such as these should send a strong message to motels and hotels that provide swimming pools. Once again, operators of swimming pools and spas should make certain that their facilities comply with the Virginia Graeme Baker Act.

Renaming Facilities: A Delicate Problem

One of the most disappointing times during my 37 years at Guilford College came unexpectedly. Our Booster Club had funded a renovation of a room in our gymnasium to honor a family whose sons had made an impact on the college during their years of dedicated service as coaches and athletics directors. These men had also gone on to later coach at a state university with unusual success. The renovated room was used when students visited campus, for meetings, hospitality functions at intercollegiate games and other special events. Everyone who frequented the room lavishly praised it.

At the time this family was to be honored by a special room, another alumnus wanted to furnish the room with expensive "high end" furniture to honor his father. This man had contributed much to his community as a family doctor, and much to the athletes in his community. He too was a distinguished alumnus of the college. The beautiful furniture was to embellish the room named for the family of the two outstanding coaches.

One day, I saw the furniture being moved from the room and was told, "We will restore it when we build our new facility." However, the new facility was scheduled to be built in three or four more years, depending on funding. The beautiful furniture was distributed over several locations on campus, and the name of the room and its accessories was eliminated.

The move of the furniture and the loss of the name of the room disappointed both the family that donated the furniture in honor of their father and the family that named the room after their sons. The new field house never provided a special room named for the family of the coaching legends. An ethical question that leads to friction and controversy can arise from an action that involves the loss of facilities that were established to honor outstanding people at a previous time in the school's history.

Retired Jerseys vs. Retired Numbers

Marquette University faced a public relations debacle over the use of a retired number by a current freshman basketball player, which damaged a strong relationship with one of the basketball program's prominent players and all-time leading scorer, George Thompson. Thompson was the late coach Al McGuire's first outstanding star who set the school's scoring record of 1,773 points. Friends teased Thompson about the un-retirement of his No. 24 jersey and this angered Thompson. Marquette's associate athletic director of marketing and communications said, "We retire jerseys but not numbers" (Wolfey, 2006).

For years, the school has honored its great players and others by retiring jersey numbers and they hang from the rafters of the Bradley Center. Confusion led to controversy over the jersey versus number retirement. It was unfortunate that the action of the school caused controversy between the athletics department and an individual they had respected and admired for years. The problem is an ethical one that needs attention on the part of everyone involved in the jersey retirement process.

Report Says Texas A&M Facility Flawed

Texas A&M hired a Houston engineering firm to evaluate its new $35.6 million tent-like athletic complex. Haynes Whaley Associates' report was obtained by *The Associated Press* under the Texas Public Information Act. The firm reported that they did not think the facility as constructed could withstand 90 mph winds. The firm's executive vice-president, Mark Thompson, informed Texas A&M that the McFerrin Athletic Center was built using a flawed design similar to the one used for the Dallas Cowboys' practice facility, which collapsed in May 2009, injuring a dozen people. In response to Haynes Whaley's concerns, Summit added a series of cables to the Texas A&M facility's steel frames (*The Associated Press*, 2009).

Connecticut Study: Turf Fields Are Safe

Four Connecticut state agencies conducted a study of artificial turf fields at a cost of $245,000. The study was made as a result of the "concern that has been raised across the country about artificial turf's safety because of industrial chemicals in crushed rubber tires." The study at four outdoor fields and one indoor field concluded that "based upon these finding, outdoor and indoor artificial turf fields are not associated with elevated health risks." The study recommended, however, that "it would be prudent for building operators to provide adequate ventilation at indoor fields." The study was conducted by "the University of Connecticut Health Center, the Connecticut Agricultural Experiment Station, the Department of Public Health, and the Department of Environmental Protection" (*USA Today*, 2010).

California Limits Lead in Artificial Turf

In California, a settlement was reached requiring "artificial turf makers FieldTurf and Beaulieu to eliminate nearly all lead from their products which are widely used by school, parks and daycare centers." Then State Attorney General Jerry Brown said that the settlement would prevent potential hazards of lead in those who are users of the artificial turfs. Brown also stated that FieldTurf, the biggest supplier of artificial turf in the United States, is required to replace artificial turfs in California at a discount if they were installed before November 2003. Michael Green of the Center for Environmental Health said, "California is now the national leader in resolving a problem that has concerned parents across the country" (McCarthy, 2010).

New Coaches and Artificial Turf

Many new coaches in basketball and football convince their administrators to convert their facilities from artificial turf to grass or vice-versa. In various cases, artificial floors in basketball are converted to wood. These changes cost considerable amounts of money. At the University of Tennessee, recently hired football coach Derek Dooley told an audience of football fans that he hoped he could have FieldTurf at Neyland Stadium the following year so he could avoid damage to the grass field. He wants to make his facility available to high school and younger teams who want to use the field without fear of damaging the facility. His former athletics director, Mike Hamilton, reportedly responded that the university has no plans to replace the grass field (*Knoxville News Sentinel*, 2010).

When Guilford College received a $1 million grant to upgrade its outdoor athletic field, they installed FieldTurf. The student body and the football, men's and women's soccer, and men's and women's lacrosse players use the field, including under the lights. When available, intramurals also use the field. The students have given positive reports regarding the new field.

Recruiting: Using Facilities to Attract Athletes

In some instances, universities provide "special admissions" to a limited number of prospective athletes with lesser credentials. Other universities appropriate millions to improve facilities designed to attract "blue chip" athletes to their schools.

The late Bill George, an All-America football standout who was also an All-Pro for the Chicago Bears, said that when he came to Raleigh, North Carolina, to visit the Wake Forest Campus, Coach "Peahead" Walker took him to Duke's campus and stadium and told him it was Wake Forest. When George committed to Wake and was met by his coach again, he was taken to the "real" Wake Forest campus. George reportedly said, "Coach, this doesn't look like the Wake Forest I saw when you recruited me." Coach Walker then said, "Bill, that was our East Campus."

Another story told was that of John Polanski, a celebrated fullback and devout Catholic, who told Coach Walker that he really liked everything about Wake Forest, but one thing was lacking and would keep him from coming: a Catholic church. Coach Walker assured him that there would be a Catholic church if Polanski came to Wake Forest. Polanski came that fall and on the outskirts of town was a small, but beautiful Catholic church. Polanski had a great career at Wake Forest and went down as one of the finest fullbacks ever to play for the Deacons.

Importance of Recruiting

Recently, several academically selective universities have gained national attention by winning football games. The question asked is how "brainiac universities" like Duke, Rice and Vanderbilt are rising in big-time football (Lederman, 2008). Factors may vary from school to school. However, "the biggest reason, often, is that the institution has suddenly started getting more good players ... [due to] a coach with a big name or whose staff is particularly good at recruiting, for instance, or players being more impressed by sparkling new practice facilities or the chance to play in front of tens of thousands more fans" (Lederman, 2008).

Duke University, known for its high admission standards, hired a well-known outstanding football coach, David Cufcliffe. He gained his reputation at Tennessee and Mississippi, where he coached Eli and Peyton Manning. Cutcliffe's hiring attracted outstanding athletes. In his second season at Duke, Cutcliffe scheduled No. 1-ranked Alabama for his third game. The game was a sell-out with extra seating added.

At Vanderbilt, credit for success in football has been given to hiring Bobby Johnson as coach and the administration's decision to stand by Johnson "despite no winning seasons." Former Chancellor Gordon Gee and Vice Chancellor David Williams "decided that he was the man for the job" because he "values academics, but as a recruiter, really seems to understand the type of scholar-athlete schools like [Vanderbilt] should recruit, but hasn't always done so" (Lederman, 2008). This confidence paid off, although Johnson resigned prior to the start of the 2010 season.

Notre Dame Is "Responsible" in Student's Death

Reverend John Jenkins, president of the University of Notre Dame, sent an email to students, faculty, staff and alumni in which he said that "the school is responsible for a student videographer's death because it failed to protect him" (*The Associated Press*, 2010). Dedan Sullivan, 20, was killed when a hydraulic lift he was on while he was filming football practice toppled over due to gusts of up to 51-mph. Jenkins added, "We at Notre Dame and ultimately I, as President are responsible. Words cannot express our sorrow to the Sullivan family and to all involved." At the same time, Jenkins praised coach Brian Kelly, who said it was his decision to practice outdoors despite the heavy winds. The state is investigating whether "a federal Occupational Safety and Health Administration rule barring workers from using scaffolds during storms or high winds" was violated. Jenkins said the school hired the former president of University of Arizona, a "world-renowned engineer," to provide an independent review of its investigation (*The Associated Press*, 2010).

Death of a Two-Year-Old Investigated

Two-year-old Lucas Anthony Tang fell about 30 feet after he scaled a glass safety guard in a luxury box at the Staples Center after a Lakers game. Anthony died from head injuries. The building is in compliance with city codes, which require guardrails to be at least 26 inches high in front of seats (Moore, 2010).

What Will It Take?

After 20 years of publishing our sport law and risk management newsletter, *From the Gym to the Jury*, several disturbing issues have been discussed repeatedly. Despite our pleas to correct dangerous situations that result in crippling injuries and even deaths to people of all ages, they persist. We have published the results of numerous court cases, often with enormous awards to injured parties and/or to families of injured or deceased victims. The ability to foresee problem areas involving unsafe facilities and equipment represents an ethical dilemma that is too often minimized and as a result, the problems continue with disastrous effects.

Ethical Questions

1. What ethical questions arise from the purchase of equipment?
2. Discuss problems that can arise when schools fail to inspect facilities/equipment on a regular basis. Give a few examples.
3. Discuss the use of ground fault interrupters.
4. Discuss safety features for school laundries and dryers. Discuss the $1 million lawsuit in a Louisiana high school.
5. Discuss safety for locker rooms, gymnastic equipment, weight rooms and spectator seating.
6. What is the problem of overlapping facilities?
7. What should be done to accommodate outside groups who use a school's facility?
8. Discuss unanchored soccer goals as a major problem.
9. Discuss the Virginia Graeme Baker law.
10. How do schools use facilities to attract "blue chip" athletes?
11. Discuss any situation you observed or experienced regarding ethical or unethical behavior dealing with equipment/facilities.

Chapter 11

Sportsmanship

"Let me win. But if I cannot win, let me be brave in the attempt."— *Motto of the Special Olympics*

Sportsmanship, good or embarrassingly bad, has been a part of my life as a participant, coach and administrator for many years. Bad sportsmanship appears to be getting the spotlight on a regular basis. During the 1992 Olympics in Barcelona, Spain, the specter of the "Ugly American" reared its head, causing marketing consultants to ask if it would hurt United States firms such as Nike, Coca Cola, Club Sports and others with Olympic ties. Critics opposed the lavish $900 per day hotel rooms for members of the basketball "Dream Team." On the other hand, the United States women's basketball team refused an offer to live in the same hotel, preferring to reside in the Olympic Village with their opponents in the games. Members of the Santa Monica Track Club rented private apartments. Dr. Leroy Walker, head of the U.S. Delegation in the Barcelona games, began a campaign to require Olympians to reside together in future Olympics. Walker emphasized the need for one Olympic team. He believed that there is a principle that goes beyond how good the participants are and winning a medal.

The Asian Tour

I, along with former University of Los Angeles at California (UCLA) sprinter Rod Richards, accompanied a group of seven outstanding track and field athletes in 1965 to Singapore for the Malaysian Games. At the end of the games, 55 Malaysian men would qualify to compete against our seven men in track and field. We represented the U.S. State Department and the Amateur Athletic Union on a goodwill trip designed to build friendship between the United States, Malaysia and other countries of the Far East. We had flown from New York to Singapore with brief stops in San Francisco, Guam and Saigon. Our men were determined to represent their country well, and determined to win every event.

Our track and field athletes and their two coaches (Richards and myself) were housed in an old schoolhouse with absolutely the poorest possible conditions. All of the athletes from Malaysia were quartered in the same conditions as our team. Our entire group was looking forward to the day when we were to be transferred to the University of Singapore. We could not wait, and the thought of air-conditioned rooms with modern conveniences got us through the stifling hot days in the school house. I heard the complaints daily, and I was just as eager to leave the windowless building where the toilet was a hole in the concrete floor under a leaky shower head.

A strange thing happened that lives in my memory as an unforgettable event. To my complete surprise and shock, each member of our group sought me out when no other person was around to make a request. The unanimous request from the nine-person team was to stay in the primitive conditions so they could be with their new Malaysian friends. The athletes were embarrassed by their request, because they had complained so much. I was caught off guard, but pleased that they were willing to sacrifice in order to remain with their friends. To our team, this was no big deal; however, it was a big deal elsewhere and reports of it were circulated throughout the Far East, and, at every new location, Asian officials praised our group for its unselfish conduct. When we returned to the United States, officials at the State Department thanked us over and over again for shedding the "Ugly American" image.

Unsportsmanlike Incidents

From 1991 to 2001, 13 incidents that illustrate a lack of sportsmanship on every level of sport were reported in *From the Gym to the Jury*:

1. In South Africa, a soccer referee shot and killed a player who protested his call in a game between neighboring towns.
2. A little league coach was awarded $630,000 by a district court after he was beaten by an opposing coach between innings.
3. A coach with a history of abuse toward players and an advocate of rough play was sued when the coach's son broke the leg of a teammate during practice by ramming his helmet into the boy's leg.
4. A player slammed an opponent into the boards after an ice hockey game, rendering the player paralyzed from the waist down. The coach of the opposing team allegedly "fanned the emotional intensity of his players" and encouraged his players to go after the leader of the opposing team.

5. A University of Evansville baseball player was beaned by an opposing pitcher from Wichita State University while he was warming up on the sidelines. A lawsuit against the coach, player and umpires followed the incident.

6. A district judge in Nebraska sentenced a football coach to 30 days in jail for assaulting a 16-year-old referee.

7. A father of four children died from injuries received after a pick-up ice hockey game in Massachusetts. The post-game fight began as a dispute over rough play.

8. A 14-year-old freshman told his football coach that another player had been picking on him. The coach told him to take care of his business. The boy responded by hitting his teammate with a weight lock he had stored in his gym bag. The coach became enraged and struck the 14-year-old with the weight lock, causing him to lose an eye.

9. A coach of a coed team in Florida became enraged when a 10-year-old boy dropped a pass during a coed football game. The coach, with a background of assault and abuse, lifted the boy to head level and slammed him to the ground. As a result, the boy broke both arms.

10. A father and uncle beat a coach after a game because they felt the coach did not give their son and nephew enough playing time. Both men were sentenced to 45 days in prison.

11. A youth league baseball coach convicted of getting one of his players to deliberately injure a teammate was sentenced to one to six years in prison.

12. An Arlington, Washington, Little League coach was accused of using some of his players to help him break into and rob an abandoned tool shop.

13. Ray Recchi, a baseball coach and journalist for the *Sun Sentinel* of Fort Lauderdale, wrote that in his league, a parent tried to scale a fence to get at a coach who ordered his son to bunt. Coaches had to be restrained after one threw a clipboard at another coach, and police were called to quell a brawl when a manager was ejected for profanity.

"No Sportsmanship Bull, Please!"

With the increase in sports violence and a concerted attempt by national governing sport organizations to emphasize the values of sportsmanship, I received a telephone call that really surprised me. A high school principal called with an unusual request. He said that his athletics teams were struggling with losing seasons, and frankly, he was tired of being a good sport. He told me in strong language that he wanted me to speak at his athletics banquet, but not about sportsmanship under any circumstances. "I don't want any of that bull if you accept this invitation." I thanked him for thinking of me, but responded that I would not be the right one for his banquet. I assured him that there were some coaches who would gladly comply with his guidelines and avoid any reference to sportsmanship.

A Souvenir of Singapore: The Influence of a 14-Year-Old-Boy

During the 1965 Asian Goodwill Tour, our men were keyed up the day of our exhibition in the Malaysian Games. I told them to relax in their room and report 45 minutes before their events. When I walked into the locker room, I noticed a 14-year-old Chinese boy quietly sitting on a bench with nine paper bags. He told me his name was Tony Lim and asked when the members of our team would arrive. I told him it would be an hour or so, and he asked if he could wait. I had no idea what was on his mind or why he was waiting for our team.

Norman Tate, our outstanding 100- and 200-meter sprinter and long jumper, was the first to arrive. Tony jumped from the bench and proudly handed Norman one of the paper bags. Norman was surprised to find a track trophy in it and asked Tony about it. Tony replied that he had no money, but when he overheard one of our men the day before saying he would like a souvenir of Singapore, he decided that he could do something that did not cost money. Tony ignored our protests against giving away his hard-earned trophies. Each team member knew that Tony would not listen to them so they accepted his gift, and in return gave him a USA hat, jersey, pin or something in exchange to express their gratitude for his gesture of international goodwill. I could not fit the entire trophy in my travel bag for my return trip home, but I was able to detach the beautiful medal from the trophy, and it occupies a very prominent and special place in my home. Tony Lim, a 14-year-old Chinese boy, will never know how much he contributed to international goodwill and sportsmanship at the start of our tour. Tony's act of sportsmanship set a positive tone for all of us.

International Rivalry Demonstrates Good Sportsmanship

In the 1960s, Manikavsagam Jegathesan (Jegar) was a world class sprinter who dominated the 100- and 200-meter events in Asia. He set a record in the 200 meters that lasted for more than a decade, and he competed in the 1960, 1964 and 1968 Olympics for Malaysia. Jegar was regarded as the fastest man in all of Asia, and his prestige was unquestioned. Malaysia's quest for a gold medal rested on his shoulders. In the Rome Olympics, Jegar reportedly advanced to the quarter finals, but tragically pulled a hamstring and was forced to withdraw. The general consensus of Asian track fans was that Jegar would have won the gold if he had not been injured.

During the 1965 Malaysian Games that we attended as part of the Asian Goodwill Tour, we watched Jegar compete in the 400-meter relay. He was so far ahead of his nearest competitor, he slowed down to a jog by the finish line and broke the tape with his fingers. The gesture did not go unnoticed by our seven men, especially Norman Tate, our outstanding sprinter. Tate turned to me and predicted that he would defeat Jegar in the 100 meters and promised to break the tape with his fingers as a payback for the cocky manner in which Jegar finished the relay. "Don't do that," I cautioned Tate, "We are on a goodwill tour and it would not be an act of sportsmanship." "Coach," Tate responded, "I know Jegar and like him, but he was showboating and I'm going to teach him a lesson."

On the day of our meet, everyone in the overflow crowd in the Singapore Stadium was buzzing about the Jegar-Tate race that featured two of the finest sprinters in the world. Just prior to the start of the meet, one of our State Department officials asked to talk to me about a very "important matter." He stressed the importance of Jegar winning in front of the crowd of fans who idolized him. "If he loses," the U.S. official said, "he will lose face and the great respect he has earned over the years. It will destroy his career." This indirect request for Tate to lose was unexpected and jolted me. At that moment, the second highest official in Malaysia told me that Jegar had decided to switch from the 100 to 400 meters, obviously choosing to avoid the confrontation with Tate. Dato Gazahli, the Malaysian official, saw the look of despair on my face, and he laughed and slapped me on the back saying that he had ordered Jegar to run the 100 meters, and that was that. He also suspected that the U.S. official had suggested that it was important for Jegar's medical career to win somehow. "I want you to tell your men to do their best to win," Gazahli said, almost ordering me to comply with his wishes. I will always respect him for taking the pressure off our man and I replied, "I assure you, Dato Gazahli, that our men did not come 9,000 miles to lose. These men only know how to strive for victory and will do everything they can to win. If we lose, it will be an honest victory for your fine Malaysian men."

I knew that Norman Tate never thought for one minute that he would not give his best effort. Even with the help of Gazahli, tension mounted as the start of the 100 meters drew near. The crowd cheered wildly as Tate and Jegar were introduced to run the 100 meters, and true to his word, Tate broke the tape with his fingers as he crossed the finish line.

What followed was spontaneous and surprised the sell-out crowd in the stadium. The other members of our American track team raced to Jegar, not Tate their teammate, hugging him and congratulating him for his superlative effort against one of the premier sprinters for the United States. The crowd exploded in joy when Tate rushed to Jegar and told him that no one in the world that year had come as close to him as he did. I can't explain the actions of our men, but the headlines in the morning paper captured the significance of the moment. The article quoted Tate and his American teammates who praised Jegar's outstanding performance. Jegar, now a medical doctor and Director of Malaysia's Institute of Medical Research and Ministry of Health, did not lose face that day in Singapore. Instead, he gained respect from his country's men and women, even in defeat. I often wonder if the action of Tony Lim an hour before the meet had anything to do with our spontaneous reaction that day.

Great Strategy or Poor Decision?

In 1953, I coached a basketball team at Chowan College that was special. The college had never had a strong basketball program before, and the student body and local townspeople were excited over this team that averaged 83 points a game in a day when low scoring was the rule, and 50 points was considered a game that featured high-powered offense. The team was on a roll and had won eleven straight games. Our next game was at Pembroke College, a predominantly Native American institution that was coached by Belus Smawley, a former star professional basketball player. The small junior college featured a 6'5", 195-pound Native American named Ned Sampson who was an unbelievable scoring machine. Rival coaches told me there was no possible way to stop Sampson, who lived up to the "Sampson" strong man image.

According to Coach Smawley, who recognized basketball talent, Sampson could have played for any college in North Carolina. In 1953, however, Native Americans were victims of discrimination, and schools refused to enroll them. Basketball coaches did not consider recruiting Sampson, although they readily acknowledged his tremendous ability. Their loss was Pembroke's gain, and Sampson scored 40 and 50 points per game. We arrived in time for a pre-game meal, confident that, despite the projected heroics of Sampson, we had the fire power to add to our winning streak. After all, we had Hilliard Greene, a 6'6" center who was leading the league in scoring, and Ken Haswell, a power forward who often took pressure off Greene when opponents double- and triple-teamed him.

When the officials took the floor, we began to feel uneasy because the two officials were local men, who we named the Sears and Roebuck boys. They worked in town, and we were warned that we might get a serious dose of home cooking. From the first tip off between Greene and Sampson, we knew we were in trouble. It was obvious that the officials did not know the rules. Two-shot fouls became one and one-shot fouls became two. To make matters worse, Greene picked up four fouls before the game was minutes old. As predicted, Sampson was a scoring machine and with Greene on the bench, there was little we could do to stop him.

At half-time, I made a decision that came out of desperation. I rationalized that the officials were unfairly penalizing our team, not intentionally, but because they just did not know the rules of the game. We felt it was unfair to stop our win streak and the momentum we had gained during the season. I called the team together and told them to listen carefully because the action we took the second half could help us win the game. I told the team emphatically, if Greene gets fouled, whoever is near him immediately raise his hand and take the foul. We must keep Greene in the game, so make sure he doesn't foul out.

At the start of the second half, Greene was whistled for his final foul, but Jerry Stokes, a guard, quickly raised his hand and Greene stayed in the game. His 55 points made the difference despite Sampson's 50+ point effort, and we narrowly won this hotly contested game. Without a doubt, Greene's continued presence ensured the victory. On the return trip, the players praised me over and over for winning the game with what they perceived to be great coaching strategy. Why is it that I think of this strategy almost 50 years later with regret, regret that I caused a great effort by a superstar and an outstanding coach to be nullified by illegal strategy? I also regret that I set an example for 12 young men who still think it was smart. Would it not have been better to take the loss and set the right example for impressionable men who would know that we lost with integrity rather than won with unsportsmanlike conduct?

Pitino's Book Changed a Flawed Strategy

A very successful veteran college basketball coach once told me about a strategy he had when he first started coaching. When a foul was called on his team, the players would huddle up and the best free throw shooter would go to the free throw line. He said that the officials never saw the wrong player go to the line to shoot the free throws. Later in his career, he read one of Rick Pitino's books, in which the outstanding coach wrote that he had used that tactic early in his career. He wrote that it was wrong (unsportsmanlike) to use such a tactic. The veteran coach later told me that after he read Pitino's book, he never again used that strategy with any of his teams. Pitino unknowingly influenced many coaches who used this strategy as an attempt to get an edge.

Golf Coach Exemplifies Good Sportsmanship

I was proud of Guilford College golf from 1979 until 1987. During this time, ten golfers won All-America honors, two were national champions and one won the World University Games in Sardinia, Italy. As a team, Guilford golfers participated in national championships with top ten finishes. Guilford was runner-up for the NAIA national title in 1985, 1986 and 1987. In 1989, the team won the NAIA national championship. The late Jack Jensen became only the second coach in NAIA history to win national championships in two sports. In 2001, the golf team finished second, and won the 2002 NCAA Division III National Championship. Jensen's basketball team won the title in 1973 when three players, Greg Jackson, "World B" Free and M.L. Carr led the team to the national championship. All three played successfully in the National Basketball League (NBA). Jensen was also a member of six Sports Halls of Fame.

Although Jensen won three national championships, he was primarily concerned with good sportsmanship. Tom Cooksey, senior rules official for the American Junior Golf Association, referred to the following anonymous poem that, in his opinion, exemplified the meaning of true sportsmanship and fair play:

> In the battle that goes on through life,
> I ask for a field that is fair.
> A chance that is equal to all in the strife,
> The courage to strive and to dare.
> And if I should win let it be by the code.
> With my faith and my honor held high
> And if I should lose let me stand by the road,
> And cheer as the winners go by.

This poem personified Jack Jensen and his attitude toward sport participation. With all of Jensen's success in basketball and golf, the following two instances are better demonstrations of his emphasis on good sportsmanship as a coach because the athletes involved overcame temptations that can any athlete can face. Instead of giving in to the temptations, these men stood tall and set an example for all to follow.

"My Ball Moved"

Jay Kennedy, a member of the Guilford College golf team, was playing in an invitational golf tournament on the Gold Course at the Camp Lejeune Marine Base. On a par-five hole, Jay sliced his ball, and it landed in the woods on the right in a pocket of leaves. Jay hit a tremendous shot out of the woods and landed on the green. The spectators applauded as he calmly sank his putt for an apparent par. The contest was close and the par was needed by Jay and the Guilford team. He quickly reported that when he set his club down to move some leaves, the ball moved. Instead of a par, he recorded a bogey six. No one, absolutely no one, knew that the ball had moved, but Jay did, and he had no hesitation in reporting the movement of the ball. Jay went on to win NAIA All America honors in 1979 and 1980.

"My Ball Moved, Too!"

Keith King, a native of Virginia Beach, Virginia, was a talented athlete. At 6'7", he was an outstanding center on the 1983 Guilford College basketball team and a two-time All America in golf in 1984 and 1985. Keith was competing with 167 qualifiers for one of only four spots to enter the Anheuser-Bush Golf Classic at Williamsburg, Virginia. This was the first opportunity he had to qualify for a spot on the professional tour, and he was determined to earn a berth. At the end of qualifying, three golfers had made the team and Keith was tied with two others for the one remaining spot. On the first hole of the playoff, Keith hit a tremendous drive on the par-five hole to outdistance his two rivals. The two hit the green, and Keith followed with another tremendous shot. The two opponents knew that Keith would be shooting for an eagle, and they would have to sink long putts for a birdie that would tie them with Keith. When he arrived on the green, they were sure he would win and qualify for the coveted spot. Instead, Keith told the men that his club inadvertently touched the ball as he got ready to hit his second shot. He didn't win the playoff and like Jay Kennedy, he admitted that the ball moved and, although no one saw the contact, he adhered to the spirit of the game rather than to the win without honor.

Umpire Apologizes as an Act of Sportsmanship

Leonard Pitts, a columnist for the *Miami Herald*, writes that "we seek examples, parables with which to teach our kids. Sports is, after all, an irresistible microcosm of life and its verities, an ongoing lesson in how to get a win and bear a loss, in the value of hard work and teamwork, in the importance of resilience and leadership, sacrifice and self-confidence." Pitts laments the fact that our "sports heroes too often behave in ways that make you want to cover your child's eyes" (Pitts, 2010).

To illustrate good sportsmanship, Pitts describes an instance where the umpire in a baseball game between Cleveland and Detroit admitted he blew a call that cost Detroit pitcher Armando Galarraga a perfect game against the Cleveland Indians. The perfect game is "perhaps the rarest occurrence in sports"; there have been only 20 in the last 130 years. Both the umpire, Jim Joyce, and Galarraga showed extreme sportsmanship in their action after the play, which was clearly called wrong: Joyce "sought out the player and apologized, weeping. And Galarraga promptly accepted: 'Nobody's perfect,' he explained." Pitts captures the result well: "The game might not have been perfect, but that response surely was. You will seldom see better definitions of integrity, civility, sportsmanship" (Pitts, 2010).

Ethical Questions

1. Discuss the examples of unsportsmanlike conduct listed above.
2. The decision to have other basketball players take a foul for an outstanding player bothered the author later and still does. However, others would consider this a good strategy. What is your opinion?
3. What is your opinion of the two golfers whose ball moved?
4. Do you have any examples of both good or bad examples of sportsmanship?

Winning at All Costs

A Player Takes Over

Our football team, a 30-point underdog, played an undefeated team that was ranked in the top ten of the NAIA. The team was undefeated, but there was a problem for their coach. Ranking was based on a power rating, and although our opponent had won its first three games against very strong teams, the margin of the three victories totaled a mere four points. Their coach realized that he had to beat us by a wide margin to advance to the top and possible playoff opportunity. Everyone in the stadium soon realized that the coach would not substitute unless he had a 40-point margin. Although it was the hottest day of the year, dangerously hot and humid, he only dressed 28 players. It was the day of one-platoon football, and he did not want to be tempted to substitute no matter what the score became.

In the third quarter, his All-America lineman collapsed from heat exhaustion. There was considerable concern as he was carried off the field in poor condition. To the surprise of everyone, he was helped back on the field after just one play. I was sure our quarterback observed this and was positive he would run the next play over the semi-conscious lineman. This was accepted strategy, and I waited to see the reaction of the heat-stricken lineman. Our co-captain, who played opposite the player, called timeout. We were moving for a touchdown, and I questioned the timeout. Our next series of plays were away from the injured lineman. I realized what was happening and it was confirmed when our quarterback told me that our co-captain called the timeout to tell the team to run away from the helpless player. He reportedly told the team that we should not compound the coach's poor judgment in putting his player back in. "This isn't the way the game is played," he said. All of us congratulated our co-captain for making a good decision. In this case, the players had the sense of sportsmanship a coach lacked.

Today, our society values winning as never before, and colleges and universities, as well as high schools, are willing and ready to reward coaches who consistently win championships. The University of Texas football coach, Mack Brown, has set a standard for winning coaches with his $5 million plus perks salary. This in spite of budget cutting at the university. Many respected sport figures emphasize the importance of winning when they say: "Winning isn't everything, it's the only thing," "Defeat is worst than death," "Nice guys finish last," and "To play the game, you have to have fire in you." Parents along with coaches play a huge part in calculating the "winning at all costs" attitude that can lead to brutality in sport (Appenzeller, 1985).

Winning Is Not the "Only Thing"

Vince Lombardi, a Green Bay Packers Hall of Fame coach, was quoted for years by people in all walks of life. Perhaps his most used quote was: "Winning is not the most important thing, it's the only thing." Quarterback Bart Starr said that Lombardi was quoted incorrectly, and that instead Lombardi had actually said, "Striving for victory is the only thing." Quite a difference!

Winning at All Costs a Reality in World Cup Games

North Korea, in the 2010 World Cup, its first since 1966, lost all three group games. Upon returning to North Korea, the team was subjected to public humiliation and forced to stand on a stage in the Peoples Palace of Culture as "400 government officials, students and journalists watched the six-hour ordeal." Coach Kim Jong-Hun was relegated to a construction job and expelled from the Worker's Party of Korea (Weir, 2010).

Other countries reacted negatively to failure after the World Cup Games. In France, all members of the team were dumped. Iraq has a history of beating and even killing players who failed to win. A source from South Korea said that the North Korea players could have been punished more severely, since past bad performances led coaches and athletes to be sent to prison camps (Weir, 2010).

Fifth Downs Fifty Years Apart: Two Coaches' Approaches

Murray Sperber, a professor at Indiana University in English and American Studies, was also a noted sport historian and author. Sperber wrote several books in which he looked critically at sport and education. In 1998, he wrote *Onward to Victory: The Crisis that Shaped College Sports*. In this book, he recalls two similar situations that were treated completely differently by two outstanding coaches that viewed winning differently: Carl Snavely, Cornell University's former football coach, and Bill McCartney, Colorado University's football coach.

In 1940, Ivy League schools competed for national championships. Cornell University, after beating Ohio State to remain undefeated, played Dartmouth for top ranking in the national poll. Underdog Dartmouth led 3–0 with a minute to go in the game. With Cornell at the Dartmouth goal line, Dartmouth held on four downs. However, confusion over the downs led the officials to rule that Cornell had a fourth down, although in reality it was a fifth down. Cornell scored on the fifth down and won the game. The following Monday, the movie newsreel film proved that the referee had given Cornell an extra down and that the touchdown came on the fifth down. The referee apologized, but he and officials of the Eastern Intercollegiate Athletic Association said that the rule prohibited a change of the 7–3 score and Cornell's victory. Cornell's athletics director and head football coach Carl Snavely "waived the victory and their hopes of a national championship" and sent a telegram to Dartmouth that read as follows: "In view of the conclusions reached by the officials that the Cornell touchdown was scored on the fifth down, Cornell relinquishes claim to the victory and extends congratulations to Dartmouth" (Sperber, 1998).

The action taken by athletics director James Lynch and Coach Carl Snavely was gracious. As one might expect, people all over the United States applauded Cornell's giving up the opportunity to finish undefeated and for a possible national championship. Sperber wrote that the action of Cornell's athletics director and head football coach was classic football and the way everyone wanted the game to be played.

Fifty years later, a similar situation occurred in the Big Eight Game between Colorado and Missouri. Colorado scored on a fifth down against Missouri to win the game and co-national championship with Georgia Tech. The difference between Snavely's decision to refuse to accept a win that came on a fifth down and Colorado's unwillingness to forfeit the game, thereby winning the game and the national championship, was Bill McCartney, Colorado's coach and leader of "The Promise Keepers," a religious organization. McCartney argued, "Only the Lord can judge me," and "I'm confident HE will find that we did the right thing" (Sperber, 1998). Today, sports fans everywhere continue to discuss the actions that both coaches took in the controversial fifth down situation.

"The Beauty of Athletics"

Gary Frederick served at Central Washington University for 40 years. He coached baseball and women's basketball for 11 years, he was assistant football coach for 17 years and athletics director for 18 years. Frederick, at 70 years of age, was in his 14th year as the women's softball coach, when a home run led to something unbelievable, something that spoke to "the beauty of athletics" (Prince, 2008).

Central Washington University was playing Western Oregon University (WOU) in a softball doubleheader. After a loss to WOU in the first game, the Wildcats needed to win to make the NCAA's Division II playoffs. WOU was on a ten-game winning streak at the time of the doubleheader. Western Oregon's Sara Tucholsky, a 5'2" senior, was getting a hard time from a group of guys who had heckled her unmercifully. A career .153 hitter, Tucholsky hit a long ball that cleared the outfield fence for a three-run home run, the first of her career. As she sprinted toward first base, she watched the ball go over the outfield fence and missed tagging the base. When she attempted to return and touch first base, Tucholsky collapsed with severe pain in her knee. Her first base coach urged her to crawl back and touch the base or be ruled out. In unbearable pain, Tucholsky crawled back to the base. Western Oregon's coach rushed to the field to talk to the umpires, and was told that she could put in a substitute for Tucholsky but she could not get credit for a home run, only a single. The umpire said that according to the rules Tucholsky could not be assisted by her teammates. "But it is her only home run in four years. She is going to kill me if we sub and take it away," her coach said (Prince, 2008).

Mallory Holtman, the greatest softball player in Central Washington's history, volunteered a simple, selfless solution for her opponent's dilemma. She asked the officials what would happen if her Central Washington teammates carried Tucholsky around the bases. There is nothing in the rule book that prohibits help from opponents, so Holtman and a teammate carried Tucholsky around the bases, giving her the opportunity to touch each base with her other, uninjured leg. When Holtman and Tucholsky reached home plate, they saw the entire Western Oregon team in tears. The Central Washington team, coach and many in the stands were also crying. Western Oregon held on to win the close game and Central Washington was eliminated from further competition.

Following the game, Holtman said, "In the end, it is not about winning or losing so much. It was about this girl. She hit it over the fence and was in pain and she deserved a home run." Holtman also commented, "We are not going to remember if we won or lost, we are going to remember this kind of stuff that shows the character of our team." Frederick later received clarification of NCAA rules, which do allow a substitute to run for a player who is injured after a home run (Prince, 2008).

An Important Change of Policy

Previously in this chapter, reference has been made to an Asian Goodwill Track and Field Tour. Many acts of good sportsmanship were exhibited on the tour; one more act may have been our most important and deserves mentioning.

One of our competitions was in Bangkok, Thailand, against the Thai National Team. Once again, our men were eager to perform well and represent out country in a proud way. We had worked out prior to the meet and we felt the meet would be extremely close. However, to our surprise, we won 12 of the 13 events. The only loss was in the 800-meter run, which we lost by a step. The Thai runner ran the fastest 800-meters ever and broke the Thai record.

After the meet, our team asked if they could have a meeting with the coaches. The members of our team decided that rather than going "head to head" against their newly found Asian friends, they wanted to train with them and demonstrate track and field tips and training methods. They felt that eliminating the competition would improve our effectiveness. The decision to go forward with that approach was unanimous and we were excited about the new policy in Hong Kong and the Philippines over the next few weeks.

As coaches, we were proud of the sentiments of our team, as "winning at all costs" became a thing of the past. At the conclusion, we all agreed that we made the right decision on behalf of our country.

Things You Can't Forget

I asked my 27-year-old granddaughter to tell me about any incident involving ethical behavior or lack of it during her career in sport. She immediately responded that one incident made an impression on her that has been impossible to forget.

As a fifth grader, she was a member of a girls' soccer team that was playing a neighborhood school team. Her coach was frustrated by a rule that prohibited him from substituting his star player unless there was an injury to one of the team members. During a timeout, he instructed one of his players, who was not very good at soccer, to fall down and clutch her leg and fake an injury. He told everyone to join in the act and pretend to be helpful to the girl who would act out a painful injury. The girl performed brilliantly, as did her supporting players, and the substitution was made. My granddaughter could not remember whether her team won or lost the game, but she never forgot the strategy of her coach, who left an indelible impression on all her teammates. As a cheer coach at a NCAA Division I school, she insists that the incident and conduct of her fifth grade coach still stands out in her memory. Was this a good strategy and part of the game, or was it an example of unethical behavior?

"Don't Tell Anyone What I Did"

I asked an outstanding freshman baseball player the same question I asked my granddaughter. He immediately replied, "I sure can tell you one that happened this year [2009]." He told me of his star pitcher at a NCAA Division I university baseball team who only attended three or four classes. The "star" did not show up for the final examination in physical education. All the classmates heard that he took a special exam later and received a very high grade. The instructor met with the class and told them not to tell anyone about her action on behalf of the "star" player. "If you do," she said, "I can be fired." The athlete told me, "All of us in the class felt that this instructor had been unfair to the rest of us who came to class and tried to do right." It is obvious that this instructor wanted the university's baseball team to win, apparently at any cost.

An Unethical Grading System

One of our football student-athletes was an exceptional student. He was clearly the top student in class and hoped to get his master's degree after graduation. He came to see me and I knew something was very wrong when I saw the expression on his face. He was certain he had earned an A in a class and was greatly disturbed when he received a B. He had been to see his instructor, who was also a football coach on our staff. The coach told him that he did in fact earn an A, but he had to give the A's to several scholarship athletes who needed an A to remain eligible in several sports. The coach said, "I can't give too many A's so I had to give you a B." Needless to say, this coach never taught another academic class at our college and his contract was not renewed the following year.

"Winning Was the Last Thing on Our Minds"

Marion Kirby, a North Carolina High School Hall of Fame football coach at Page High School in Greensboro, North Carolina, had an unexpected experience that caused him to make an important decision. Page was trailing a strong North Mecklenburg High School team in Jamieson Stadium by seven points. With three minutes remaining in the hard fought game, Page began a rally that enabled them to move down the field and get in scoring position. Suddenly, Coach Kirby sensed that something was terribly wrong when he saw the face of one of the officials. When he turned toward the sidelines, he saw Milton "Buck" Hines, a veteran and highly respected official, lying face down on the turf. At that time, Page High School, as the host team, had three medical doctors at the game with two certified athletic trainers and one volunteer athletic trainer. The outstanding medical staff worked on Hines for over 40 minutes in a valiant attempt to save the official, who had suffered cardiac arrest. It was apparent to all that Hines had suffered a fatal heart attack and was dead.

Coach Kirby, whose team was in position to win the game, made a decision that was later criticized by some fans to call the game, even though his team could have won the game. The next day he and the athletics director for the Guilford County School System went to the home of Hines to offer condolences to his family. Hines was a Hall of Famer at Guilford College and his daughter was also a student of mine at the college.

Coach Kirby has a special letter from Hines's daughter that he treasures as part of his long career as a coach. There were those who were critical of his decision not to continue playing, but Coach Kirby never gave that a second thought. "In light of things that night, we lost a great man, winning was the last thing on our minds and that of our players." His record was 219–51–2 in 23 seasons at Page and he won a record 46 straight games. He also won four state championships, 18 playoff appearances and 14 conference titles.

Ben Hartman's Nightmare

Ben Hartman, a field goal kicker, became East Carolina's all-time leading scorer at the Liberty Bowl against Southeastern Conference opponent Arkansas. This should have been a night to celebrate his achievement, but it turned out to be one of the lowest moments in his career as an exceptional place-kicker. Hartman had three chances to win the game for East Carolina, a major victory in the school's program. Hartman missed two 39-yard field goals with 1:03 left in regulation. He then missed a three-yard winner in overtime. Hartman finished the night one for five, an exception to his usual accuracy.

The result was a loss to Arkansas, 20–17. Instead of a young man who should have gone down in East Carolina history, Hartman has been the victim of an ugly backlash from disappointed fans. Anti-Hartman Web sites appeared and the comments were derogatory and menacing. He made the mistake of turning on his cell phone. His number had been given to the public via the internet and his voice mailbox was full of hatred comments that were too obscene to print. One such message read: "I'm going to kill your mother and brother in front of you and then kill you." Someone posted on Facebook: "I hope you burn in hell, Ben Hartman." The reaction to a true hero's failure to make three game-winning field goals in a Liberty Bowl is very sad and unfortunate for all concerned, but it is also evidence of the winning at all costs mentality.

"I Didn't Catch the Ball—I Trapped It!"

Bud Wilkinson's Oklahoma football team was on a winning streak when they played a Texas Christian University (TCU) team determined to pull an upset. Late in the game, TCU's quarterback threw a pass to wide receiver Tim Crouch. The crowd realized TCU would win the game that Oklahoma led 6–0. Tim Crouch gave the ball to the referee and surprisingly said, "I didn't catch the ball—I trapped it!" Oklahoma escaped from an upset win by TCU and kept its wining streak intact. When asked about his action, Crouch said, "I didn't want to win a game when I did not catch the ball within the rules." Many people criticized Crouch for his decision to admit that his catch was really trapping the ball. This act of sportsmanship is an interesting ethical question and one that has been discussed by many people for years.

Ethical Questions

1. Discuss the fifth down situations at the Cornell and Colorado games. What would you have done if you were Cornell or Colorado?
2. Comment on the Central Washington versus Western Oregon softball game.

3. Comment on the "winning at all costs" attitude.
4. In the Oklahoma versus Texas Tech game, did you agree with Tim Crouch's action? Should he have told the referee that he trapped the ball?

Epilogue

The Roman poet Martial wrote *Nec tecum possum vivere sine te*, which means, "I am able to live neither with you nor without you." This describes America's love affair with sport. *Ethical Behavior in Sport* documents many events over a 70-year period to illustrate the state of affairs of sports, both good and bad, as they exist in the 21st century.

Many historians believe that there is a dangerous parallel between the fall of the Roman Empire and the direction the United States is heading in its sports programs. There is a strong belief that Rome left more than its legal genius as a legacy to follow. The historians suggest that America needs to heed the lessons exemplified by the Romans in the sports arena.

Arnold Beisser, in *Madness and Sport*, deplores the fact that "while Romans cheered their games and gladiators, there empire was crumbling." Beisser warned that:

> The lessons of ancient Rome should be justification for close examination of America's athletic interest and motivation. There are many parallels between our sports and those of the declining years of the Roman Empire. A single coliseum may have served Roman spectators; today thousands of stadiums and their satellite television sets serve about everyone in the United States. (*Sports and the Courts* 1980)

Sports in America, with its mega stadiums and arenas and unprecedented growth and popularity, have led to an emphasis on winning at all costs, and, unfortunately, to unethical behavior, greed, uncontrolled spending and multi-million dollar salaries. Many of these incidents raise questions for the reader to discuss, as they mirror society as we know it. On the other hand, there are numerous examples of courage, honor, loyalty and high moral conduct in sport.

Duke professor Edwin Cady described the relationship between spectators and sports as "an affair of the people who mirror society in the United States." Cady raises the question, "Where indeed can you find and hear a hard hat who never finished high school and a scientist with three degrees stand side by side and sing the foolish and vulgar tune of *alma mater* with fervor and unction for a Bach Chorale sung by believers?" (*News & Record* 1978).

Wilt Browning, the former sports editor of the *News & Record*, wrote an outstanding column based on the research of Dr. Tom Appenzeller, professor at Catawba College. Browning's column based on Appenzeller's findings regarding the status of sport in America sends an important message to all who are involved in sport.

"The 60-Year Torment of Chicken Little" by Wilt Browning

There it is in black and white, confirmation that Chicken Little is right. In the world of college athletics, especially football, "the sky is falling." The confirmation comes in a study by Thomas Appenzeller, a professor at Catawba College and the son of Dr. Herb Appenzeller, former athletic director at Guilford College. The younger Appenzeller was careful in his analysis of the state of college football and what writers, educators and coaches—the Chicken Littles among us, I suppose—have been fretting about. It is not a pretty picture. Zeroing in on the emotions which reached print in one of the single years included in the study, Appenzeller's findings are the reflections of a nightmare. Here are some of them: "Never before had football as a spectator sport been so popular, never had the public been so insatiable, and never had the gate receipts been so high." College football had become "forever linked with money." He discovered concern that college football was "becoming too professional, that it was becoming more than just a game."

Appenzeller, in the report, quotes the lament of the President of the United States: "Athletics is the side show of academic life, but today football tends to be the main show." Ah, and he discovered that "a majority of college football players did not enjoy playing the game." There was in the Appenzeller report these haunting words of an unidentified college football player: "You can't play the game and smile both." And exploitation. There is in the Appenzeller report this charge: "The innocent athlete found himself not so much a sportsman as a benefactor of his alma mater. He was exploited ... The public paid immense sums for the privilege of seeing him muff a punt or sprain a knee." And stuff that must make the NCAA cringe like: "One alumnus of a certain college discovered a promising young football player in a prep school and persuaded this youth to come to his alma mater. The athlete made a brilliant record on the gridiron but did not show up for his sophomore year." The young star wound up on another campus, playing for another college football team.

"What did you change for?" The student answered, "$1,000 this year, $2,000 next year and $3,000 in my senior year in addition to my tuition." ... He quotes an educator in another ... portion of the report concerning the evils of recruiting. "It is a disgrace to modern college life, securing promising athletic material by competitive bidding for high school athletes. [Recruiters] have begun to outbid each other while the high school athlete stands back, receives all the bids and chooses the highest, and best offer."

Appenzeller's report goes on. It addresses the relationship between athletes and other students. "The need to bring in gifted athletes resulted in abuses within the system," he wrote. Not omitted in the academic review of college football were coaches and the pressure under which they operate. "The football coach ... was also caught up in the commercial, or shall we say profit-making, enterprise that was dominant in college football. If the coach did not win, he was fired, and if he won, he advanced to another position where critics said he was being paid too much."

Not surprisingly, Appenzeller uncovered concern about coaching salaries. "One source of evils of present day football," he quoted one educator, "is the high salaries of coaches and directors." The educator, according to the report, was "in favor of making every such official a member of the college faculty with a salary no greater than that paid to professors and corresponding length of service. "As long as coaches ... have before them the possibility of very high salaries, there will be plenty of reasons found for their favoring unethical practices to produce winning teams."

But one publication, addressing the subject according to Appenzeller, pointed out that "a winning coach had greater cash value than the president of a university." Lordy! And the alumni. They'll do anything to fire a losing coach and will stop at nothing to help the old alma mater land a winner. Furthermore, "if the coach lost, no consideration was taken for the character of the coach; he may have had the finest influence in shaping the characteristics of his pupils."

Among Appenzeller's conclusions was this: "The uneasy suspicion smoldered in the breast of many serious minded persons that there was something distinctly rotten in the state of college football." And he pointed out that there was a move afoot calling for "desperate remedies" to cleanse college athletics.

Oh ... maybe I failed to mention up front that Appenzeller's study was based upon the 1925—one, nine, two, five—season.

References

Chapter 1

Appenzeller, Herb. (2003). *Managing Sport and Risk Management Strategies* (2nd ed.). Durham, NC: Carolina Academic Press.

Appenzeller, Herb and Tom Appenzeller. (2008). *Successful Sport Management*. Durham, NC: Carolina Academic Press.

Brennan, Christine. (2011, March 9). Armor of integrity falls from Ohio State coach Jim Tressel. *USA Today*.

Debbie Yow warns sport agents. (2010, July 14). *News & Record*.

Football Bowl Subdivision coaches salaries for 2010. (2010, December 9). *USA Today*.

Haglan, Dennis. (2011, May 25). Letter: Rules and regulations that govern college sports are a problem. *The Washington Post*.

Knight Commission on Intercollegiate Athletics. (2010, June). *Restoring the balance: Dollars, values, and the future of college sports*. Miami, FL: John S. And James L. Knight Foundation.

Malekoff, Robert. (2010, August 4). Agents not only threat in college sports. *Charlotte Observer*.

Maltz, David. (2010, August 18). Up, up and away. *Inside Higher Ed*.

McCormack, Mark H. (2000). *Staying Street Smart in the Internet Age: What Hasn't Changed About the Way We Do Business*. New York, NY: Viking Press.

Regulating sports agents: a problem. (2010, July 13). *News & Record*.

Sport administration described. (2009, Winter). *Interscholastic Athletic Administration*.

Status of sports today. (2010, November 10). *News & Record*.

Tide's Dareus ruled ineligible for 2 games. (2010, September 3). *The Associated Press*.

Whiteside, Kelly. (2011, March 22). Ohio State case casts doubt on power of school presidents. *USA Today*.

Wieberg, Steve. (2011, January 15). NCAA considers academic crackdown in basketball, football. *USA Today.*

Chapter 2

45–0 in third inning. (2010, April 25). *News & Record.*

An analysis of salaries for college basketball coaches. (2010, April 1). *USA Today.*

Appenzeller, Herb. (2003). *Managing Sport and Risk Management Strategies* (2nd ed.). Durham, NC: Carolina Academic Press.

Appenzeller, Herb. (1987). *Pride in the Past: Guilford Athletics, 1837–1987.* Greensboro, NC: Quaker Club, Guilford College.

Appenzeller, Herb. (1985). *Sports and Law: Contemporary Issues.* Charlottesville, VA: LEXIS Law Pub.

Applebome, Peter. (2009, October 21). In basketball, troubles spill off the court. *The New York Times.*

Berkowitz, Steve. (2009, December 2). As teams achieve, college football coaches see payoffs. *USA Today.*

Berkowitz, Steve. (2011, June 14). Auburn football staff to make $4 million; Gus Malzahn receives big raise. *USA Today.*

Berkowitz, Steve. (2010, March 10). Salaries spike for college football assistants, successful coaches. *USA Today.*

Binghamton coach claims discrimination for his firing. (2009, October 15). *From the Gym to the Jury.*

Brown, Marquita. (2010, November 12). Officials mum on fate of coach accused of whipping players. *USA Today.*

Carey, Jack. (2010, April 28). Ex-coaches try other courts for wins: when firing leads to litigation. *USA Today.*

Carey, Jack. (2009, December 15). South Florida to probe claim that football coach slapped player. *USA Today.*

Coach presents boy with the "Cry Baby Award." (2004). *From the Gym to the Jury.*

Coach sues parent for defamation. (2003, August 7). *Good Morning America.*

Cost of football questioned. (2008, September 28). *News-Sentinel.*

Curliss, J. Andrew. (2010, June 9). Coach K's pay: $4M. *The News & Observer.*

Do coaches' salaries compare to entertainers? (2010, June 10). *News & Record.*

Dyed hair and playing time problems. (1999, Vol. 8, No. 2). *From the Gym to the Jury.*

Elliott, Doug. (2007, May 10). An unusual proposal. *News & Record.*

Football coach with history of player abuse back on the field. (2010, April 13). *FOXNews.com.*

Funk, Abigail. (2009, July). Coach-athlete boundary lines. *Athletic Management.*

Funk, Abigail. (2009, October). Signed, sealed, and … debating. *Athletic Management.*

Grade changing. (2009, November 15). *San Antonio Light.*

Harris v. McCray, 87 So. 2d 188 (Miss. 2003).

Helling, Dave and Diane Stafford. (2009, November 18). Aggressive coaching is a growing problem, but how much is too much? *The Kansas City Star.*

I'll be suing you coach. (2003, August 7). *ABC News.*

Jenkins, Sally. (2009, November 29). Does football cost too much? *Parade.*

McGhee v. Miller, 753 S.W. 2d 354 (Tenn. 1988).

Miller, Jeff. (2010, June 23). Disgraced ex-Baylor coach Bliss gets a shot at redemption. *USA Today.*

Motivation or abuse? (2009, November 2). *News & Record.*

Phelps, Mike. (2010, January 11). Blowout sparks fight, controversy. *Athletic Management.*

Rutherford v. Cypress Falls Independent Sch. Dist., U.S. Dist. Court, So. Division of Texas, Civil Action No. 96-3953, Feb. 1988.

Schrotenboer, Brent. (2010, March 1). Point Loma Nazarene dropping 4 sports to stay equitable. *The San Diego Union-Tribune.*

Smith, Alphonso. (2010, Winter). Coach Hood changed my life. *Tribute to Wake Forest.*

Vawter, Vince. (2010, January 30). Citizen's Voice: Put caps on college coaches' salaries. *Knoxville News Sentinel.*

Wieberg, Steve. (2009, October 12). Thompson strongly supports Binghamton coach Broadus. *USA Today.*

Winning coach in 100-point win fired. (2009, January 27). *The Oak Ridger.*

Chapter 3

ACC signs deal for $1.86 billion. (2010, Vol. 20, No. 4). *From the Gym to the Jury.*

Appenzeller, Herb. (1975). *Athletics and the Law.* Charlottesville, VA: The Michie Co.

Appenzeller, Herb. (2003). *Managing Sport and Risk Management Strategies* (2nd ed.). Durham, NC: Carolina Academic Press.

Appenzeller, Herb and Tom Appenzeller. (2008). *Successful Sport Management*. Durham, NC: Carolina Academic Press.

Berkowitz, Steve. (2010, September 29). California to cut five varsity sports, including baseball. *USA Today*.

Berkowitz, Steve, Jodi Upton, Michael McCarthy and Jack Gillum. (2010, October 6). How student fees boost college sports amid rising budgets. *USA Today*.

Bohls, Kirk and Mark Rosner. (2010, June 24). Big obstacles, big money await Longhorn network. *American Statesman*.

Brady, Erik. (2008, April 9). Pickens backs Okla. State at all costs. *USA Today*.

Brennan, Christine. (2011, March 30). NCAA sports in 2010–11: a school year for scandal. *USA Today*.

Carey, Jack. (2010, June 18). Knight Commission: Athletics vs. academic spending too unbalanced. *USA Today*.

Carey, Jack and Steve Wieberg. (2009, November 3). Faculty group wants Cal to end subsidies for athletics department. *USA Today*.

Cherry, Blair. (1951, October 20). Why I quit coaching. *The Saturday Evening Post*.

Finger, Mike. (2011, June 15). Longhorn Network developing programs. *The Houston Chronicle*.

Garcia, Marlen. (2010, June 12). New alliances, league affiliation ready to reshape college sports. *USA Today*.

Georgia signs $92.8 million media rights deal. (1999, Vol. 8, No. 2). *From the Gym to the Jury*.

Hacker, Andrew and Claudia Dreifus. (2010, September 12). Colleges: where the money goes. *Los Angeles Times*.

Hacker, Andrew and Claudia Dreifus. (2010). *Higher Education?: How Colleges Are Wasting Our Money and Failing Our Kids–and What We Can Do About It*. New York, NY: Holt/Times Books.

Hiestand, Michael. (2010, June 16). Top college football schools need a league of their own. *USA Today*.

High school signs deal with Nike. (2008, March 12). *News-Sentinel*.

Iowa Hotel Association v. State Board of Regents, 114 N.W.2d 539 (1962).

Laguna development signs $2.5 million pact with UNM athletics. (2008, February 14). *The Associated Press*.

Lewis, Michael. (2007, November 11). Serfs of the turf. *The New York Times*.

McCarthy, Michael and Steve Wieberg. (2009, November 13). SEC, Big Ten set the standard for media rights money. *USA Today*.

Michael Jordan aids middle schools. (2010, Vol. 21, No. 4). *From the Gym to the Jury*.

Morgan, Marlon W. (2009, August 24). In reversal, beer to be sold at Memphis Tigers football games. *Memphis Commercial Appeal.*

Moye v. Board of Trustees of University of South Carolina, 177 S.E.2d (S.C. 1970).

Murphy, Austin. (2010, June 21). What just happened to college football. *Sports Illustrated.*

Nike deal: just do it bigger. (2011, Vol. 21, No. 4). *From the Gym to the Jury.*

North Carolina legislature attempted to save booster clubs $9.4 million. (2010, June 20). *News & Record.*

O'Toole, Thomas. (2010, August 19). WAC commissioner Karl Benson fires back, says league will target new members. *USA Today.*

Patton, Maurice. (2008, May 21). Vandy commits $60M to sports. *The Tennessean.*

Ramirez v. Malone, 141 S.W.2d 713 (Tex. 1940).

Smith, Erick. (2011, May 17). Fiesta Bowl keeps license but organization will be on probation. *USA Today.*

Smith, Erick. (2010, June 17). Utah officially accepts invitation to become 12th member of the Pac-10. *USA Today.*

Sperber, Murray. (2000). *Beer and Circus: How Big-Time College Sports Is Crippling Undergraduate Education.* New York, NY: Henry Holt and Company.

Sperber, Murray. (1998). *Onward to Victory: The Crises that Shaped College Sports.* New York, NY: Henry Holt and Company.

Spurrier's unusual proposal. (2011, June 4). *News & Record.*

Superconference chaos postponed, for now. (2010, Vol. 20, No. 4). *From the Gym to the Jury.*

Tennessee wants out of UNC series. (2010, August 18). *News & Record.*

Tresolini, Kevin. (2010, June 21). Del. school home to 13-year-old USC recruit comes under fire. *USA Today.*

Tysiac, Ken. (2009, September 13). Hotel stays for teams are under the gun. *The Raleigh News & Observer.*

UNC signs lucrative pact with Nike. (2010, Vol. 21, No. 4). *From the Gym to the Jury.*

USC athletics assist academics. (2010, December 27). *News-Sentinel.*

Wetzel, Dan, Josh Peter and Jeff Passan. (2010). *Death to the BCS: The Definitive Case Against the Bowl Championship Series.* New York, NY: Gotham Books.

White, Ryan. (2004, April 18). The high price of recruiting. *The Oregonian.*

Wieberg, Steve. (2011, May 11). Fiesta Bowl to stay in BCS after being hit with $1 million fine. *USA Today.*

Wieberg, Steve. (2011, March 30). NCAA president: time to discuss players getting sliver of revenue pie. *USA Today.*

Wieberg, Steve and Steve Berkowitz. (2009, April 2). NCAA, colleges pushing the envelope with sports marketing. *USA Today.*

Witt, Gerald. (2011, April 2). Fiesta event drew ACC coaches, ADs. *News & Record.*

Chapter 4

Acosta, R. Vivian and Linda Jean Carpenter. Title IX in a nutshell. http://www.acostacarpenter.org/Title%20IX%20in%20a%20nutshell.pdf.

Alaskan girl wins state H.S. wrestling title over boys. (2006, February 6). *Sports Illustrated.*

Appenzeller, Herb. (2003). *Managing Sport and Risk Management Strategies* (2nd ed.). Durham, NC: Carolina Academic Press.

Appenzeller, Herb. (1983). *The Right to Participate: The Law and Individuals with Handicapping Conditions in Physical Education and Sport.* Charlottesville, VA: Michie Co.

Appenzeller, Herb. (2002). Roses in December. In Jack Canfield & Mark Victor Hansen (Eds.), *Chicken Soup for the Teacher's Soul* (pp. 34–36). Deerfield Beach, FL: Health Communications, Inc.

Appenzeller, Herb. (1980). *Sports and the Courts.* Charlottesville, VA: LEXIS Law Pub.

Batista, Paul. (2002). Balancing the First Amendment's establishment and free exercise clauses: a rebuttal to Alexander & Alexander. *Journal of Legal Aspects of Sport.*

Belk, Jeremy. (2010, October 30). Soddy-Daisy group prays at football game. *Chattanooga Times Free Press.*

Bishop v. Colaw, 450 F.2d 1069 (8th Cir.1971).

Brayton, Ed. (2009, July 28). Fired wrestling coach files suit against Dearborn Fordson. *The Michigan Messenger.*

Chase, Chris. (2009, October 6). Raiders cornerback thinks he was flagged because of his religion. *Shutdown Corner: A Yahoo! Sports Blog.*

Court voids kicker's award. (2002, November 16). *The News & Observer.*

Duke University ordered to pay female kicker $2 million. (2000, October 13). *The News & Observer.*

Evans and Redding v. Looney, No. 77-6052-CV-SJ, U.S. Dist. Court (for the W.D. of Missouri, Sept. 2, 1977).

FHSAA settles Title IX suit. (2009, October 15). *Miami Herald.*

Funding for injured veterans approved by USOC. (2009, October 21). *USA Today.*

Galloway, Jim. (2009, September 30). No more on running through Scripture on football Friday. *Political Insider with Jim Galloway*.

Glier, Ray. (2010, August 5). Savannah State faces two lawsuits with race at center. *USA Today*.

Halley, Jim. (2009, August 6). Handicapped coach inspires from the sidelines. *USA Today*.

Hollonbeck v. United States Olympic Committee. Nos. 07-1053, 07-1056. January 16, 2008.

Katz, Andy. (2010, May 18). Negedu moves on after brush with death. *ESPN.com*.

Kirkpatrick, Christopher D. (2010, August 1). Whitmer basketball coach Bruce Smith faces accusations of bias. *Toledo Blade*.

Klemko, Robert. (2009, September 16). Deaf athletes hurdle barriers, achieve goals in college sports. *USA Today*.

LA Clippers fined. (2009, Vol. 20, No. 5). *From the Gym to the Jury*.

Lieber-Steeg, Jill. (2008, June 18). Fresno State settles suit with ex-coach Johnson-Klein. *USA Today*.

Man with cerebral palsy. (2009, August 7). *USA Today*.

McCarthy, Michael. (2009, October 22). Kevin Laue inspires, motivates on the court at Manhattan. *USA Today*.

McNabb, David. (1992, April 21). UT orders coach not to use player with heart problem. *The Dallas Morning News*.

Morino, Douglas. (2009, September 14). Title IX complaint brings improvements. *Daily Breeze*.

Mullen, Bryan. (2009, September 5). Minority coaches shut out. *The Tennessean*.

NFL urges equal access to women. (2010, October 26). *Charlotte Observer*.

Roberts, Steven V. (1978, June 19). The handicapped are emerging as a vocal political action group. *The New York Times*.

Schrotenboer, Brent. (2009, December 4). Former coach at Mesa wins Title IX-based suit. *The San Diego Union-Tribune*.

Smith, Cameron. (2010, October 11). Arkansas player with cerebral palsy scores in wheelchair. *Prep Rally: A Yahoo! Sports Blog*.

Steinbach, Paul. (2010, July). College coaches still lack Title IX knowledge. *Athletic Business*.

Storms, Tommie. (2007, Summer, Vol. 23, No. 3). The wheels of justice turn in adapted interscholastic sport—making progress. *Palaestra*.

Supreme Court denies review of Hollonbeck. (2008, March 1). *STLToday.com*.

Wagner, Dennis. (2010, October 15). Blind hikers know no limits at Grand Canyon. *USA Today*.

Ward, Paula Reed. (2009, December 22). Slippery Rock University agrees to additional Title IX improvements. *Pittsburgh Post-Gazette*.

White, Joseph. (2010, March 12). DC high school football team gets female coach. *The Associated Press*.

Witt, Gerald. (2010, February 28). Guilford player nearly died playing a game he loves and had to fight for the right to play baseball. *News & Record*.

Yellow Springs v. Ohio High School Athletic Association, 647 F.2d 651, 653 (6th Cir.1981).

Chapter 5

Alic, Steve. (2010, November 10). USA Football Rules Committee approves four rule changes for 2011 youth football rulebook. *USA Football*.

Appenzeller, Herb. (2005). *Risk Management in Sport: Issues and Strategies* (2nd ed.). Durham, NC: Carolina Academic Press.

Awareness of sickle cell trait saves athlete. (2010, October 26). *News & Record*.

Coach defends heat training. (2010, August 14). *News & Record*.

CPR saves coach's life. (2007, Vol. 18, No. 2). *From the Gym to the Jury*.

Defibrillator saves life. (1997, Vol. 9, No. 2). *From the Gym to the Jury*.

Family of Korey Stringer suing Riddell. (2009, July 14). *USA Today*.

Fitzpatrick, Frank and Sam Wood. (2009, December 1). La Salle to pay $7.5 million to brain-injured football player. *The Philadelphia Inquirer*.

Healy, Melissa. (2010, August 29). ER visits for concussions soar among child athletes. *Los Angeles Times*.

House panel acts on student athlete concussions. (2010, September 16). *The Associated Press*.

I'll make the team or die trying. (2010, August 21). *News & Record*.

Keating, Peter. (2010, June 29). Researchers find brain trauma in Henry. *ESPN The Magazine*.

Kendall, Adam. (2009, September–October). Concussion in sports. *Sports KidsPlay*.

Lawsuit over high school football player's death settled. (2010, September 17). *The Associated Press*.

McCloskley, John. (2007, February 17). Heart device couldn't be found. *Houston Chronicle*.

Mihoces, Gary. (2010, August 20). In NFL training camps, heatstroke awareness rises. *USA Today*.

Missouri to pay $2M to Aaron O'Neal's family in death settlement. (2009, March 13). *The Associated Press*.

Mueller, Frederick O. (2008, Vol. 19, No. 3). Heat Stress and athletic participation. *From the Gym to the Jury.*

National Athletic Trainers Association. (2009, June). Preseason heat-acclima-
tization guidelines for secondary school athletics. *Journal of Athletic Training.*

NFL officials to take proactive role in guarding players from big hits. (2010,
August 6). *The Associated Press.*

NFL, union begin approving independent neurologists for each team. (2009,
November 23). *The Associated Press.*

Pickeral, Robbi. (2009, August 12). North Carolina football players testing pill
that can give body temperature readings. *The News & Observer.*

Prep running back suffers post-TD cardiac arrest. (2010, September 15). *AB
Newswire.*

Rawe, Julie. (2007, September 6). Football's $1,000 Helmet. *TIME Magazine.*

Schmutz, James. (2010, May 20). *The Impact of Concussions on High School
Athletes.* Testimony before the US House of Representatives Committee
on Education and Labor.

Smith, Jeniece. (2010, June 11). Trial date set in athlete's case against Ashford.
Clinton Herald.

Spokane Valley football player dies of injury. (2009, September 28). *The Associated
Press.*

Sport physicals need to include an electrocardiogram. (2010, July 15). *The
Morning News.*

Stanmyre, Matthew and Jackie Friedman. (2010, January 4). Kids and concussions: the effects of head injuries in young athletes. *Newark Star-Ledger.*

Walker, Don. (2010, July 13). Area study suggests more caution with athletes'
concussions. *Journal Sentinel.*

Chapter 6

Another view on free speech: curb lawsuit abuse. (2010, June 8). *USA Today.*

Appenzeller, Herb. (1975). *Athletics and the Law.* Charlottesville, VA: The
Michie Co.

Appenzeller, Herb. (2003). *Managing Sport and Risk Management Strategies*
(2nd ed.). Durham, NC: Carolina Academic Press.

Appenzeller, Herb. (1978). *Physical Education and the Law.* Charlottesville,
VA: LEXIS Law Pub.

Appenzeller, Herb. (2005). *Risk Management in Sport: Issues and Strategies*
(2nd ed.). Durham, NC: Carolina Academic Press.

Appenzeller, Herb. (1980). *Sports and the Courts*. Charlottesville, VA: LEXIS Law Pub.

Appenzeller, Herb. (1985). *Sports and Law: Contemporary Issues*. Charlottesville, VA: LEXIS Law Pub.

Braesch v. DePasquale, 265 N.W.2d 842 (Neb. Sup. Ct. 1978).

Brown v. Wells, 181 N.W.2d 708 (Minn. 1970).

Crace v. Kent State Univ., 185 Ohio App.3d 534, 2009-Ohio-6898.

Dunham v. Pulsifer, 312 F. Supp. 2d 411 (D. Vt. 1970).

Foley, Ryan. (2009, January 27). Cheerleading is a contact sport, Wis. court rules. *The Associated Press*.

Goss v. Lopez, 419 U.S. 565 (1975).

McFarlin v. Newport Special Sch. Dist., 980 F.2d 1208, 1211 (8th Cir.1992).

Neuhaus v. Torrey, 310 F.Supp. 192 (N.D. Cal. 1970).

New Jersey State Interscholastic Athletic Association Handbook. (2010).

Noffke v. Bakke, 308 Wis. 2d 410, 748 N.W.2d 195 (2008).

Our view on free speech: want to complain online? Look out. You might be sued. (2010, June 8). USA Today.

Students have a constitutional right. (1975, January 23). *Greensboro Daily News*.

Taylor v. Wake Forest University, 191 S.E.2d 379 (1972).

Thompson v. McNeill, 53 Ohio St.3d 102 (1990).

Welch v. Sudbury Youth Sport Soccer Association, 901 N.E.2d 1222 (Mass. 2009).

Wellsand v. Valpariso Community School Corp. Case No. 71 H122 (21U.S.D.C. Ind. 1971).

Chapter 7

Additional hazing incidents reported. (2008, Vol. 19, No. 5). *From the Gym to the Jury*.

Allan, Elizabeth & Mary Madden. (2008). *Hazing in View: College Students at Risk. Initial Findings from the National Study of Student Hazing*. www.hazingstudy.org.

Anderson, Charis. (2008, February 15). Family of hazing victim seeks $1 million from town. *The Standard-Times*.

Bell, Robert. (2008, January 29). Hazing prompts Asheboro to fire wrestling coach. *News & Record*.

Carroll, Michael S. and Daniel P. Connaughton. (2010, September 1). Bullying and legal liability. *Journal of Physical Education, Recreation and Dance*.

Catholic forfeits three women's lax games over party photos. (2006, August 8). *The Associated Press.*

Gonzalez, Marci. (2008, June 22.) High school students allege sexual hazing. *WPTV.com.*

Hazing leads to $3 million in medical bills. (2008, Vol. 19, No. 5). *From the Gym to the Jury.*

Hoover, Nadine & Norm Pollard. (2000). *Initiation Rites in American High Schools: A National Survey.* www.alfred.edu/hs_hazing.

Hoover, Nadine & Norm Pollard. (1999). *Initiation Rites and Athletics: A National Survey of NCAA Sports Teams.* Alfred University and Reidman Insurance Co., Inc.

Hopf, Joelle & John T. Wolohan. (2010, July). Title IX assists hazed high school student-athlete. *Athletic Business.*

Huckabee, Charles. (2008, December 2). 6 are arrested in possible hazing that put 2 Southern U. band members in hospital. *The Chronicle of Higher Education.*

Irvine, Martha. (2010, May 2). Teen's suicide prompts schools to take on bullying. *The Associated Press.*

Kalil, Mike & Todd Dewey. (2006, February 21). A special report: hazing. *Las Vegas Review-Journal.*

Lipkins, Susan. (2007, Fall). Hazing—kill the myth. *NFHS Coaches' Quarterly.*

Loudon, Bennett J. (2008, September 12). Henrietta justice hears RIT hazing case. *Rochester Democrat and Chronicle.*

Mack, Kristen. (2009, August 19). Paralyzed teen's parents sue Chicago school over alleged hazing. *Chicago Tribune.*

Mangan, Katherine. (2008, October 24). Texas fraternity ordered to pay $16.2-million to parents of pledge who died. *The Chronicle of Higher Education.*

Marblehead soccer coach hit by hazing claim. (2008, September 9). *The Daily Item.*

Matlock, Staci. (2008, September 3). Fourth student suspended in Robertson case. *The New Mexican.*

McGlone, Colleen. (2005). *Hazing in N.C.A.A. Division I Women's Athletics: An Exploratory Analysis.* Unpublished doctoral dissertation, University of New Mexico.

McGlone, Colleen & Nathan Martin. (2006, April). *Hazing and Sport Clubs: Are you and your athletes protected?* Presented at the National Intramural Recreational Sports Association Conference, Louisville, KY.

McGlone, Colleen. (2008, Vol. 19, No. 4). Hazy viewpoints: administrators' perceptions of hazing. *From the Gym to the Jury.*

Meyer, Ed. (2008, April 28). Tallmadge teen gets probation in hazing case. *Beacon Journal.*

Mullen, RoNeisha. (2008, July 1). Shaved heads for sports teams: Do they promote unity or are they hazing? *The Flint Journal.*

National Federation of High Schools. (2009). Hazing information. http://www.nfhs.org/Activity3.aspx?id=3784&terms=hazing.

Nuwer, Hank. (2008). High school hazing. www.stophazing.org.

Nuwer, Hank. (2000). *High School Hazing: When Rites Become Wrongs.* New York, NY: Franklin Watts.

Nuwer, Hank. (1999). *Wrongs of Passage: Fraternities, Sororities, Hazing, and Binge Drinking.* Bloomington, IN: Indiana University Press.

Ousted athletics director gets $567,500 settlement. (2008, Vol. 19, No. 5). *From the Gym to the Jury.*

Patterson v. Hudson Area Schools and Mainar, 551 F3d 438 (6th Cir. 2009).

Prank leads to tragedy. (2008, Vol. 19, No. 4). *From the Gym to the Jury.*

Six band members arrested. (2008, Vol. 19, No. 5). *From the Gym to the Jury.*

Stripling, Jack. (2008, October 7). Bands gone wild. *Inside Higher Ed.*

Teen gets nine-month sentence for hazing. (2009). *Journal Northern Bureau.*

Wilson, Aaron. (2008, August 17). Halting hazing tradition. *Carroll County Times.*

Chapter 8

Appenzeller, Tom. (2011, Vol. 22, No. 2). Sport in America: a new crisis. *From the Gym to the Jury.*

Adult attacks 17-year-old referee. (2011, January). *Referee.*

Appenzeller, Herb. (1980). *Sports and the Courts.* Charlottesville, VA: LEXIS Law Pub.

Appenzeller, Herb. (1985). *Sports and Law: Contemporary Issues.* Charlottesville, VA: LEXIS Law Pub.

Brady, Erik, Bob Kimball and Michael McCarthy. (2011, April 20). Tell us: do you feel safe at the stadium? *USA Today.*

Buchwald, Art. (1977, October 23). Beginners Watching Football. *Atlanta Journal and Constitution.*

Fried, Gil. (2011, Vol. 21, No. 5). Can sports kill you? *From the Gym to the Jury.*

Hackbart v. Cincinnati Bengals, 43F. Supp. 32 (D.C. Colo. 1977).

Lipsyte, Robert. (2010, November 22). Only we can save the NFL from itself. *USA Today.*

Livingstone, Seth & Bob Nightengale. (2010, May 6). Was Taser too much? Incident at Phillies game stirs debate. *USA Today.*

McLeod v. Grant County School District, No. 128, 255 P. 2d 362 (Wash. 1953).

Mihoces, Gary. (2010, October 25). James Harrison, NFL defenders transition to gentler side of rules. *USA Today.*

Mother charged with assault. (2009, February). *News & Record.*

Penalties to prevent liability. (2010, October 25). *Monday Night Football.*

Player gets 10-year prison term for assault on official. (2010, September). *Referee.*

Schiano, John. (2010, May 24). New York: Allegany-Limestone baseball coach suspended. *MaxPreps.com.*

Stoops calls Oregon about injury. (2009, November 24). *The Associated Press.*

Tutko, Thomas & William Bruns. (1976). *Winning Is Everything and Other American Myths.* New York, NY: Macmillan.

Two Houston-area peewee teams suspended after brawl. (2010, September 30). *The Associated Press.*

Where's the will to enforce child athlete abuse and neglect by juvenile/family court systems. (2010, September 23). *CAPPAA.*

Woman gets 20–40 years in Sox-Yankees dispute. (2010, April 13). *The Associated Press.*

Chapter 9

Appenzeller, Herb. (2003). *Managing Sport and Risk Management Strategies* (2nd ed.). Durham, NC: Carolina Academic Press.

Barba speaks out on firing. (2009, May 6). *Santa Maria Times.*

Coach resigns because of parents. (2010, July 25). *News & Record.*

Clotfelter, Charles. (2010, December 31). Stop the tax deduction for major college sports programs. *The Washington Post.*

Dad pulls .357 Magnum at pee wee game. (2006, October 26). *MSNBC.com.*

Dominic v. Wyoming Valley West High School, et al., 362 F. Supp. 2d 560 (Wyo. 2005).

Hyman, Mark. (2009, April 13). The kids aren't alright. *Sports Illustrated.*

Kniceley, Andy. (2009, November 19). Kniceley issues an apology. *The Times West Virginian.*

Knight Foundation Commission on Intercollegiate Athletics. (1991, March). *Keeping Faith with the Student-Athlete: A New Model for Intercollegiate Athletics.*

Knight Foundation Commission on Intercollegiate Athletics. (2001, June). *A Call to Action: Reconnecting College Sports and Higher Education.*

Hook, Debra-Lynn B. (2006, February 19). Parent urges emphasis on good character and behavior in youth sport. *Milwaukee Journal.*

Parents: have faith, don't hover. (2010, November 14). *News & Record.*

Pennington, Bill. (2008, March 10). Expectations lose to reality of sports scholarships. *The New York Times.*

Report: costs, risks high in youth sports. (2010, August 30). *USA Today.*

West, Kay. (2001). *How to Raise a Gentleman.* Nashville, TN: Rutledge Hill Press.

Youth Sport: A Search for Direction (1980, November 20). Greensboro Printing Company.

Chapter 10

Appenzeller, Herb. (2003). *Managing Sport and Risk Management Strategies* (2nd ed.). Durham, NC: Carolina Academic Press.

Beasley v. Morton, 564 So.2d 45 (Ala. 1990).

Burke v. Seacrest, Inc., Docket # 99-438 Court of Common Appeals, 2003.

Engineering firm says Texas A&M facility not built to code. (2009, November 4). *The Associated Press.*

Kingsley v. Ind. Sch .Dist., Hill City, No. 12. 251 NW 2d, 635 (Minn. 1977).

Leasing facilities require adult supervision. (1990). *From the Gym to the Jury.*

Lederman, Doug. (2008, October 10). Turnarounds at Traditional Underdogs. *Inside Higher Ed.*

Massey v. Persson, 729 SW2nd, 448 (KY. App.1987).

McCarthy, Michael. (2010, July 16). FieldTurf, Beaulieu to eliminate lead from products in California deal. *USA Today.*

Moore, David Leon. (2010, November 24). Investigation ongoing in toddler death at Staples Center. *USA Today.*

New coaches and artificial turf. (2010, June 31). *Knoxville News Sentinel.*

Notre Dame president: School responsible in student's death. (2010, November 5). *The Associated Press.*

Provide and maintain safe equipment and facilities. (1990). *From the Gym to the Jury.*

Safety device could have prevented a death. (1991, June 14). *News & Record.*

Student manager awarded $1 million for injury due to school's dryer device. (1990, Vol. 1, No. 3). *From the Gym to the Jury.*

Turf fields are safe. (2010, August 3). *USA Today.*

Unanchored soccer goals a problem. (2009, Vol. 20, No. 1). *From the Gym to the Jury.*

Use UL approved laundries. (1990, Vol. 1, No. 3). *From the Gym to the Jury.*

Vargo v. Svitchan, 100 Mich App. 809, 823; 301 NW2d 1 (1980).

Virginia Graeme Baker entrapment lawsuit filed. (2010, Vol. 21, No. 3). *From the Gym to the Jury.*

Welch v. Sudbury Youth Soccer Association, Inc., 453 Mass. 352 (2009).

Wolfey, Bob. (2006, November 16). '24' rerun angers Thompson. *Journal Sentinel.*

Woodring v. Board of Education of Manhasset, 435 NYS2d 52 (NY App. Div. 1981).

Chapter 11

Appenzeller, Herb. (1985). *Sports and Law: Contemporary Issues.* Charlottesville, VA: LEXIS Law Pub.

Pitts, Leonard. (2010, June 9). Imperfect call, perfect reaction. *The Herald-Sun.*

Prince, Seth. (2008, April 28). Softball opponents offer unique display of sportsmanship. *The Oregonian.*

Sperber, Murray. (1998). *Onward to Victory: The Crises that Shaped College Sports.* New York, NY: Henry Holt and Company.

Unsportsmanlike incidents. (2009). *From the Gym to the Jury.*

Weir, Tom. (2010, July 30). North Korea shames its World Cup losers. *USA Today.*

Index